The Transformation of the Classical Heritage

Peter Brown, General Editor

I   *Art and Ceremony in Late Antiquity,* by Sabine G. MacCormack

II *Synesius of Cyrene: Philosopher-Bishop,* by Jay Alan Bregman

III *Theodosian Empresses: Women and Imperial Dominion in Late Antiquity,* by Kenneth G. Holum

IV *John Chrysostom and the Jews; Rhetoric and Reality in the Late Fourth Century,* by Robert L. Wilken

V   *Biography in Late Antiquity: The Quest for the Holy Man,* by Patricia Cox

VI *Pachomius: The Making of a Community in Fourth-Century Egypt,* by Philip Rousseau

VII *Change in Byzantine Culture in the Eleventh and Twelfth Centuries,* by A. P. Kazhdan and Ann Wharton Epstein

VIII *Leadership and Community: The Transformation of Late Antique Gaul,* by Raymond Van Dam

IX *Homer the Theologian: Neoplatonist Allegorical Reading and the Growth of the Epic Tradition,* by Robert Lamberton

X   *Procopius and the Sixth Century,* by Averil Cameron

XI *Guardians of Language: The Grammarian and Society in Late Antiquity,* by Robert A. Kaster

XII *Civic Coins and Civic Politics in the Roman East, 180–275 A.D.,* by Kenneth W. Harl

XIII *Holy Women of the Syrian Orient,* Introduced and Translated by Sebastian P. Brock and Susan Ashbrook Harvey

XIV *Body, Soul, and Spiritual Progress in Gregory the Great,* by Carole E. Straw

XV *Apex Omnium: Religion in the* Res gestae *of Ammianus,* by R. L. Rike

APEX OMNIUM

R. L. RIKE

· *APEX OMNIUM* ·

RELIGION IN THE
RES GESTAE OF AMMIANUS

UNIVERSITY OF CALIFORNIA PRESS
Berkeley · Los Angeles · London

University of California Press
Berkeley and Los Angeles, California

University of California Press, Ltd.
London, England

© 1987 by
The Regents of the University of California

Library of Congress Cataloging-in-Publication Data

Rike, R. L.
  Apex omnium.
(The Transformation of the classical heritage ; 15)
Bibliography: p.
1. Ammianus Marcellinus—Religion. 2. Ammianus
Marcellinus. Rerum gestarum libri. 3. Rome—History—
Empire, 284–476. I. Title. II. Series.
DG206.A4R55 1987   291'.0937   86-16030
ISBN 0-520-05858-5 (alk. paper)

Printed in the United States of America
1 2 3 4 5 6 7 8 9

If I tell you that the city towards which my journey tends is discontinuous in space and time, now more tenuous, now more concrete, you must not believe the search for it can stop. Perhaps while we speak it is about to rise, scattered within the confines of your empire; you can look for it, but only in the way I have said.

Le Città Invisibili,
Italo Calvino

TO
PETER GARNSEY
MOSES FINLEY

CONTENTS

ILLUSTRATIONS		xi
ACKNOWLEDGMENTS		xiii
INTRODUCTION	*MEDIUS*	1
CHAPTER ONE	THE GODS	8
CHAPTER TWO	CULT: JULIAN *SIDUS SALUTARE*	37
CHAPTER THREE	JULIAN *MINAX SIDUS*	52
CHAPTER FOUR	THAT THEY COME TO THE GODS: PHILOSOPHERS IN A NEW RESTORATION	69
CHAPTER FIVE	COMPARISON OF RELIGIONS	87
CHAPTER SIX	THE SHIELD OF ACHILLES	112
CONCLUSION	ROME	134
	BIBLIOGRAPHY	139
	INDEX	145

ILLUSTRATIONS

ROMAN BRONZE TOKENS OF THE LATE FOURTH CENTURY A.D.

All from *Die Kontorniat-Medaillons*, ed. by A. and E. Alföldi (Berlin, 1976), Plates 2, 27, 38, 52, 152, 163, 184. Reproduced with the kind permission of the Deutsches Archäologisches Institut and Walter de Gruyter and Co., Berlin.

SERAPIS	Title page
THE CIRCUS MAXIMUS	1
SOL INVICTUS	8
JULIAN	37
ATTIS	52
APOLLONIUS OF TYANA	69
JASON	87
THE SHIELD OF ACHILLES	112
THEODOSIUS I	134

ACKNOWLEDGMENTS

This book is the outcome of work performed at Cambridge University under the supervision of Peter Garnsey, who gave me freedom and instruction that will not be forgotten. I must also honor the utterly indispensable assistance given by my wife, Elizabeth, and her parents, Jane and Bernard Koopman. Peter Brown, Geoffrey Harrison, and Doris Kretschmer have been enlightening sources of advice to whom I will link in gratitude the Department of Classics, Leland Stanford Jr. University, and the Andrew W. Mellon Foundation.

· INTRODUCTION ·

MEDIUS

When the warriors of late paganism gather in the square—Julian, Libanius, Eunapius, Praetextatus, the two Flaviani, and Symmachus—we do not see Ammianus, whom custom holds to have been no such *miles*. Scholars, to be frank, are bored by the personal religion of Ammianus after they have learned their catechism from Julian: the emperor's paganism strikes out from his own writings with the speed and immediacy of an electric impulse; the historian, though, seems to black himself out in whispering moderation. Both are cherished for contrary reasons—one for his embattled devotion to the old cults, the other for his lack of attachment to them. The Ammianus we usually meet in the writings of others has offered a parole of absolute toleration and been allowed to pass quickly through the lines of any committed religious group. His *Res gestae* is no lance raised on behalf of Rome's pagan senators. If he enjoys a special reputation for independence, however, it has cost him much, for we instinctively pay more attention to those who are ideologically committed than to those who are not. And we want to learn our paganism, understandably, from Julian, not the quiescent Ammianus.

The spectrum of old and current opinions includes all of the following: Ammianus was a Christian, a monotheist inclined toward Christianity, a vague monotheist, a polytheist aspiring toward monotheism, a pagan hostile to any excess, a superstitious pagan, or a man unattached to any religion but still pious and highly receptive to superstition. At other places along this road of disengagement stand the philosophic Ammianus, intent upon reason and practical ethics, not gods; the tolerant, moderate, prudent empiricist; or descending, the intellectually confused and rhetorical writer apathetic to all religion. If he was actually coerced into reticence on the matter—another theory—then of course our ground for choosing any of the other interpretations will cave into blackness as well.

Of all these opinions, only one—that Ammianus was a Christian[1]—is no longer alive, and only two others—that his monotheism was more Christian than pagan[2] and that imperial coercion stunted the religious content of the *Res gestae*[3]—appear to be less than thriving. Scholars mix the rest so freely that we may believe it is impossible to contradict oneself when discussing the historian's religious beliefs. Such freedom to move in two directions at once, toward engagement and disengagement as one pleases, arises from the historian's persisting reputation for neutrality. There is no better point than the center after all for moving in any direction, and that power for omnidirectional movement inherent within this central position has become the primary shaping force of scholarly discussion: comments about Ammianus often go everywhere and nowhere at the same time as they turn about the *meta* of ideological equilibrium. Nothing appears fixed but the turning point which is itself simply a mark for zero.

Three centuries of assertion and denial of the historian's involvement with religion, frequently within the same argument, have effectively drained the question of its vitality. The possible Christian of Chifflet was the tolerant but devoted pagan of de Valois, then Gibbon's philosophical soldier lifted by Reason beyond the reach of any religion.[4] To Heyne (1802), Ammianus walked prudently between surrounding superstitions—if he just escaped them—neither abandoning Rome's ancestral cults nor condemning the new state religion.[5] Gimazaine (1889) alloyed

---

1. The argument usually turned upon Ammianus' praise of provincial bishops, 27.3.15. See those favorable opinions of Pierre Pithou and Claude Chifflet (both remarks of uncertain date) and their rebuttal by Henri de Valois in his 1681 edition of the *Res gestae*. The preface to this edition is most readily available among those documents that Wagner and Erfurdt collected to preface their own edition of the History (*Res gestae*, by Ammianus Marcellinus [Leipzig, 1808]), xlii–iii, xcii. Gimazaine (*Ammien Marcellin*, 68–85) discusses this earliest question about Ammianus and his religion with specific reference to Pithou, Chifflet, and de Valois.

2. Demandt, "Zeitkritik und Geschichtsbild im Werk Ammians" (diss., Marburg University, Bonn, 1965), 82.

3. Thompson, *Historical Work*, 26–31.

4. *History of the Decline and Fall* 3:122. Cf. the assertion of MacKail (*Last Great Roman Historian*, 173–74) that a desire for absolute toleration placed Ammianus "far in advance of his age"; he had no interest in doctrine and took no side in religious controversy.

5. Wagner and Erfurdt, *Res gestae*, cxxxiii–iv. For a similar assertion of Ammianus' independence from an alleged miasma of superstition, see the preface to Yonge's transla-

Introduction: *Medius* 3

this estimable prudence with baser suggestions of indifference and superficiality. Paganism in the *Res gestae* was merely a rhetor's stroke of greasepaint. Neither philosopher, nor Christian, nor pagan, "*ce Protée insaissisable*," eluded his academic pursuers.[6] By the time Witte (1891) published the first, and only, monograph exclusively devoted to religion in the *Res gestae*, negative definition had become the prevailing mode of description. Like God, Ammianus was to be most readily perceived by what he was not. Slicing away all pagan attachments, Witte left him a neutral monotheist, although one (oddly) *pius*, who cultivated philosophy, not religion.[7] Paganism vanished into philosophical symbols, and so discussion of religion quite understandably turned into a quest for specific philosophical influences. Scala (1898) felt the "spirit of Posidonius,"[8] while Ensslin (1923), author of the most respected study of Ammianus' religion, mined the Neoplatonists.[9] But then how did Ammianus rank as a Plotinus, Porphyry, or Iamblichus? We see the approaching wreck: unable to stand such comparison—unless someday the *Enneads* should be

---

tion of the *Res gestae* (London, 1862), vi–vii, although the historian in this case does not entirely escape the "contagion."

6. *Ammien Marcellin*, 67, 77, 83, 85, 105, 358.

7. "Ammianus quid iudicaverit," 12, 18, 28–29, 37, 40–44, 48–50, 57–59. Witte explicitly borrowed the judgment of Teuffel (*History of Roman Literature* 2:429) that Ammianus held to a "confused and colorless" polytheism, which really amounted to neutral monotheism, deleting from his own argument, however, Teuffel's initial supposition of polytheism. By "piety" (*pius atque tamen religiosus*), Witte may have meant Ammianus' affection for the supposed superstition of divination (p. 59). Critics have traditionally distinguished, improperly so, a belief in divination from an attachment to religion per se, making it fall rather under the heading of lingering superstition. Of course, perfectly conventional Greco-Roman religion had always consisted of such practices. In older works paganism often seems to be thought of as the sum of monotheism plus superstition(s). Boissier (*La fin du paganisme*, 227), for example, criticized Ammianus' "great theories" about God when these were mixed with so many "puerile superstitions." We can sense the bifurcation and will recognize, too, its logical import: if superstition is by definition not religion, then the only (real) religion Ammianus *could* have had was monotheistic! Dill (*Roman Society*, 120) also employed Teuffel's formula: adherence to traditional Roman religion combined with a "real creed" of vague monotheism.

8. "Doxographische und stoische Reste," 150.

9. *Zur Geschichtsschreibung und Weltanschauung des Ammianus Marcellinus* (Leipzig, 1923). Ensslin produced a far more probing analysis than Witte's yet employed much of his argument—for example, the impossibility of attaching Ammianus to any cult; the need for explicit statements of personal involvement (*Wir-berichte*); invalidation of religious material on the ground of rhetorical or poetic usage; the historian's susceptibility to superstition amid a "dying syncretism"; and Teuffel's formula. See pp. 48–53, 64, 84, 96. While Ensslin did pursue his *Quellenforschung* with vigor, he could not be said to have made any original contribution to the essential methodology of the problem.

tested for its historiographical quality—Ammianus was marked as "no philosopher."[10] If the valuation of Ammianus' religion should indeed depend upon his proficiency in formal philosophical canons as this model taught, then there was little incentive to probe him further.

When a question is still alive, it generates original ideas and new detailed studies, two vital signs we scarcely see after Ensslin. Thompson (1947) contributed his famous theory of Christian coercion, but, as I have pointed out, any further discussion of religion should then have to be surrendered to the Great Secret.[11] Refusing the customary stroke at Ammianus' affection for "tainting superstition," Fontaine (1969) resurrected the thoroughly legitimate connection between divination and a sound Greco-Roman religious mentality by grounding the intellectual drive of Ammianus, his *curiositas*, within a sensitivity to divine manifestations of all sorts.[12] The only lengthy treatment of religion in the *Res gestae* to appear since 1923 has been that of Camus (1967), yet this is simply a recycling of older views: praise for the historian's philosophical monotheism and condemnation for his sterile paganism.[13] Familiarity dogs the rest of our critics as well. Demandt has returned to Chifflet for his Christian hook. Laistner chooses the "no philosopher" approach, stressing Ammianus' uncertainty.[14] Blockley (1975) takes confusion and

---

10. After Gimazaine, Dautremer (*Ammien Marcellin*, 64–69) employed this phrase in his own description of Ammianus' philosophic paganism. Glover (*Life and Letters*, 37–40) picked up the refrain as did Laistner (*Greater Roman Historians*, 158–60). Despite Ensslin's caveat (*Zur Geschichtsschreibung*, 76) that one should not expect a philosophical system from Ammianus, this did not alter his choice of method: Ammianus was essentially evaluated as a philosopher.

11. Against the originality of his coercion theory stands Thompson's refusal (*Historical Work*, xi) to enter into any general discussion of religion in the *Res gestae*, believing Ensslin had already done this adequately.

12. "Ammien Marcellin," 426–27. Sabbah (*La méthode d'Ammien Marcellin*, 202, 493, 546–48) followed Fontaine in defining the historian's "profound religiosity" against his belief in divination but returned the conceit of superstition to its former place. That Ammianus opened his account of Julian's Persian expedition to so many portents was a proof of his "superstitious devoutness."

13. Camus, *Ammien Marcellin*. Camus' ingredients are toleration, moderation, indifference, ethical pragmatism, attachment to the old cults, aspiration to monotheism, "pacified" paganism, and the shackle of an "inorganic pagan credo." See pp. 133–34, 140, 143–44, 199, 267–68. Such a farrago exemplifies the tendency to toss just about any idea into a description of Ammianus regardless of the jolts.

14. Laistner (*Greater Roman Historians*, 158–59) offers a noteworthy example of that style of negative definition by which Ammianus can often appear to turn into a sum of denials: "He is in short no philosopher. . . . Although his own religious beliefs were not inspired by implicit faith in any one cult or doctrine, but show some fluctuation, he was not an atheist nor even an agnostic."

rhetorical superficiality;[15] Browning (1982), gratuitous erudition and a detachment from Rome's traditional religion "verging on contempt."[16]

Today the most widely recognized opinions on Ammianus are probably those of Momigliano (1974), who has shaped our long-standing methodology of detachment into the theme of the Lonely Historian.[17] Momigliano's conviction that we should ignore Ammianus' many religion-packed digressions when seeking a precise description of his personal religious beliefs—religion was "not the business" of classical historians—drives the venerable principle of separation to a point where we will begin to ask whether two different men did not write the book.[18]

Or perhaps the problem of religion in the *Res gestae* is rightly dead. Consensus has certainly been achieved, or rather, never lost: Julian was the living, Ammianus the dying, pagan. When considering whether this verdict should stand, however, we may point to a distinct set of difficulties and biases. The perennial recirculation of a small group of ideas is striking. Much of this tendency results from the absence of works, save one, completely devoted to religion. Scholars of Ammianus typically undertake several topics at once, a distracting responsibility that probably inclines one to take the religious interpretation at hand, usually that of Ensslin. In the same vein, religious views are most often relegated to short comments or a few paragraphs, which are not enough to convey

15. "Ammianus Marcellinus, A Study of His Historiography and Political Thought," *Latomus* 141 (1975): 168–69, 175–76. "Ammianus was a pagan and apparently a monotheist. But his religious system (if one can speak of such) seems to have been rather confused. His philosophy, as far as it is discernible, was both confused and eclectic, showing strong traces of Stoicism and Neoplatonism, where the two can be separated. At times, Ammianus' language, which is often vague, rhetorical, and poetical, makes it impossible to be certain exactly what he is saying, or if he really means what he appears to say. Moreover, his desire to display his learning sometimes causes him to utilize passages from authors whom he has read, passages which he seems not fully to have understood or the implications of which in his *History* he has not fully considered."

16. *Cambridge History*, 2:746–47.

17. "Lonely Historian," 134–35. Cf. Gimazaine's *"étranger à toute religion"* (*Ammien Marcellin*, 392). See, of course, Momigliano's highly influential essay, "Pagan and Christian Historiography," with particular reference to pp. 95–97.

18. "Popular Religious Beliefs," 142, 148. In his desire to make Ammianus an isolated figure, Momigliano is far too quick to neutralize the ideological import of the excursuses and too eager to prevent the historian from choosing sides. I do not see the point, for example, in stating that Ammianus was openly pagan, an admirer of Julian, and yet "refused to choose," although not emotionally indifferent ("Lonely Historian," 134). Any open pagan in the late fourth century had made a choice.

genuine argument. Beyond this poverty of specialized studies lies the very fundamental impediment of Ammianus' renowned neutrality or fairness, for it seems to be impossible to form a major opinion about him without somehow beginning here. The notion that his peculiarities proceed from an estimable personal ideal, an essential goodness, has been an article of faith present in varying degrees at the inception of every study. Of course Ammianus stands alone among his contemporaries, but this difference of character may have had comparatively little to do with superior ethics. Against such a favorable predisposition stands the tendency to criticize Ammianus for failing to provide his religious or philosophical system *en bloc*. He is expected to prove his convictions and enthusiasms—or stand "confused"—far beyond what is demanded of other ancient historians in this respect. However, the intelligibility of any argument within a text cannot be fairly judged without due respect for that particular literary genre that has influenced the shape and dispersion of the argument's various parts. The *Res gestae* is a history, not a theological treatise; we should keep in mind that such patterns of religious thought as are present will have to be carefully elicited from reorganized material.

It is obvious that we are frequently dealing with a severely biased model of late paganism, which depicts monotheism as progressive or at least inevitable while paganism is made to lose its internal cultic distinctions (and any desire to make them), its social purpose, and either to collapse into superstition or to evaporate into philosophy.[19] The desire to convert Ammianus into an aspiring, and failed, philosopher owes much to the assumption that late paganism was the chattel of Neoplatonism. But to measure his success in adopting and conforming to the canons of one late antique philosophical school is scarcely identical to the task of seeking to identify Ammianus' religious beliefs and their cultic expression. If the historian's way was different from that of correct Neoplatonism, although establishing contact with it at various points, does this signify intellectual confusion? One suspects that scholarly esteem for Ammianus' philosophical aspirations, his progress toward reason or objectivity, may mask a bias against religious involvement per se. In the

19. See Blockley, *Ammianus Marcellinus*, 105, "By the fourth century A.D. superstition and belief had to a considerable extent replaced reason"; also Chesnut, *First Christian Historians*, 51–52, "In Ammianus' work, one had reached the twilight of paganism, and there one moved through a particularly dim and gloomy world." A fine example of this old-fashioned approach to late paganism can be found in Dill, *Roman Society*, 3, 7–8, 75–76, 105, 112.

apparent search for a less religious and more philosophical explanation of the historian's paganism, cult-related material has often been discarded and religious neutrality achieved in a self-fulfilling manner by sterilizing that which is most obviously pagan. Seeing the operation of such habits within former interpretations, we are entitled to question the extent of Ammianus' religious detachment, whether he truly belongs in a "vast zone of silence."[20]

If there is reason to suspect that his voice has been artificially muted, a new attempt should be made to reconstruct the historian's religion from the beginning and to examine his relationship to traditional paganism. Here narrative and digression will be yoked, not divided, for only against the total background of Ammianus' Roman and barbarian or ethnic religions, in which his digressions are rich, is it possible to see clearly into the respective merits of Christianity and the *cultus deorum* as he envisioned them. I believe that in Rome, ultimately, we find a militant pagan who was striving to rescue the pieces of her heroic religion out of the shattering crash of Julian. Despite the existence of an enthusiastic defense of paganism in his apologetic work, the *Res gestae* yet retains its balanced character. Ammianus was deliberately attempting to lay a bridge between the *cultus deorum* and Theodosius I, who for a brief period between A.D. 388 and 391 opened himself to reconciliation with Rome's pagan senators. And if this study is a just witness to that critical labor, we will in the matter of religion call him not *medius* but *miles*.

20. Momigliano, "Pagan and Christian," 96.

· CHAPTER ONE ·

THE GODS

To reconstruct the religion of Ammianus, we should begin by studying the many divine beings he mentions, for these suggest possible candidates for his personal devotion and house the elements of his theology. Gods are everywhere: emperors invoke them in speeches, honor them with monuments, and give thanks to them—or try to turn away their anger—with actual sacrifices. In the excursuses lie accompanying theology, myths, heroic legends, divine foundation stories, as well as descriptions of temples and cult. Such multifarious references obviously call out to be put together, and scholars, however varied their final conclusions on the subject, have never denied that a description of Ammianus' religion could be synthesized from them. Potential wholeness is waiting.

However, we cannot go on to press our fingers into the raw textual material without first considering how we will address the troubling power of literary convention. Ammianus wrote as a traditional, Greco-Roman historian who endeavored to set his own work beside that of Tacitus and his eminent predecessors, the *maiores stili*,[1] back to Herodotus. So there are plenty of exciting descriptions of battles as well as long digressions about interesting peoples and regions within or around the empire. How then can we tell when Ammianus is speaking personally or "ancestrally"—that is, introducing elements whose main function is to help him play the elegant literary mimic before his Roman audience? Anyone who assembles a complex theology for Ammianus out of the *Res gestae* does so under this sword. At its most devastating, the invocation

---

1. "Scribant reliqua potiores aetate et doctrinis florentes. quos id, si libuerit, aggressuros procudere linguas ad maiores moneo stilos," 31.16.9. Clark's edition of the *Res gestae* (Berlin, 1910–15) will be used for all textual citations. All translations, from Ammianus or any other author mentioned, will be my own.

of rhetorical influence has been a critical knife that cuts from his work its digressions, poetic statements—customarily those referring to a specific pagan god—and opinions attributable to other sources. This method allegedly leaves us with the real Ammianus, whose paganism was a bland literary fragment, a borrowed, secondhand religion. Neutral monotheism is necessarily victorious. But that idea is more than a statement about his religion; it embodies the methodological precept that we dare not take at face value a very large portion of the *Res gestae*.

Although no one would question his zeal to create something worthy of the *maiores stili* of Greece and Rome, we should reject any method of analysis that threatens the basic integrity of the historian's work: he wrote all of it, selected each statement, and meant everything he said, *opus veritatem professum numquam, ut arbitror, sciens silentio ausus corrumpere vel mendacio.*[2] The dichotomy between a genuine and some "literary" Ammianus is, fundamentally, a false one. He did not add digressions to have them discarded; that material most obviously supports and deepens kindred subjects within the narrative portion. Indeed the historian's religious argument cannot be understood without studying this interplay between narrative and excursus. Our particular but essential sense of the history as an extended sum of personal choices should make us feel bolder as we assemble the references before us into a personal theology.

There is more encouragement to offer. When considering Ammianus' place among the recognized trends of fourth-century paganism—Hellenism, scholasticism, or theurgy to name a few—it will be helpful, if obvious, to remember that these trends as we know them now are at root the projected experiences of a relatively small group of surviving authors whose personal forays onto the great social landscape of the Mediterranean hardly accounts for all possible and plausible theologies: they do not make a closed shop. Let us adopt the premise then that each author first and foremost bears witness to his own theology without laying necessary bonds on the particular religious experience of his neighboring author. Ammianus is under no compulsion to "equal" Julian or Iamblichus, and he should in no way be penalized if his own vision of the gods diverges from precise Neoplatonic canon. Acknowledging the important operations of individual choice and initiative in forming religious concepts, we will put the question of trends somewhat differently:

---

2. 31.16.9. Certainly an author can borrow an idea and still mean it. Originality has nothing to do with belief.

what obstacles were there in the fourth century to the creation of *any* personal theology from traditional religious elements? Imperial Christianity became the decisive block, of course, but Ammianus would have had no difficulty imbibing pagan beliefs from many sources, however much imperial legislation—only fitfully so during his lifetime—and the rare destruction of a temple might limit the external expression of this pagan viewpoint in public worship. Considering that Eunapius, his contemporary, was quite able to publish blatantly pagan works in the more thoroughly Christianized East, we have all the more reason to doubt that in Rome, Christian coercion would have frightened Ammianus into making a radically different presentation of his own religion.[3]

Granting that it does not have to beggar itself before the beliefs of others, or vanish into rhetoric, or dissipate among *Quellen,* would such a historiographically transmitted statement of personal belief really have mattered to anyone anyway? Our interest in discovering the historian's religion unquestionably grows or diminishes in relation to our assumptions about his senatorial audience. If we assume the least interesting audience possible—usually one of intellectually supine, "literary" pagans—the ideological volume (to use Momigliano's language) of religious items in the text must drop accordingly.[4] We believe that they heard nothing and consequently—flipping our logical switch—that Ammianus must never have intended to tell them anything. If we imagine the historian reciting his *Res gestae* among the senatorial literati of Macrobius' *Saturnalia,* religion will seem no more daring than a *codex.* But what if we leave that fictive, dreamy symposium created by Macrobius in the fifth century and think instead of the real, acutely tense political environment of Rome in the last two decades of the fourth century? That is where Ammianus actually read, before many who wanted not simply to experience paganism as a literary fantasy but to enact it as a way of life. Surely at no other time would a Roman audience have heard more audibly, and listened more attentively to, the religious notes within a work.[5]

3. For the continued survival of paganism, see chap. 4 of Geffcken's *The Last Days,* esp. 223–40.

4. See Cameron, *Claudian,* 190: "The answer is that in literature the old mythology had long since become merely decorative, and in any case bore so little relationship to contemporary paganism, that none but a few extremists gave its pagan associations a thought."

5. When encountering Ammianus' criticism of the worst Roman nobles for their bolted libraries and hate for learning (14.6.18, 28.4.14), we should remember that this reveals only those whom he did *not* expect to attend his recitations. Let us not look for his actual *auditores* among this apathetic group. See below, p. 137. For discussions of the historian's Roman audience, refer to Thompson, "Ammianus Marcellinus and the Romans," 130–34; Pack, "Roman Digressions," 181–89; Neri, "*Ammiano e il cristianesimo Religione,*" 86–100; Matthews, *Western Aristocracies,* 1–12; Brown, *Religion and Society,* 161–82.

In sum we have several reasons to pursue a fresh theological synthesis with vigor, since Ammianus may have intended to deliver a politically engaged religious message before an audience that itself was fully engaged. Accordingly, we should be particularly sensitive to the cultic implications of his theological scheme as we attempt to construct entire portraits of Ammianus' gods and the principles by which they are related: where and how is cult being directed? Emerging details will occasionally be highlighted against a select background of pagan writers: Iamblichus, Sallustius, Plotinus, the Hermeticists, Julian, and Eunapius. But the purpose of such external comparison is not to find every possible connection, for this would distract us into a self-consuming *Quellenforschung* and away from the first principle of this study, which is that more effort can be profitably concentrated upon the history in its own right.

Adrasteia and Themis are without doubt the most important personifications in the *Res gestae*, for their excursuses furnish two complementary hierarchies and the first principles of Ammianus' theology. That on Adrasteia follows notice of the execution of Gallus and those forthcoming deaths of his betrayers, Scudilo and Barbatio, all turning under the gaze of the supreme Numen:

> But the just and celestial Godhead stood at its post, looking everywhere. For Gallus was crushed to death by his bloody acts; and both of those who led him to this fatal smashing, plying the man—guilty enough to be sure—with fawning lies, died wretchedly not long after. . . . Adrasteia, the avenger of impious deeds and rewarder of the good, often involves herself in innumerable actions of this sort, and may she always do so! She, whom we call too by the name of Nemesis,[6] men think of as some high law of the creating Godhead, set beyond the moon, or, as others understand her, a guardian more immediately connected with our own realm of substance who is generally empowered to govern the life of each and every man. The old theologians used to paint her as the daughter of Justice, and they say she gazes down upon everything that is earthly from some hidden recess in eternity. As queen of causes and judge of events, this goddess gathers lots from the urn of fate[7]. . . . and legend has given her a rudder and set her upon a wheel

---

6. Cf. Eunapius' description of the divinely writ death of Valens's inquisitor Festus in *Vitae sophistorum*, ed. J. Giangrande (Rome, 1956), 481. Festus dropped paralyzed at a temple of Nemesis after condemning the philosopher Maximus to death. Ammianus, of course, offers his own example of ominous death on the steps of a temple, 23.1.6, that of a priest at the *Tychaion* of Antioch.

7. An intervening section simply expands the image of changing fortune, Ammianus then proceeding to the props accorded to the deity by the "storied past"; first, wings for swift execution.

so that no one would fail to recognize that she runs through all the elements, ruling the universe.[8]

Between the attributions to external authority, extended imagery of revolving fortune, and mythical props, there is a trail of theological details that clearly reveals attention to the structure and operation of a divine hierarchy: *superni numinis aequitas; aliquotiens operatur Adrastia; ius quoddam sublime numinis efficacis; lunari circulo superpositum; substantialis tutela generali potentia partilibus praesidens fatis; Iustitiae filiam; ex abdita quadam aeternitate; regina causarum; universitatem regere per elementa discurrens omnia*. Adrasteia is subordinate to a supreme Numen,[9] whose epithet *efficax* distinctly evokes the fabricating character of the Platonic Demiurge. Below Numen and Adrasteia are *fata* and *elementa*, which the latter administers in her capacity of *substantialis tutela*. The phrase *generali potentia* partakes both of *ius quoddam* and *universitatem*.

If Adrasteia governs fates—men—this occurs through the markedly physical or "substantial" character of the deity's guardianship. Here Ammianus is discussing terrestrial life, and he most probably intends to identify this particular set of controlled elements with the world of earthly substances—that is, matter. Such a materialistic view of divine administration as the penetration of matter by law, Adrasteia, would be in harmony with that conventional description of Heimarmene as the exercise of God's providence upon physical bodies that we have from Sal-

8. "Sed vigilavit utrubique superni numinis aequitas. Nam et Gallum actus oppressere crudeles et non diu postea ambo cruciabili morte absumpti sunt, qui eum licet nocentem blandius palpantes periuriis ad usque plagas perduxere letales. . . . Haec et huiusmodi quaedam innumerabilia ultrix facinorum impiorum bonorumque praemiatrix aliquotiens operatur Adrastia—atque utinam semper!—quam vocabulo duplici etiam Nemesim appellamus, ius quoddam sublime numinis efficacis humanarum mentium opinione lunari circulo superpositum vel, ut definiunt alii, substantialis tutela generali potentia partilibus praesidens fatis, quam theologi veteres fingentes Iustitiae filiam ex abdita quadam aeternitate tradunt omnia despectare terrena. Haec ut regina causarum et arbitra rerum ac disceptatrix urnam sortium temperat accidentium. . . . Pinnas autem ideo illi fabulosa vetustas aptavit, ut adesse velocitate volucri cunctis existimetur et praetendere gubernaculum dedit eique subdidit rotam, ut universitatem regere per elementa discurrens omnia non ignoretur," 14.11.24–26.

9. *Ius quoddam, filia Iustitiae*; this is the language of subordination, of participation within an embracing whole. *Regina* itself naturally calls forth the *rex*, Jupiter; cf. Themis, *cognominatam in cubili solioque Iovis, vigoris vivifici*, 21.1.8. By my reckoning, Iustitia here is identical to the *aequitas superni Numinis* and, ultimately, should be regarded as equivalent to the supreme Numen itself. In this sense, Adrasteia would be the "daughter" of her *pater* (*deorum*), Jupiter. Note the parallelism bonding Jupiter *vivificus* to Numen *efficax* through that demiurgical idea of making, *facere*. See Iamblichus' *De mysteriis*, ed. E. des Places (Paris, 1966), 8.3, where the Demiurge is called a molder of living substance, *zōtikēn ousian*.

Iustius.[10] Whatever the historian's uncertainty about the primary location of Adrasteia—and given the deity's wide-ranging role as a mediator, this is a legitimate *aporia*, not just "confusion"—his system operates clearly enough, nor is there an obvious need to invoke Neoplatonic hypostases to explain what is happening.[11] The details at the core of this excursus form an intelligible personal point of view. Moreover, they also suggest the sort of theological problems that were of interest to Ammianus, such as the physical integration of deities with the world or their location with respect to it.[12]

When, in Book 21, good omens rouse Julian to move against Constantius, Ammianus provides a long description and defense of divination: "Because malevolent people charge an emperor who was intellectually refined and eager for all such discoveries with practicing the evil arts of predicting future events, it must be considered briefly how this important branch of learning also adorns a wise man."[13] Introducing the various methods is their unifying principle, Themis, who not only underpins these techniques but does so in an excursus that is explicitly apologetic and that unquestionably shows the historian's personal enthusiasm:

> There is an essence of life present within all the elements which, surely because they are eternal bodies, is always in motion between them and everywhere strong in its capacity to indicate future events. When we bring knowledge from various sources to the task of analyzing these elements, this spirit shares with us the gifts of divination. And the powers of natural substances, when men please them with various rituals, bear prophetic words as if along ever flowing streams. The divine being which presides over these powers is called Themis, for she publishes

---

10. *De deis et mundo*, ed. A. Nock (Cambridge, England, 1926), 9. The handbook of Sallustius offers a quick and useful introduction to contemporary Neoplatonic theology. See as well Chapters 1 and 2 of Wallis's excellent *Neoplatonism* on the aims and sources of this philosophical school.

11. E.g., Dautremer, *Ammien Marcellin*, 87; Ensslin, *Ammianus Marcellinus*, 76; Jannacone, *Ammiano Marcellino*, 80. *Substantia*, as here in the phrase *substantialis tutela*, is regarded as a precise translation of the Greek *hypostasis*, that Plotinian metaphysical term denoting one of three levels of reality. But Ammianus elsewhere uses *substantia* in the more ordinary way to mean simply a physical substrate, matter: [*Neptunus*] *umentis substantiae potestas*, 17.7.12. Cf. *elementorum omnium spiritus* and *substantiales potestates*, 21.1.8. We should not want to rush straightaway then into the assumption that Adrasteia must represent some Neoplatonic overseer of the Hypostases without further evidence.

12. Momigliano, "Lonely Historian," 134, incorrectly accuses Ammianus of having "no very clear ideas about the numen to which he so frequently alludes . . . or about Adrastia, the goddess of Justice [sic, *filia Iustitiae*] to which he pays homage in a famous passage."

13. 21.1.7.

beforehand those decrees fixed by the law of Fate, that is, *tetheimena* as they say in Greek. And so the old theologians have said that she shares in the bed and throne of Jupiter, the life-making force.[14]

This passage is free of embellishment and dense with theology. Again the components of a divine hierarchy are at hand. An omnipresent force of undiminished vigor, Jupiter,[15] links the eternal elements to one another, simultaneously dispersing a network of communication, or prophecy, powered from within itself. The elements that thus embody prophecy are also those upon which men are to focus the techniques (rites) of divination. Inasmuch as Ammianus calls these powers eternal, living entities infused with *spiritus,* they are of course gods.[16] Although Ensslin identified them with Neoplatonic demons[17]—that is, the lowest grade of divinity—the theological purview of this passage actually embraces much more of the divine cosmos, envisioning Jupiter as the great Lord of Substance[18] with all of his substantial dependents, including the celestial deities, arrayed below. Ammianus has a type of cultic activity in mind that cannot be limited simply to demon worship. Themis monitors that returning flow of divine communication that follows correct placation, and her lofty rule in this respect allows the goddess some special association with the ultimate source of life and fate, Jupiter. However rationalized such theology may appear, it is by no means sterilized of religious content: we are offered a hierarchy of explicitly vital deities whom men are to seek by cult.

The two hierarchies within which Ammianus places Adrasteia and

14. "Elementorum omnium spiritus utpote perennium corporum praesentiendi motu semper et ubique vigens ex his, quae per disciplinas varias affectamus, participat nobiscum munera divinandi et substantiales potestates ritu diverso placatae velut ex perpetuis fontium venis vaticina mortalitati suppeditant verba, quibus numen praeesse Themidis, quam ex eo, quod fixa fatali lege decreta praescire facit in posterum, quae τεθειμένα sermo Graecus appellat, ita cognominatam in cubili solioque Iovis, vigoris vivifici, theologi veteres collocarunt," 21.1.8.

15. Sc., *elementorum omnium spiritus . . . motu semper et vigens = Iovis, vigoris vivifici.*

16. Cf. Neptune, *umentis substantiae potestas,* 17.7.12; Mercury, *mundi velociorem sensum,* 16.5.5; Sol's *scintillae* turning into mortal minds, 21.1.11; Iris, the prophetic rainbow, 20.11.30. As for the presence of *poetae* in Ammianus' references to Neptune (where they are paired with *theologi*) and Iris, such attributions should not distract us, for poetic evidence need hardly be synonymous with "doubtful" in the *Res gestae.* Homer is called to witness on the subject of *genii* with every indication of seriousness, *Itidem ex sempiternis Homeri carminibus intellegi datur,* 21.14.5.

17. *Ammianus Marcellinus,* 66.

18. The Ousiarch of the Hermetic tract, *Asclepius, Hermetica,* ed. W. Scott (Oxford, 1924), 3.19b, "Caeli, vel quidquid est quod eo nomine conprehenditur, οὐσιάρχης est Iuppiter ⟨ὕπατος⟩; per caelum enim Iuppiter omnibus praebet vitam." Cf. Ammianus' *vigor vivificus.*

Themis are obviously related. Each is tripartite with a mediating deity set between the *elementa* she administers and that highest god who creates the entire apparatus. Jupiter the *vigor vivificus* neatly matches the Numen *efficax*, who is similarly "vigorous."[19] Although Adrasteia and Themis share a mutual concern for substance in its variously divine and mundane grades, they are not the same goddess. Ammianus states clearly that the province of Themis is *vaticina verba* and so restricted to the control of words. Men learn the letter of divine decrees through her but, unlike Adrasteia the Queen of Causes, she does not actually implement them. Limited in this manner, Themis may suggest that bodiless providence of the gods that Sallustius coordinates with the material activity of Heimarmene.[20] And gradually we become aware that our two divine hierarchies are not only similar in certain respects but complementary, two aspects of a single theological scheme, which the historian first describes from the viewpoint of *aequitas*, the descent of Fate upon men, and then from that of *benignitas*,[21] the religious and intellectual ascent of men to the gods through a generously shared knowledge of divine will. Their fabrication from kindred forms of celestial and terrestrial substance, *elementa*, binds deities to men who may then successfully exploit the former if they do so in the proper spirit of piety, *affectio*.

Adrasteia and Themis are well-delineated examples of abstract or personified deities; in them we have no trouble seeing *numina*. But theological concepts of this sort in the *Res gestae* can be numinous—that is, intended to be read as characterizations of actions taken by other gods— without necessarily being *numina* in themselves. This distinction is worth noting when we are confronted by Ammianus' many references to Fatum, Fortuna, and Iustitia. Should we conceive of each as a deity? Yes, if we follow the history of Roman religion as a whole. Not necessarily so, if we let ourselves be guided into their personal signification for this particular man by the best evidence for it, his own text. Leaving external authorities aside, let us consider, for example, whether Ammianus himself offers any cultic base to set beneath the concept in question: are there *templa*; does he call it a god; do people pray to it (with any striking effect)? Allowing the values of individual deities to float freely in this

---

19. *Vigilavit*, 14.11.24; see above, p. 12, n. 8.

20. *Hē asōmatos pronoia*, 9. Cf. Sallustius' ascription of oracles to the "good providence" of the gods, and Ammianus' own invocation of the *benignitas numinis*, 21.1.9, in a similar context.

21. "For the kind Godhead, whether because men deserve its favor or because it is touched by affection for them, desires by these methods also [augury and auspice] to reveal future events," 21.1.9.

way provides an important point of ontological leverage beneath our burden of abstractions.

Both Fatum and Fortuna are protean terms that appear variously in singular and plural forms to designate events, death, and the occasional demon. As Ammianus presents the former idea, it is simply a characterization of divine activity. Any independent cultic base is lacking and Fatum properly amounts to no more than divine writ, "predestined order."[22] Fortuna in the *Res gestae* should be similarly interpreted as an expression of divine writ but with the important difference that this communication from the gods is, unlike Fatum, always unknowable before the event, *caeca*.[23] Note that Ammianus distinctly separates his excursus on *fortuna mutabilis* from that on Adrasteia, whose subject is the administration of *fata*. Coinlike then they portray the obverse and reverse faces of divine activity, but they are not identical to each other.[24] While no one would question the well-established popularity of Fortuna as an object of cult,[25] the most useful question to be asked in this instance is what evidence the historian himself can provide. Then the case in support of Fortuna is actually thin. Ammianus may use the term frequently, but he never refers specifically to a temple of Fortuna, instead choosing the word *genius* when he speaks of those *Tychaia* in Alexandria and Antioch.[26] Such discrimination in usage—and, I would argue, conception—is thoroughly consistent with the historian's stated dislike of Fortuna but his reverence for great *genii*.[27] Taking Fortuna's contextual similarity to the cultically inanimate Fatum together with our several

22. *Praescriptus ordo fatorum*, 15.3.3.
23. Insofar as Fate (*fata*) is the proper subject matter of divination—Fortuna, significantly, passes entirely unmentioned in Ammianus' description of the *doctrinae genus haud leve*, 21.1.7–14—it could be said to possess this quality of potential intelligibility that Fortuna lacks. Notice Julian's suggestion that the understanding of Fatum through divination was a victory over blind, and blinding, Fortuna: "Steti fundatus turbines calcare fortuitorum assuefactus . . . nec fateri pudebit: interiturum me ferro dudum didici fide fatidica praecinente," 25.3.18–19.
24. This may be one answer to the query of Naudé, "Fortuna in Ammianus Marcellinus," 85: "One great problem in studying *fortuna-tyche* in Ammianus is to decide its relation to Adrasteia and Ammianus' belief in the all-controlling factor of justice." Note, too, the conventional location of Fortuna at, and below, the moon (Sallustius, 9) and Ammianus' description of Adrasteia, *lunari circulo superpositum*.
25. Sallustius, 9, particularly favors the worship of Tyche in cities inasmuch as these required some common focus of ritual for their highly diverse populations.
26. 22.11.7, 23.1.6.
27. E.g., "Tu hoc loco, Fortuna orbis Romani merito incusaris," 25.9.7; "de te, Fortuna, ut inclementi querebatur," 31.8.8. See Naudé, 83: "By far the most common occurrences in Ammianus are of *fortuna* personalized as the hostile and unpredictable power." The excursus on glorious *genii*, 21.14.3–5.

signs of aversion to her, there is reason to refuse this specific abstraction a temple within the personal array of Ammianus' deities.

Iustitia joins Fatum and Fortuna in its frequency of appearance and, emotional invocations notwithstanding, absence of explicit cult. It is distinguished from them, however, in establishing contact with three of Ammianus' most important gods, the supreme Numen, Adrasteia, and Themis. Two passages dealing with Iustitia's punishment of Valens and the *Magister officiorum*, Remigius, reveal its connection with Numen and Adrasteia:

> The unsleeping eye of Justice, the eternal judge and avenger of deeds, watched searchingly. For the last curses of those who were cut down, moving the eternal Godhead by the very just reason of their groans, set fire to the torches of Bellona so that the truth of the oracle was confirmed: no crime would go unpunished. . . .
>
> While Africa suffered one catastrophe after another and the souls of the Tripolitan envoys were still wandering without revenge, the eternal power of Justice, the sometimes slow but piercing inquisitor of right and wrong, avenged them in this way.[28]

In these we will recognize several links with the excursus on Adrasteia: the vigilance of the supreme Numen, Adrasteia's delayed or occasional activity, and her role as judge.[29] Of course, Ammianus titles her the *filia Iustitiae* where it is understood that Iustitia represents his supreme diety.[30] As for Themis, she shares in, or receives power from, Jupiter just as Adrasteia participates in Iustitia-Numen. Iustitia's timely revelation of the Gothic plot to capture Hadrianople, *quod ipsa indicante Iustitia publicatum est*,[31] recalls, moreover, that job of releasing prophecy that Ammianus has assigned to Themis. Considering that Adrasteia and Themis do not elsewhere appear in the *Res gestae* outside of their respective excursuses, we may choose to regard Iustitia as a surrogate for them within the narrative portion of the text. But its prime duty probably lies not so much in representing two intermediate deities as in summoning up the supreme Numen itself, a view encouraged by their joint share in "perpetual vigor."[32]

---

28. 29.2.20, 30.2.9.
29. *Vigilavit attente*, 29.2.20: *vigilavit utrubique superni numinis aequitas*, 14.11.24. *Aliquotiens serus*, 30.2.9: *aliquotiens operatur*, 14.11.25. *Arbitra . . . rerum*, 29.2.20: *arbitra rerum*, 14.11.26.
30. See above, p. 12, n. 8.
31. 31.15.7.
32. Iustitia: *perpetuus . . . vigilavit*, 29.2.20; *sempiternus vigor*, 30.2.9. Numen-Jupiter:

When moving our discussion of Ammianus' divinities away from his personifications and into the nonabstract gods, we may be tempted to start immediately with the humble *genii* given to all men and ascend steadily through more important gods until we stand with Numen at the summit. But an interesting gathering of creatures would then be missed, for guardian spirits are not the only divine beings that cling to the soul:[33]

> During these humiliations, even when nature should have tendered him [Gallus Caesar] the truce of sleep, his senses were continually slashed by terror as his victims' ghosts surrounded him in a shrieking mob led by Domitianus and Montius—he was grabbed, or so he thought in his dreams, and they kept trying to shove him onto the claws of the Furies. For a soul freed from bodily connections and the waking thoughts and cares that disturb mortal minds is always tirelessly in motion and gathers nocturnal visions which we call *phantasiai*.[34]

These are the *larvae, imagines, visa,* and *manes inulti,* who attach themselves to the soul like *genii,* but not for life; their duration there is fleeting. Like *genii,* too, they dispense a special type of admonishment, and their participation in Themis' communication of Fate through the "fixed and certain trustworthiness of dreams" may also be said to give specters a share in teaching *maiora.*[35] If by a pure life one gained assistance from his *genius,* then the vulnerability of the soul to threatening or, if lucky, benign visions provided an additional reason to keep the soul pure. This is the lesson of Gallus' haunting: mortal actions determined *fata,* which in their turn were the ultimate source of these nocturnal encounters. A good life should act as some brake upon those *imagines* that were actually *terrores.*

Ammianus' specters, then, are not simply dramatic props but grounded securely within his general theology. His belief is real. Gallus' fear of *larvae* is matched by Constantius' terror at *nocturnae imagines,*

---

vigilavit utrubique, 14.11.24; *motu semper et ubique vigens,* 21.1.8; *vigoris vivifici,* 21.1.8. Cf. the soul, *semper vigens motibus indefessis,* 14.11.18.

33. *Quibus primordiis hi genii animis conexi mortalium,* 21.14.5.

34. "Inter haec tamen per indutias naturae conquiescentis sauciabantur eius sensus circumstridentium terrore larvarum interfectorumque catervae Domitiano et Montio praeviis correptum eum, ut existimabat in somniis, uncis furialibus obiectabant. Solutus enim corporeis nexibus animus semper vigens motibus indefessis ex cogitationibus subiectis et curis, quae mortalium sollicitant mentes, colligit visa nocturna quae phantasias nos appellamus," 14.11.17–18.

35. 21.1.12; for oneiromancy, see *De mys.,* 3.2. "[Genii] docentque maiora, si senserint puras et a colluvione peccandi immaculata corporis societate discretas," 21.14.5.

which in fact introduces the excursus on *genii*. This is the medium of the Furies, whom the historian identifies with *imagines*.[36] Nor are specters only private afflictions, for the entire city of Antioch was haunted before the battle at Hadrianople: "Beyond these signs of Valens's imminent death, the ghostly image of the King of Armenia and the wretched shades of those killed a little while before in the affair of Theodorus afflicted many during the night with ominous fears as they screeched out the horrifying verses of their laments."[37] These, it should be noted, are among those signs that Ammianus explicitly refers to the "clear evidence of omens and portents."[38] Although Julian listened to the favorable prophecy of a shining *imago* in Gaul,[39] this too was a nocturnal image connected with death, that of Constantius. As such incidents steadily accumulate over the course of the *Res gestae*, we cannot avoid the impression that Ammianus himself must have been genuinely in awe, or afraid, of specters variously associated with the dead. This is evident from his repeated references to necromancy: Sapor's consultation with Tartareal shades; Maximinus' Sardinian conjuror "extremely well versed in calling forth evil spirits and exciting prophecies from the ghosts of the dead"; the tribune Numerius' evocation of infernal shades; Paulus' prosecution of any trivial offense as if the accused were a *veneficus* "gathering horrors from tombs and the empty, garish costumes of the souls that walk there."[40] In his commentary on the *Somnium Scipionis* of Cicero, Macrobius thinks that it is safe to deny the realm of prophecy to some kinds of apparition.[41] In the divine world of Ammianus, however, there can be no such limit on the night.

Just beyond these animated cartoons, which flick menacingly upon the surfaces of divine and human substance, are their benign counter-

36. As in the *uncis furialibus* above; "[Peleus] horrendis furiarum imaginibus raptaretur," 22.16.3.
37. 31.1.3.
38. 31.1.1.
39. "Item cum apud Viennam postea quiesceret sobrius, horrore medio noctis imago quaedam visa splendidior hos ei versus heroos modo non vigilanti aperte edixit eadem saepius replicando," 21.2.2.
40. "Consilia tartareis manibus miscens et superstitiones omnes consulens de futuris," 18.4.1; "eliciendi animulas noxias et praesagia sollicitare larvarum perquam gnarum," 28.1.7; "intempestive partu extracto infernis manibus excitis de permutatione imperii consulere ausus est," 29.2.17; "ut veneficus sepulchrorumque horrores et errantium ibidem animarum ludibria colligens vana," 19.12.14.
41. *Commentarii in somnium Scipionis*, ed. J. Willis (Leipzig, 1963), 1.3.3, "Ultima ex his duo cum videntur, cura interpretationis indigna sunt, quia nihil divinationis adportant, ἐνύπνιον dico et φάντασμα." On *phantasmata* as deceptive imitations of reality, see *De mys.*, 2.10.

parts living in the realm of true *numina*, guardian spirits. Considering their many appearances, together with Ammianus' sincere belief in their existence, we must study them seriously as well. The correct starting point is the excursus on *genii* that follows Constantius' feeling that some vague presence was no longer with him:

> For theologians assert that certain divinities of this sort are joined to all men at birth to be, as it were, helmsmen of their acts, although they leave the bonds of Fate untouched. But only a few men of manifold virtue have actually seen them. And this, oracles and illustrious authors have taught, among whom we find the comic poet Menander who has written these two *senarii*: "By each man a spirit is placed / When first he is, guide of his life." So too it is given to be understood by the eternal songs of Homer that celestial gods themselves did not speak with those brave men, or stand by them, or help them when they fought, but rather their own guiding spirits. Confiding in their remarkable aid shone Pythagoras, it is said, and Socrates, Numa Pompilius, Scipio the Elder, and, as some judge, Marius, Octavian, who was first honored with the title of Augustus, Hermes Thrice-Greatest, Apollonius of Tyana, and Plotinus. The last of these ventured to give certain inspired opinions on this subject and to demonstrate in a profound manner by what primordial essences these spirits are connected with the souls of mortals and how, just as if clasping souls to their breasts, they watch over them and, as far as it is permitted, show them greater things if they feel that their wards are pure, free from wrong, and living in a stainless relationship with the body.[42]

Here Ammianus again reveals his interest in elemental connections, special behavior with respect to deities, or placation, and the transmission of *fata*. Man's necessarily continuous link with the gods and Fate, Heimarmene, is contrasted to the discontinuous nature of his moral or intellectual chain.[43] The presence of such rigid and flexible connections ensures a securely defined divine hierarchy that can yet offer the

---

42. "Ferunt enim theologi in lucem editis hominibus cunctis salva firmitate fatali huiusmodi quaedam velut actus rectura numina sociari admodum tamen paucissimis visa, quos multiplices auxere virtutes. Idque et oracula et auctores docuere praeclari, inter quos est etiam Menander comicus, apud quem hi senarii duo leguntur: ἅπαντι δαίμων ἀνδρὶ / συμπαρίσταται / εὐθὺς γενομένῳ, μυσταγωγὸς τοῦ βίου. Itidem . . . sempiternis Homeri carminibus intellegi datur non deos caelestes cum viris fortibus collocutos nec affuisse pugnantibus vel iuvisse, sed familiares genios cum isdem versatos, quorum adminiculis freti praecipuis Pythagoras enituisse dicitur et Socrates Numaque Pompilius et superior Scipio et, ut quidam existimant, Marius et Octavianus, cui Augusti vocabulum delatum est primo, Hermesque Termaximus et Tyaneus Apollonius atque Plotinus ausus quaedam super hac re disserere mystica alteque monstrare, quibus primordiis hi genii animis conexi et quod licitum est, docentque maiora, si senserint puras et a colluvione peccandi immaculata corporis societate discretas," 21.14.3–5.

43. See above, pp. 12, 15.

variety of personal responses appropriate to Iustitia: the supreme Deity issues different verdicts as men commit themselves to virtuous or vicious actions.[44] *Primordia* is our key to the physical basis of the *genii*, and this term is clearly related to the *elementa* controlled by Adrasteia and Themis.[45] The *genii* are also representatives of Ammianus' *substantiales potestates*, but we should carefully note that they are only one type of the latter. For all deities in his cosmos, both high and low, consist of substance in varying degrees of refinement; *substantialis* must denote an entire family, not a species as Ensslin thought.[46] In the same vein, when the historian claims that *genii* assisted the Homeric heroes instead of *dii caelestes*, this assertion is bound by one particular, historical if you will, context. It is not identical to a claim that divinities that are not *genii* do not or cannot project themselves onto the earth.[47]

If *genii* are inevitably connected to men at birth, further contacts are limited by the specific character of the individual; the greater his virtue, the more assistance he will receive. The Homeric heroes, *viri fortes*, were particularly great men and so possessed remarkably active relationships with their *genii*. On the other hand, Constantius, an emperor of consid-

44. Ammianus believed that the Creator and His universe were just even if frequently undecipherable to human wit, the failing of *hominum coniectura*, 21.1.14. Fortuna is accordingly no *true* part of the divine apparatus but only a sign for that screen which separates men from the comprehension of thoroughly rational and appropriate *fata*. On divine justice, see *De mys.*, 4.4–5; so too on the reconciliation of Fate with the presence of a guardian spirit, 9.2–3.

45. The historian's choice of *primordia* over *elementa* in this particular context may have been made out of consideration for the association of men with their *genii* at birth, *primo*. Despite his suggestive allusion to a more thorough discussion of these *primordia* by Plotinus, the latter does not describe the nature of such connections as a distinct topic per se in that portion of the *Enneads* (ed. P. Henry and H.-R. Schwyzer [Oxford, 1964], 3.4) specifically given to guardian spirits. There Plotinus' concern lies more obviously with the moral growth of the soul than the elemental modes of articulation between soul, body, and demon to which Ammianus draws attention.

46. See p. 14 above. This simple picture of Jupiter with his single block of *substantia* from which he strikes off gods and men, ether, the other elements, and so forth is an accurate rendering of Ammianus' particular universe. See God's division of substance in the *Hermetica*, *Libellus* 3, 1b–3a, 8, 3–4. The richly, or fiendishly if you will, schematic world of the Platonic philosophers would, of course, be something far different. The apparent absence of supracosmic Intelligibles and One in the *Res gestae* will be discussed below, pp. 33–34.

47. See Mars's aid to Fabricius, 24.4.24, where the question remains distinctly open: "Existimabatur Mars ipse, si misceri hominibus numina maiestatis iura permittunt." In a famous incident, *Vita Plotini* (*Enneads*), 10, the guardian spirit of Plotinus was summoned forth by an Egyptian priest. To everyone's shock, a god appeared rather than a demon. On this subject of epiphanies and the *dōra* men might expect from them, see *De mys.*, 2.6 and 2.9. For an assessment of two different but complementary views of the relation between demons and gods, see Rochefort, "La Démonologie de Saloustios," 53–61.

erably less virtue, merely had an obscure impression of something.[48] To those who strive for moral purity, *genii* teach *maiora*, an exchange that is but another variety of that process of supplication by which Themis conveys *vaticina verba* through properly placated divinities. The variable assistance of the *genius* thus becomes one way of representing a man's responsibility for his own fate. Like Themis, the *genius* holds offerings, *maiora*, which can contribute to greater harmony between men and the divine decrees they receive, but this instruction must be actively sought, partly at least, along cultic paths.

The historian offers a very favorable assessment of *genii* in his excursus, but to what degree do we find it realized within the work as a whole? *Genii* appear to three emperors. Both Constantius and Valentinian receive theirs as *omina mortis*, while Julian twice sees the *Genius publicus*, first in order to receive its exhortation to seize his approaching opportunity and then to watch it depart, grieving, on the night before he died.[49] Only one of these four appearances is actually benign, and in fact they better suggest our earlier incidents of menacing nocturnal specters. If use and theory seem out of balance in this respect, however, Ammianus' criterion of personal virtue is yet discernible. Only the three most prominent emperors in the extant narrative receive *genii*. Gallus, Jovian, Procopius, and Valens, all undistinguished or badly so, do not. Of the former group, the best alone, Julian, receives positive encouragement, and that his *genius* is made identical to that of the public weal can only be regarded as a particularly outstanding honor. The difference be-

---

48. On the occasion of the accidental death of a personal enemy, Amphilochius, which Constantius believed he had foreseen, Ammianus ridicules the emperor's pretension to sacred understanding: "unde Constantius ut futurorum quoque praescius exsultabat," 21.6.3. Of course we already know, 21.2.2, that a shining specter has foretold Constantius' own death to Julian in the clearest terms, even using epic verses. When at the Hippodrome of Constantinople Amphilochius fell through that railing opposite the emperor, to whom did prophecy speak?

49. "Namque et nocturnis imaginibus terrebatur. . . . post haec confessus est [Constantius] iunctioribus proximis, quod tamquam desolatus secretum aliquid videre desierit, quod interdum affuisse sibi squalidius aestimabat," 21.14.1–2; "nocteque, quam lux ereptura eum vita secuta est, ut per quietem solet, videbat [Valentinianus] coniugem suam absentem sedere passis capillis amictu squalenti contectam; quam aestimari dabatur Fortunam eius esse cum taetro habitu iam discessuram," 30.5.18–19. "Nocte tamen, quae declarationis Augustae praecesserat diem, iunctioribus proximis rettulerat [Iulianus] imperator per quietem aliquem visum, ut formari Genius publicus solet," 20.5.10; "obscuro noctis altitudine sensus cuiusdam philosophi teneretur [Iulianus], vidit squalidius ut confessus est proximis, speciem illam Genii publici . . . , velata cum capite cornucopia per aulea tristius discedentem," 25.2.3.

tween this distinct vision and the squalid thing of Constantius' experience is in harmony with their contrasting virtues.[50]

On the edge of combat near Strasbourg, Julian's men felt themselves drugged with the presence of his *genius:*

> Grinding their teeth and showing their eagerness to fight by pounding their lances upon their shields, they kept pleading to be led against the enemy who was now in plain sight, strengthened by the favor of heavenly God, their own self-confidence, and the proven talents of their well-omened leader. And, as the event showed, there was some guardian spirit standing by, whenever he was present, that kept compelling them to battle.[51]

Here finally is a straightforward case of divine assistance involving a tutelary *genius:* two divinities, supreme and subordinate, cooperate with a mortal. Moreover, Julian's explicit connection with the ancient heroic spirits[52] brings him into precise alignment with those Homeric *viri* to whom Ammianus refers in the excursus on *genii*. But in order to find the example that best enunciates the historian's theory of benign guardian spirits, we then must seem to leave behind those instances, oddly enough, in which *genii* make themselves most explicitly perceptible as *imagines*. This could mean that Ammianus, although personally enthusiastic about the gifts of a genius *praesens* that flowed invisibly from the unique character or genius, *ingenium,* of a general on the battlefield, in fact responded with some aversion to *genii* as fully emerged divinities to be seen, *visa*.

Let Julian be our mystagogue for the rest of Ammianus' deities up to the highest. He attracts gods, and we are perhaps already beginning to sense that this is to be his chief glory. Julian is the religious hero of the *Res gestae,* by which I mean specifically that even if Ammianus neither accepts that emperor's personal mix of cult nor its public implementation, he yet esteems him as a champion of Rome who conscientiously strove to define his achievements and *imperium* according to the *cultus deorum*. Seen in this way, the emperor's life itself must be an *indicium,* a

---

50. And intellects. No wonder that Constantius with his *ingenium obtunsum,* 21.16.4, could not "see" as well as his philosophically adept cousin. See above, p. 22, n. 48.

51. 16.12.13.

52. *Heroicis connumerandus ingeniis,* 25.4.1; cf. Julian's deployment of his troops in a *Homerica dispositio* outside Ctesiphon, 24.6.9.

light falling upon a series of gods that unifies and draws attention to them: in Gaul—Hercules, Mercury, and Bellona; at Pessinus—Mater; in Antioch—Venus, Apollo Daphnaeus, Zeus Casius, Apis, the urban Genius, and Apollo Palatinus; during the Persian expedition—Luna, Apollo Palatinus and Mater again, Mars Ultor, Jupiter, and Mars again. His imperial journey forms in effect a cultic spine within the *Res gestae*, which spreads obvious points of attachment toward other references to the same deities, many of which are alive with ominous intensity.

Julian is, for example, quite clearly joined with the hero and god, Hercules, fighting tyranny and savagery on behalf of civilization. The excursus on Gaul, which immediately follows Julian's appointment as Caesar, speaks of the ancient overthrow of Geryon and Tauriscus by Hercules, together with his construction of the port at Monaco and a road through the Alps.[53] Such references prefigure Julian's good works in the prefecture: an end to Gaul's suffering from barbarians and the misrule (tyranny) of Constantius. When hurrying to Constantinople after the death of his cousin, Julian passes through one of Hercules' famous foundations, Perinthus (Heraclea).[54] Hercules and the Argonauts appear several times again in the Black Sea excursus that preludes Julian's departure for Antioch—where some of his critics are in fact called Pygmies around a Hercules.[55] As the emperor shifts his victorious struggles from west to east, the historian is seen to present Julian, and successors worthy of him, with a heroic, divine mandate to fight in that direction. It would be a serious mistake in these instances to underrate or rather write off the power of *exemplum*, adopting that negative and anach-

---

53. *Saevum tyrannorum perniciem*, 15.9.6, 10.9. Libanius, as we might expect, himself draws Julian into the Herculean ethos: Julian followed the choice and path of Hercules, Oration 12.28, *Opera Libanii*, ed. R. Foerster (Leipzig, 1909–27). In Gaul he was Hercules serving a lesser man, ibid., 44; suffering people everywhere—including Libanius—invoked him as they did Hercules, 15.36, 47; 18.186. Bowder (*Age of Constantine*, 118) refers to coins of Julian minted at Arles and Siscia, which bear the eagle of Jupiter or, of special interest to us, the club of Hercules as part of their mint marks. As Bowder suggests, these evoke the ruler symbolism of the Tetrarchs, Jovius and Herculius.

54. 22.2.3; "quam Hercules conditam Perinthi comitis sui memoriae dedicavit," 22.8.5. See Julian's Herculean restoration of Gallic Heraclea (Castra Herculis, *R.G.* 18.2.4), Libanius, 18.87.

55. Diomedes, 22.8.3; Perinthus, founded by Hercules, 5; Amycus, the tyrant overthrown by Pollux, 14; Harpies, 14; Symplegades, 15; tomb of Sthenelus, Hercules' comrade, 22; the "Pygmies" of Antioch, 22.12.4. On the peculiar religious signification of the *Argonautica* for contemporaries, see Geffcken, *The Last Days*, 188: "Now, in this late period, Orphic poetry made another advance upon epic poetry. It took up the *Argonautica* of the Alexandrian poet Apollonius and attempted, by giving a leading part to Orpheus, who in the *Argo* appears only incidentally, to endow the epic with a spiritual and mystical content."

ronistic modern view that tends to oppose a living present to an ever more deadened or deadening past. By this theory of receding vitality, "Hercules" ought to mean not much more than a name scratched in wax to please some *grammaticus*. That response of course will hardly do justice to the great tensions that the past exerted upon those who read about the triumphs of their illustrious fellow competitors, men or gods, in the *agōn* of great deeds. Could Julian be another Hercules; would *he* overthrow tyrants and liberate peoples?[56] Ammianus continually goads with his *exempla* at that ever raw nerve of *aemulatio*, for Romans, never healing, and we must feel the argumentative line of the *Res gestae* grow stronger in intelligibility as it flexes between (far) past and present.

The textual currents flowing between narrative and excursus, present and past, and man and god, strengthen the vitality of two more divine Argonauts as well, the Castores. Pollux ends the *saevitia* of the tyrant Amycus,[57] while Castor and he both reach out through the medium of cult to free Rome from a threatening famine, quieting natural rage:

> And soon by the decree of that divine Godhead which has given Rome increase from the moment of her birth and pledged that she should exist forever, tranquility stilled the sea while Tertullus sacrificed at the temple of Castor and Pollux in Ostia; and after the wind changed its direction to blow gently from the south, with full sails the ships entered the harbor and refilled the storehouses with grain.[58]

Although Mars and Bellona have conventionally been discounted as simple flourishes of rhetoric,[59] Julian's serious attention to both in Gaul and Persia[60] should warn against assuming such a low value out of hand. Consider two examples of apparently rhetorical usage, [*dirae*] *Bellonae accenderant faces* and *Martius furor incendio insolito miscendo cuncta concivit*. They point in fact to explicitly trustworthy omens: the wrath of Mars that would consume Valens—by fire—was precisely forecast by the seers Hilarius and Patricius;[61] Bellona's torches were lit at the Battle of Hadria-

---

56. See the final *comparatio*, or *aemulatio*, of Eunapius, *Fragmenta historicorum Graecorum*, ed. K. Mueller (Paris, 1841–72), fol. 23: no less than a god would have been required to succeed the dead Julian.
57. *Et Amyci saevitia Bebryces exempti virtute Pollucis*, 22.8.14.
58. 19.10.4.
59. Witte, "Ammianus Marcellinus," 42; Ensslin, *Ammianus Marcellinus*, 52; Thompson, *Historical Work*, 114; Camus, *Ammien Marcellin*, 144.
60. In Gaul, "placata ritu secretiore Bellona," 21.5.1; Persia, "complures hostias Marti parabat ultori," 24.6.17; "horroreque perfusus est, ne ita aperte minax Martis apparuerit sidus," 25.2.4.
61. Given twice, 29.1.33, 31.14.8.

nople, "so that the truth of the oracle was confirmed." The *minax Martis sidus* is certainly no gratuitous element from the viewpoint of religion when Ammianus himself wonders whether Mars might not appear on the earth—a true possibility in a cosmos of intimately connected *elementa*.[62] Whatever the cases of purely dramatic usage, it would be incorrect to deny that Bellona and Mars are cultic realities in the *Res gestae*. Gods of war are indeed as genuine a concern to Ammianus' heroic emperor, whom we shall soon meet at the obelisk of Rameses, as they are to the Alans.[63]

Another deity made ritually active by Julian is Mercury, who shares in Jupiter's vivifying role through the stimulation of minds—here, that of Julian—and as a *sensus* evokes those elemental connections between gods and men that encourage supplication of the substantial powers.[64] That the historian awards Julian with Mercury's emblem, the *caduceus*, is evidence of a particularly vital and successful relationship of this sort: "while he was on the earth, all its peoples remained at peace, moving nowhere to create a disturbance, as if some earthly *caduceus* were soothing them."[65] Mercury's authority in the *Res gestae* then stands firmly upon the twin validation of theology and cult.

Less benign is Venus, who appears twice in connection with Adonis: once during the funeral of Grumbates' son at Amida and again for Julian's inauspicious *adventus* at Antioch.[66] In both cases Ammianus states that the rites of the festival of Adonis symbolize the harvest, citing "mystic religions" as his authority on the earlier occasion and myth, *fabulae*, on the other. This emphasis upon teaching, *indicia*, has much to say to the credibility of the historian's traditional deities, for it is not his intent to reduce the importance of *mysticae religiones* by speaking symbolically but rather to enhance the connection between divine and hu-

62. See p. 21, n. 47.
63. "Sed gladius barbarico ritu humi figitur nudus eumque ut Martem regionum, quas circumcolunt, praesulem verecundius colunt," 31.2.23. Cf. the Scordisci, "Bellonae litantes et Marti," 27.4.4.
64. "Occulte Mercurio supplicabat, quem mundi velociorem sensum esse motum mentium suscitantem theologicae prodidere doctrinae," 16.5.5.
65. 25.4.14.
66. "Feminae vero miserabili planctu in primaevo flore succisam spem gentis solitis fletibus conclamabant, ut lacrimare cultrices Veneris saepe spectantur in sollemnibus Adonidis sacris, quod simulacrum aliquid esse frugum adultarum religiones mysticae docent," 19.1.1. "Evenerat autem isdem diebus annuo cursu completo Adonea ritu vetere celebrari, amato Veneris, ut fabulae fingunt, apri dente ferali deleto, quod in adulto flore sectarum est indicium frugum. Et visum est triste, quod amplam urbem principiumque domicilium introeunte imperatore tunc primum ululabiles undique planctus et lugubres sonus audiebantur," 22.9.15.

man activity. Such symbols would be valueless without their divine bases, and Venus is surely one of these.[67] Ultimately, it is the gods themselves who are teaching through religion. When Julian arrived at Antioch during this festival—the pivotal moment of his religious career—he was surrounded by an *indicium* of his own approaching death *in adulto flore*, a sign that in its truth yet confirmed, if ironically, the not-to-be-ignored life and power of Venus.

But it is Julian's contact with Apollo that carries us to the most abundant source of religious connections. Given Ammianus' great esteem for the *munera divinandi* and his anxiety over Rome's present failure to maintain proper—that is, imperially supported—communication with the gods,[68] it can hardly be surprising that the chief Greco-Roman god of prophecy permeates the history. His shrines appear often—at Delphi, the Palatine Hill, Daphne, Tenedos, and Seleucia.[69] Delos is "famous for the birth of gods," and the rites once used by the Athenians to purify it were later employed by Julian at Daphne. Moreover, important omens are associated with these temples. The burning of the Palatine and Daphnaean shrines—remembering too that unfavorable reply of the Sibylline Books kept in the former—were warnings to Julian that he entered Persia *nondum pace numinum exorata*.[70] Ammianus significantly ends his description of the fire at Daphne with two other disasters from that same year, a serious drought and now the total destruction of Nicomedia by an earthquake.[71] Similarly, the looting of the Temple of Apollo Comaeus

---

67. Ammianus describes Paphos on Crete as famed for its temple of Venus, 14.8.14.

68. See his response to the monstrous birth reported at the Antiochene suburb of Daphne—remember, Ammianus was a native of Antioch: "This twisted birth warned that the State itself was turning into an unnatural organism. Portents of this type are frequently born beneath our eyes as signs of the outcome of various events, but because they are no longer investigated by ritual as our fathers used to do, they pass unheard of and unknown," 19.12.20.

69. Delphi: mentioned with regard to the trials of Paul, 19.12.15. The Palatine: the burning of the imperial chapel and repository of the Sibylline Books, 23.3.3; the translation there of the cult statue of Apollo Comaeus taken at Seleucia, 23.6.24. Daphne: the burning of the Temple of Apollo Daphnaeus, 22.13.1–3. Tenedos: the Temple of Apollo Smintheus mentioned in the Black Sea excursus, 22.8.3. Seleucia: the sack of Apollo's shrine by the men of Lucius Verus, 23.6.24.

70. "Eisdem diebus [before the expedition] nuntiatum est ei per litteras, Romae super hoc bello libros Sibyllae consultos, ut iusserat, imperatorem eo anno discedere a limitibus suis, aperto prohibuisse responso," 23.1.7. "Litteras tristes Sallusti Galliarum praefecti suscepit [at Cercusium] orantis suspendi expeditionem in Parthos obtestantisque, ne ita intempestive nondum pace numinum exorata irrevocabile subiret exitium," 23.5.4.

71. 22.13.4–5. Nicomedia had suffered an earthquake in 358, 17.7.1–8, and still not been repaired by the time Julian passed through his onetime home in 362, 22.9.3–5; he allotted a generous sum of money for its restoration.

at Seleucia by the soldiers of Lucius Verus (its cult statue was reerected within the Palatine temple) brought a universal plague on the empire.

That the historian is actually hurling this last incident as a barbed *exemplum* into the differing natures of Julian and Constantius, the virtuous Marcus Aurelius and his undistinguished brother, Verus,[72] appears a particularly attractive possibility when we reflect upon Apollo's identification with a more recent plague, that at Amida: "many [Achaeans] died by the arrows of Apollo, who is reckoned as the Sun."[73] This statement from the accompanying excursus on *pestilentiae* is no throwaway line. *Piaculum*, the abuse of Apollo's priest, had originally brought on the Achaean plague, and in the case of Constantius we have a choice of such sins against traditional religion: the spoliation of temples by this emperor's *palatini* or, more directly, Constantius' culminating part in the theft of the obelisk of Sol by his father.[74] Ammianus makes the crime of Constantine stand in contrast to the reverence for the same monument shown by Augustus, Apollo's most distinguished imperial patron and he who was responsible for removing the Sibylline Books to his Palatine temple.[75] From the later books of the *Res gestae* we will note other Apollo-

---

72. See above, p. 23, n. 50. Julian and Gallus are explicitly paired with Titus and Domitian, 14.11.28.

73. 19.4.3.

74. "Pasti [palatini] enim ex his quidam templorum spoliis et lucra ex omni odorantes occasione," 22.4.3. "Verum Constantinus id parvi ducens [quod deo Soli speciali munere dedicatus] avulsam hanc molem sedibus suis nihilque committere in religionem, recte existimans, si ablato uno templo miraculum Romae sacraret, id est in templo mundi totius, iacere diu perpessus est," 17.4.3. Lest there by any confusion about the meaning of *recte existimans* in this context, Ammianus is *not* condoning Constantine's theft on the ground that, when all was said, the obelisk was now on its way to the Temple of the whole World. Rather, we have two sentiments: he thoroughly disapproves of the act; he *does* agree with Constantine's thought, and a very traditional one, that Rome was just such a lofty *templum*. Cf. Cambyses' spoliation of the temples at Thebes, *ne deorum quidem donariis parcens*, for which that Persian ruler paid with his life, 17.4.3–4 (Libanius, *Opera Libanii*, 17, 32). The lesson is clear: emperors like Constantine and Constantius are no better than Persian *latrones*. In a similar ascription of imperial calamities to imperial sins, Libanius, 24, 32, uses this same figure of Apollo's wrath against the Achaeans to describe how the East must continue to feel great disasters until Julian's murderer was found by Theodosius. Many years before, he had invoked the same sin when trying to assuage "the wrath of Achilles" against his fellow Antiochenes, 15, 33–34, and again before that identified himself with Apollo's outraged priest, Chryses, in his lament over the ruined temple of Apollo Daphnaeus, 60, 14. See below, pp. 117–19.

75. For Augustus, Apollo, and the Sibylline Books, see Liebeschuetz, *Continuity and Change*, 82–86; Boissier, *La religion Romaine*, 80–82; Bouché-Leclerque, *Histoire*, 4:286–317; Wissowa, *Religion und Kultus*, 537. After arranging for the transportation of the obelisk from Egypt, Constantine died: *quibus ita provisis, digressoque vita principe memorato*, 17.4.14. It is interesting to compare Ammianus' juxtaposition of this emperor's death with two similar presentations from Zosimus' *Historia nova*, ed. L. Mendelssohn (Leipzig, 1887), 4.36,

nian references in the accurately spoken fate of Valens cast in Pythian and Branchidaean verses. An oracular deity such as Apollo reaches out not only to mortals but to other gods as well; divination's traditional role as a broker between many deities should not be forgotten. Thus Mater acquires religious significance in the *Res gestae,* not only through Julian's pious attention to her at Pessinus, but also through the goddess' important connection with the Sibyllines[76] and Apollo, Rome's salvation through prophecy.[77] By means of such extended ramification then, the historian creates a thoroughly vital divine identity.

Apollo leads naturally to Sol, the *Mens mundi,* source of mortal minds and of the flames within the Sibyls.[78] We are again in the presence of a *substantialis potestas* opened to cult. Although Ammianus once says very simply that Apollo is the Sun, this oneness may be better understood as some collegiate relationship on the order of Julian's *mia dynasteia.*[79] Sol makes his most important contribution to the religious argument of the *Res gestae* through that obelisk raised in the Circus Maximus whose inscription—one of Ammianus' two surviving religious *documenta*[80]—makes Apollo the son of Sol and identifies him with King Rameses, recipient of Sol's gift of universal rule. This potent, holy monument is the greatest religious symbol of the history, for what it tells of the unequal relationship between Constantius and Julian, the donation of *imperium* to a pious (pagan) emperor, and a new meeting between

---

59: Gratian's rejection of the reverend title of *Pontifex maximus,* and Theodosius' alleged withdrawal of financial support from traditional cults, both of which are directly joined to notices of their deaths. Note again that it is earlier in this same excursus that Ammianus shows us Cambyses dying as his men plunder the temples of Thebes.

76. "Unde dextrorsus itinere declinato Pessinunta convertit visurus vetusta Matris Magnae delubra, a quo oppido bello Punico secundo carmine Cumano monente per Scipionem Nasicam translatum est Romam," 22.9.5.

77. Bouché-Leclerque's work is a handy compendium of information on the oracular deities mentioned by Ammianus: Apollo Branchos, pp. 229–48; Apollo Claros, pp. 249–55; Apollo Daphnaeus, pp. 267–69; Aesculapius, pp. 272–307; Serapis, pp. 381–88; Besa, pp. 394–95; Jupiter Casius, pp. 400–401; Dea Caelestis, pp. 410–11.

78. "Sol enim, ut aiunt physici, mens mundi nostras mentes ex sese velut scintillas diffunditans, cum eas incenderit vehementius, futuri conscias reddit, unde Sibyllae crebro se dicunt ardere torrente vi magna flammarum," 21.1.11.

79. *Works of Julian,* ed. C. Lacombrade, Oration 11, where Apollo is described as seated by Helios, 136a; elsewhere, as sharing in his thoughts, 149c, and ruling with him, 152d. "For this god too [Apollo] is with Helios and shares with him his thoughts, substance, and activities," 144a. In that inscription from the obelisk of Rameses which Ammianus cites, Apollo (Rameses) is referred to as the All-radiant Son of Helios, 17.4.20. Cf. Themis sharing in the bed and throne of Jupiter, 21.1.8.

80. The other being Hilarius' complete description of that unlucky rite by which he and his fellow seer, Patricius, revealed the name of Valens's supposed successor, Theodorus, 29.1.29–33.

Egyptian and Roman religion—the Serapeum that comes to the Capitolium[81]—cannot be matched elsewhere in the text. The taint of Constantine's *piaculum*, so different from the piety of Augustus,[82] descended to his son who gained no benefit from erecting the obelisk in Rome: its acroterial orb was struck by sacred lightning[83] and replaced with a torch, an act symbolizing not only Sol's rule over the world but Constantius' own replacement by the true torchbearer, Apollo and Rameses, Julian, he who was "chosen for Mars."[84] Later Constantius would dream that a child took his orb.[85] The inscription itself fulfills the function of a theological document or rather that of an oracle that speaks for an earthly and a heavenly Heliopolis. One city is a solar pantheon,[86] the other is an *imperium*, or city, of the world, Sol's gift to an emperor known as his son and Apollo, who will honor the gods.[87] Here Ammianus summons a

81. "In addition to these monuments [at Alexandria] there are temples breathed upwards to lofty roofs where the Serapeum stands preeminent. Words only weakly convey the impression made by its vast columned spaces, living statues, and crowd of other adornments, so that, with the exception of the Capitolium through which venerable Rome exalts herself unto eternity, the world knows nothing so magnificent," 22.16.12.

82. "Discant, qui ignorant, veterem principem translatis aliquibus hunc intactum ideo praeterisse, quod deo Soli speciali munere dedicatus [obeliscus] fixusque intra ambitiosi templi delubra, quae contingi non poterant, tamquam apex omnium eminebat," 17.4.12.

83. *Vi ignis divini contacta*, 17.4.15; cf. the earthquake at Nicomedia, *dein velut numine summo fatales contorquente manubias*, 17.7.3.

84. Cf. *tamquam apex omnium eminebat*, 17.4.12. Apollo leads on Julian in Libanius, e.g., 12, 62, who also makes him Ares, ibid., 45.

85. "Nondum penitus mersus in somnum umbram viderat patris obtulisse pulchrum infantem eumque susceptum et locatum in gremio suo excussam sibi proiecisse longius sphaeram, quam ipse dextra manu gestabat. Id autem permutationem temporum indicabat," 21.14.1. Cf. the similar *omen mortis* of Jovian, an orb falling from the hand of a statue of Galerius at Antioch, 25.10.2.

86. Ammon, Heron, Hephaestus, and Ares are also mentioned in the inscription.

87. A selection of significant excerpts from the inscription: "Helios to King Rameses: I have granted that you should rule over all the earth in joy, you whom Helios cherishes," 17.4.18; "[Mighty Apollo] who bestowed many gifts upon the gods settled in the city of Helios," 19; "[Mighty Apollo] who filled the temples with the fruits of the palm. . . . who guarded Egypt by conquering other nations," 20; "[Mighty Apollo] who erected statues of the gods in this realm of Egypt's lord, and he adorned the city of Helios just as he did Helios himself, the Lord of Heaven; he finished a worthy task, the child of Helios, ever living king," 21. That the king is specially chosen for Ares occurs four times, 18, 20, 22, 23. For a similar sort of Egyptian, didactic communiqué from god to king that is also expressed as a form of inscription, see the Hermetic *horoi* of Aesculapius to King Ammon, *Lib.* 16, where there is much on the Sun. Ammianus' esteem for Hermes Thrice-Greatest is plain from his presence on the list of particularly virtuous men who had been in close contact with their *genii*, 21.14.5. By the late fourth century, of course, Sol had been the special *comes* of many Roman emperors including Constantine. See Halsberghe, *Cult of Sol Invictus*, and especially Nock, "Emperor's Divine *Comes*," 108, 114–15. Studying the Neopla-

new Golden Age, the *gens aurea* of Apollo, as once did his own revered prophet Virgil.[88]

There has never been any difficulty in locating a candidate for the highest place in Ammianus' hierarchy. This is the anonymous, explicitly supreme Numen, also to be identified with a similarly anonymous Deus.[89] Both terms appear most frequently in connection with imperial speeches.[90] By whatever criterion one uses, this Numen-Deus, to be referred to hereafter simply as Numen, participates fully within the text and can only have been intended by Ammianus to represent a genuine deity. But even if that is true, what remains of the god's character beyond this point is scarcely transparent. What, precisely, is the kind of supremacy with which we are dealing?[91]

To proceed straightaway to the anonymous, transcendental One of the Neoplatonists, while ignoring Jupiter's claim, would be rash, for the historian surrounds the revered Father of the Gods with theology,

---

tonists and Julian, Nock could find no evidence for any use of the Sun's preeminent position within the cosmos as an analogy for earthly monarchy: "he [Julian] says nothing of any intrinsic relationship of earthly kingship to Helios." Perhaps Ammianus' inscription is such a guide.

88. *Eminentissimus vates*, 31.4.6; *Eclogue* 4, 8–10: "Tu modo nascenti puero [cf. *Heliou pais*, above, and Julian as a *pulcher infans*, taking the orb from Constantius], quo ferrea primum / desinet ac toto surget gens aurea mundo, / casta fave Lucina: tuus iam regnat Apollo." *Aeneid* 6, 791–93: "Hic vir, hic est tibi quem promitti saepius audis, / Augustus Caesar, Divi genus, aurea condet / saecula." See Liebeschuetz, *Continuity and Change*, 55–100, on the Augustan religious revival; additionally, Boissier, *Religion Romaine*, 79–80, for Mars Ultor, the other deity particularly associated with Augustus' patronage.

89. *Summum*, 15.8.9, 21.13.14. See Ensslin's discussion of Numen-Deus, *Ammianus Marcellinus*, 48–51.

90. Constantius in Rauracum, *secunda numinis voluntate*, 14.10.12; at Milan, appointing Julian as Caesar, *arbitrium summi numinis, prosperante deo, nutu dei caelestis, deus modo velit*, 15.8.9–14; in Sarmatia, *si placuerit numini sempiterno, deumque ex usu testata*, 17.13.28, 33; at Nicopolis, *favore summi numinis*, 21.13.14. Julian: at Strasbourg, *pace dei, caelestis dei favore*, 16.12.12, 13; at Vienne, *arbitrio dei caelestis*, 21.5.3; near Dura, *adiumento numinis sempiterni*, 23.5.19. Valentinian: at Amiens, appointing Gratian as co-Augustus, *deo spondente, propitia caelestis numinis . . . voluntas*, 27.6.6, 8. Other occurrences of Numen and Deus: the execution of Gallus, *superni numinis aequitas*, 14.11.24; the victory at Strasbourg, *favore superni numinis*, 16.12.62; the siege of Amida, *caeleste numen*, 19.1.4; the excursus on divination, *benignitas numinis*, 21.1.9; the capture of Anatha, *dei caelestis . . . curam*, 24.1.12; the Persians' unexpected move to parley with Jovian, *numen dei caelestis aeternum*, 25.7.5; provincial bishops, *perpetuo numini*, 27.3.15; Count Theodosius' capture of Conta, *magni numinis adiumento*, 29.5.40.

91. MacMullen, *Paganism*, 88: "We must confront the very term 'monotheism.' Like most big words, and '-isms' worst of all, it is no friend to clear thought. It indicates acknowledgement of one god only. Very good. But it suggests no definition of 'god.'"

temples, legends, important connections to the heroic Julian, and overall, obvious respect. Constantius' tour of Rome's great monuments begins with his wonder at the Temple of Tarpeian Jupiter, "towering as divine things do over those that are earthly."[92] Within the Egyptian excursus, Ammianus praises the Capitolium "through which venerable Rome exalts herself unto eternity."[93] The shrine of Zeus on Mount Casius achieves prominence in the *Res gestae* through Julian, not just because he, Ammianus' chief pagan, worships there, but for the more interesting reason that this is his only act of cult in Antioch that receives the historian's entire approval. Julian prays to Zeus, forgives an enemy (Theodotus), and immediately receives a good omen; a letter arrives reporting that the long-sought Apis Bull is found, oracular symbol of plenty. Clearly this happy result must reflect upon not only the emperor's virtue but also the god's.[94] When Julian later swore by Jupiter after his marred sacrifice to Mars Ultor, we are explicitly told that he did not swear in vain.[95] Along another strand in this skein of references to Jupiter lies Julian's burial at Tarsus, a city bound by tradition to this god's own son, the hero Perseus.[96] This is a good example of the way in which references from all quarters of the work, narrative and digression both, lend religious vitality to one another. Thus the portrait of a god, and a religion, overspreads its immediate scene, gaining in depth while denying a complete surface to the observer in any single reference.

Jupiter's status rises as we pursue the cultic implications of Numen's anonymity. Despite those many invocations of Numen in the course of imperial speeches, such vague references do not indicate any specific cultic apparatus—a drawback for the social intelligibility of a god: where do his worshippers pray; what ritual do they use? Quintus Aurelius Symmachus may have argued that there was more than one way to the "great secret"; he did *not* say that the ways themselves were therefore unimportant, that cultic paths could be dispensed with in the pursuit of deity: "Each has his own custom and ritual: the Divine Mind has allotted the various cults to be guardians over their cities."[97] But Numen never

92. 16.10.14.
93. 22.16.12.
94. 22.14.4–6. Cf. a similar proof of divine vitality, or the continued relevance of traditional deities, in connection with Venus, pp. 44–45. Theodotus, an ex-governor, was a virulent partisan of Constantius and had asked that the emperor give him the head of Julian.
95. *Nec resecravit celeri morte praereptus*, 24.6.17.
96. 14.8.3. Cf. Julian's *heroicum ingenium*, 25.4.1.
97. From his plea on behalf of Rome's pagan nobles that Valentinian restore the altar of Victory to the senate house, *Relatio* 3, sec. 8, ed. O. Seeck (Berlin, 1883). See Barrow's usefully annotated text and translation of this letter in *Prefect and Emperor*, 32–47.

offers this kind of precision—no one sacrifices at a temple of nondescript Numen—and imperial invocations notwithstanding, the term by itself leaves something out of our grasp. Those who have reconstructed Ammianus' religion about a predominantly philosophical matrix, satisfied with the result of "vague monotheism," have perhaps unconsciously absorbed some measure of their Neoplatonic exemplars' aloofness from public religion.[98] For few, certainly not those who believed in *ritus* as *custodes urbis*, could dialectic, contemplation, and assent make a whole religion. However much Ammianus appreciates philosophy, he exhibits no sign of that sort of *autarkeia;* he loved the temples. If the historian's frequently alleged monotheism appears vague and detached, this is not the case at all when we examine his presentation of traditional polytheism. To bring our portrait of Numen to completion then, we should look for some cultic complement, and one lies very close at hand in Ammianus' several references to Jupiter.[99] Stated in other words, if someone had asked the historian where specifically he should go to worship Numen, Ammianus would most probably have responded by pointing to a temple of Jupiter or Zeus.

There still remains the question of theological parity, whether Jupiter, for all his cultic attractiveness, might have been for the historian simply a cultic stepping-stone to a higher *summum Numen*. Zeus was commonly regarded as a cosmic Demiurge operating at the behest of a transcendental Monad, the One, and below the hypercosmic Intelligible Deities.[100] But this status was not necessarily fixed. In several Middle Platonic theologies the Demiurge was not distinguished from the supreme god.[101] The Hermeticists identify God with his creating, demiurgic activity to such a strong degree that it is often not clear when they mean to signify a subordinate Demiurge.[102] Porphyry asks how it is that Egyptian theology is built entirely about cosmic substances, *physika*, without

---

98. This philosophical detachment from public cult will be discussed in Chapter 4.

99. Consider that at Nicomedia, Numen shows itself hurling Jupiter's sacred lightning: *numine summo contorquente manubias*, 17.7.3; also that in the oath of Procopius' troops, *testati more militiae Iovem, invictum Procopium fore*, 26.7.17, Jupiter occupies that position in the formula otherwise reserved for Numen.

100. *Enneads*, 4.4.10, 5.1.7. In the *De mys.*, 8.3–4, the Demiurge appears like Ammianus' Jupiter as a *vigor vivificus* (*zōtikēn dynamin*) and a molder of living substance. Zeus is one of three cosmic, creating (*poiantes*) gods in *De deis*, 6.

101. Dillon (*Middle Platonists*, 254, 355) mentions those of Atticus, Moderatus of Gades, and Nicomachus of Gerasa. With respect to this enhancement of the role of the Demiurge, see *De mys.*, 8.4, where the Egyptians are said to place a new Demiurge anterior to the other one as its "father."

102. *Lib.* 11(ii), 17c: "For it is just as if it were the very essence of God to move everything and give it life" (cf. Ammianus' *vigor vivificus*); 9, 5: "God is the Demiurge of all"; 11(ii), 22a: "for nothing is invisible, not even that which is incorporeal."

allowing for those that are incorporeal [103]—the Demiurge is victor again. In various ways Jupiter might climb to the highest position within a divine hierarchy, Platonic or otherwise, and this realization lessens the security to be derived from applying the customary triplex division of deities to the *Res gestae*. Ammianus' many references to a specifically celestial Numen or Deus [104] may well mark it for the cosmically contained— but supreme—Demiurge, that is, Zeus. As for the Intelligibles, there is simply no sign of them in the text. Without distorting our evidence then, we have good reason to believe that in both theology and cult Jupiter was the historian's highest divinity. His terms *Numen* and *Deus* will subsequently stand best as innocuous synonyms courteously offered before a mixed audience of pagans and Christians. [105]

Looking along the band of divine faces that ends now with the freshly set *tesserae* of Jupiter, we have no doubt to whom the historian has given the most complexity and color: Apollo and Sol. Theirs is the cultic focus of the *Res gestae*. If this means, and by my system of textual measures it should, that Ammianus himself was particularly drawn to solar worship, [106] we will of course want to know what he might share with another *cultor Solis*, Julian. In the *Hymn to King Helios* the emperor connects the Sun with such divinities as the One, Zeus, Apollo, Aesculapius, Ares, and Serapis [107]—all, with the exception of the first, demonstrably impor-

---

103. *Epistola ad Anebonem*, 37, ed. G. Parthey (Berlin, 1857).

104. See above, p. 31, n. 90.

105. To a lesser degree, we may want to consider the possible influence of that literary convention whereby "God" was simply shorthand, a placeholder, for "any of the gods you, the *auditor*, wish to understand in this context." *Theos* is equivalent to *theōn tis* where, as Misson stated (*Recherche*, 40), "there is no reason to give one name or another." See chap. 2 of his work, "Le sens de ΘΕΟΣ," pp. 23–49. Misson (p. 67) observed that, after Zeus, the gods who most preoccupied Libanius were Apollo and Helios. Note the kindred emphases of Ammianus.

106. The Sun was commonly, and enthusiastically, associated with the Demiurge and made the peculiar emblem of God. In the *De mys.*, 7.2, 8.3, he appears as the helmsman of the cosmos and source of *physis*, ruling the elements and everything material. The Hermeticists are particularly strong in praise of Sol: *Lib.* 1, 6, Light is Mind, the first god; 5, 3, greatest of the gods in heaven; 16, 5–6, the Demiurge who brings down substance and leads up matter, the barb, *ongkos*, of intelligent substance (cf. Ammianus' *scintillae* and *Sibyllae*, 21.1.11). In such phrases as "the first god" and, *Lib.* 16, 16, "the sunbeam of God" there exist opportunities for confusion between the supreme Deity and his Demiurge similar to those which I discussed in connection with Jupiter. In the *Res gestae*, by contrast, we should note that Sol is never found acting in any symbolic capacity for another, loftier god, whether Jupiter or some nonsubstantial godhead.

107. *Works of Julian*, ed. C. Lacombrade, Oration 11: 132c–6a, 143d–44c, 149b, 153b.

tant to Ammianus. After the customary allusions to light's origin in Mind and the demiurgic functions of Helios, Julian describes the god's joint rule with Apollo, whose gifts of oracles, wisdom, laws, and colonies sown throughout the world—civilization—will recall similar impressions of heroic cult and the *munera divinandi* met in Ammianus. There is a particularly close correspondence where the emperor explains how Helios abides at Rome: if Zeus, the father of all things, dwells on its acropolis (the Capitolium) then Helios too, his dynastic colleague and he who holds the Palatine Hill as Apollo, must be honored as a founder of Rome. This felicitous and necessary presence of Sol in Rome is precisely what the historian himself communicates through the episode of the obelisk, and that symbolically struck orb on top of the monument even fastens a last link: Julian will be Rome's torchbearer. But such connections must be handled with restraint if we are to respect Ammianus' intellectual independence, for there are several reasons not to push him into Julian's religious corner. A similarly transcendent superstructure of Intelligible Deities and One does not of necessity exist within the *Res gestae*.[108] Egypt is a firm point of reference for the historian's conception of Sol, but Mithras, the special solar deity of Julian,[109] is not—an important difference. Mithras is entirely omitted from the history even where Julian's religious preoccupations are described. As for Egypt, the emperor says nothing here of that land's religion, priesthood, or special relations with Sol.[110]

A better parallel to the divine hierarchy found in Ammianus emerges from Julian's oration against the Cynic philosopher Heracleius. He rebukes his opponent for degenerate myth-making and retorts with an original myth about a child (himself) whom Zeus commanded to punish the impiety of a certain *plousios anēr* (Constantine) and his family.[111] Briefly put, the Father of the Gods consulted his son Helios about a remedy for this man's sins. When the Moirai were asked whether one was

---

108. For contrast, see Eunapius' history, f.11, where the Germans Cercio and Charietto are said to have come together in the same way as the Pythagorean Monad and Dyad. See the statement of Misson (pp. 82–83) that Libanius employed none of the elaborate, heliatric metaphysics of the Neoplatonists, "preferring not to venture with them to the summits."

109. Oration 11: 130c, 155b.

110. He refers three times to Egypt: a simple identification of Serapis with Hades (136a) and two allusions to Egyptian calendration (155a–b, 156b). Note Julian's claim for the kinship between Greek and Roman law (152d) and the way in which Ammianus brings Egypt into the story: "et Solon sententiis adiutus Aegypti sacerdotum latis iusto moderamine legibus Romano quoque iuri maximum addidit firmamentum," 22.16.22.

111. *Works of Julian*, ed. C. Lacombrade, Oration 7: 227c–34c.

permitted, they pledged their obedience to Dike and Hosiotes, who in their turn bowed to Zeus: "Then the Fates came to his side and allotted everything as their Father willed."[112] Helios, Hermes, and Athene were to nurture the avenging child, and Helios later told Julian how an illustrious reward would follow his victory when he, a god himself now, beheld the Father. For the coming struggle, Helios would give him a torch; Athene, a helmet and the Gorgon's head; Hermes, a golden scepter.[113] In this myth, which the emperor composed for Heracleius, we see quite clearly Ammianus' array of Jupiter, Adrasteia (Moirai), Themis (Hosiotes), Iustitia, and Sol. The donation of a *caduceus* by Hermes harmonizes with the historian's claim that a *caduceus mundanus* pacified the world while Julian was alive. Julian's picture of Moirai obedient to the Father mirrors Adrasteia's subordination to Numen (Jupiter), and the elevation of Justice over Fate similarly renders the rule of Iustitia over her own *filia*, Adrasteia, and so Fate, in the *Res gestae*.

Our survey of deities should indicate that thought-provoking differences do exist between them. They can hardly be described as essentially ornamental, nor will "scientific" do justice to the vital connections to traditional cult that appear everywhere in the history: Ammianus offers religious presentation in depth. What he does not provide—and we would not expect it in any event where individual preferences are engaged—is a row of completely uniform deities. His paganism is not distributed everywhere equally and indeed, "one god should not be invoked for another."[114] We have, in sum, a personal religious argument whose modulations suggest not intellectual confusion or apathy but rather the exercise of decision.

112. 229b–29c.
113. 234a–34c.
114. "Thus ritual and pontifical laws enjoin that priests, since it is unclear which one of the gods might be shaking the earth, be careful to avoid committing impieties by invoking some other god in place of the correct one," 17.7.10. Wardman (*Religion and Statecraft*, 160) misconstrues Ammianus' solicitous concern for proper ritual as despair over the inadequacy of traditional religion: "The older pagan books were no better than the new; one could not have much confidence in the lore of the pontifical books when they declined to say anything specific about earthquakes for fear of naming the wrong god." The historian's point at 17.7.10 is simply that priests must be extremely careful; that is the only way to realize the *munera divinandi*.

· CHAPTER TWO ·

CULT: JULIAN *SIDUS SALUTARE*

Cultus is the practical complement to theology. With the most theoretical components of Ammianus' religion in our grasp, we should focus our attention more directly upon paganism in action, the manner in which ritual activities within the narrative portion of the *Res gestae* convey an ideal of proper cult. Although the historian centers his incidents of pagan activity almost exclusively about two points, magic and Julian, only Julian can have been meant to bear the ideological burden. Many think Ammianus' frequent magic trials are best interpreted as a general indictment of imperial injustice, offerings of corrupted politics rather than religious persecution.[1] That his trials indeed do not amount to an apology for paganism will become obvious when we reflect upon the type of cult they disclose. This is not religion pursued at a heroic, imperial level that embraces great civilizing divinities such as Jupiter, Sol, or Mater but rather religion that concerns trivial, manipulative, or clearly pernicious forms of cult—from his point of view, the least inspiring grade of private religion. With the exception of Demetrius Cythras' disinterested devotion to the god Besa at Abydus,[2] none of the defendants was involved in ritual activity that Ammianus himself would have judged praiseworthy.[3]

---

1. See Blockley, *Ammianus Marcellinus*, 119, 120–22, and "Tacitean Influence," 74; Funke, "Majestäts- und Magieprozesse," 165–66, 170, 175; Seyfarth, "Glaube und Aberglaube," 382–83; Maurice, "La terreur," 184. Straub, however, disagrees: *Heidnische Geschichtsapologetik*, 71–72.

2. *Propitiandi causa numinis*, 19.12.12, only as Demetrius had always done from his youth, not for any ulterior motive.

3. Harmful activity: Serenianus' consultation *de imperio* by means of an enchanted cap, 14.7.7–8; the wild claim of Africanus' drunken guests that *imperium* was foretold them *maiorum augurio*, 15.3.7; the *veneficia* of the charioteers Hilarinus, 26.3.3, and Auchenius,

Only one of these incidents actually carries a significant portion of his religious argument. This is the trial of Hilarius, who explains in complete detail how he and Patricius consulted the gods about Valens's successor. Just as that other *documentum* taken from the obelisk of Sol speaks importantly to a solar *imperium*, "Heliopolis," so this testimonial yields another message of religion, an *indicium* that carries beyond its immediate, and illegal, context. The explicit connections with Apollo[4] should, in terms of our previous assessment of Ammianus' deities, lead us to expect a particularly important prophecy here. In fact there are three accurate predictions: the death of Valens, those of Patricius and Hilarius, and, most significantly, the eventual accession of Theodosius.[5] Sol points forward to an emperor who may, like Julian, become the new torchbearer of Rome.[6] At the end of Valens's necrology Ammianus fur-

---

28.1.27; Lollianus' possession of a *codex noxiarum artium*, 28.1.26. Trivial instances: Barbatio's consultation about the bees nesting in his house, 18.3.1–4; the use of innocuous amulets, *remedia*, 19.12.14; the healing of Festus' daughter through a *leve carmen*, 29.2.26; a young man who similarly cured his stomachache with a simple spell, 29.2.28; Bassianus' consultation about the sex of an expected child, 29.2.5. A less than praiseworthy attempt to manipulate divine forces for personal ends appears in Hymetius' consultation of the *haruspex* Amantius, 28.1.17–21. Although these two did not want to harm Valentinian but only to lessen his unjust wrath against Hymetius through a specially concocted prayer, their ceremony was nevertheless intended to spellbind the emperor and would hardly have been regarded by Ammianus as a proper display of reverence for divine power. On Roman attitudes toward magic, see MacMullen, *Enemies*, 95–128; Pharr, "Interdiction of Magic," 269–95; Momigliano, "Popular Religious Beliefs," 141–59.

4. [*Mensulam*] *ad cortinae similitudinem Delphicae*, 29.1.29; *Pythici vel ex oraculis editi Branchidarum*, 29.1.31.

5. That contemporaries understood this widely broadcast oracular fragment, "Theod . . . ", to point to Theodosius I is confirmed by an anonymous breviary in Greundel's edition of Aurelius Victor (Leipzig, 1970), 48.3–5: "There was also an oracle revealed in Asia which said that Valens would be succeeded by one whose name began with the letters TH and E and O and D. As a blood relative of the emperor, Theodorus deceived himself into thinking it was he. . . . But the man signified was in fact Theodosius, bringer of increase to the State and its outstanding defender."

6. On one important occasion at least, Theodosius had pointed himself to Sol—our *mia dynasteia* proclaimed on the obelisk and by Julian (above, pp. 43, 47)—"You reared up in the East, a second Sun, / Theodosius, bearer of light to mortals, the center of the universe, Gentle one / Having Ocean at your feet beyond the boundless land, / Rays dancing everywhere from your helmet; and the shining horse / Wild though he is, Great-souled one, you easily restrain," *Anthologia Graeca*, ed. H. Beckley, 16.65, from the base of an equestrian statue in the Forum of Theodosius at Constantinople. On this forum, see Holum, *Theodosian Empresses*, 11–13. The obelisk that Theodosius raised in the Hippodrome at Constantinople following his victory over Magnus Maximus (Holum, 14) will obviously bring to mind the one erected in the Circus Maximus by Constantius after his own defeat of a usurper, Magnentius (16.10.1, 17).

ther enhances the position of this unique ceremony by drawing attention to the emperor's mounting fear of it.[7]

Otherwise, the inhering unsuitability of Ammianus' magic trials as a medium for his religious apology effectively reduces our focus to Julian, the historian's least inhibited and most fully described *cultor*, and his best witness for the loftier grades of paganism. But we are then compelled to seek illumination in an emperor whom Ammianus judged to have been more superstitious than pious.[8] This great drop immediately runs our search for principles of cult into the complex polemical environment of the *Res gestae*. Here we see how the historian not only managed the task of warding off Christian attacks upon the *cultus deorum*, more particularly the *munera divinandi*, but also struck at the fatalism of Julian's more fervid supporters who believed that paganism's last hope was gone. In his several orations, Libanius for one seemed to understand no difference between the fates of Julian and paganism: character and cult, *ethos* and *nomos*, fell together.

Speaking for a different religious outlook, but still very much that of a *legitimus observator*, Ammianus fully appreciated the dangerous consequences for pagan apology that must follow from thus subordinating the fate of traditional religion to the (variable) career of any one emperor. In this sense he had good reason to adopt a strategy of religious presentation that steadily divorced *ethos* from *nomos*: while the *cultus deorum* is made responsible for what was best in Julian's character, his failings are yet portrayed as unrepresentative, personal deviations from what it properly enjoined. Our examination of pagan worship in the *Res gestae*, therefore, inevitably turns into a study of that particular strategy that Ammianus displays before the problem of Julian. In this chapter and the next his presentation of Julian's cultic activities will be discussed by locale, each scene then being considered through the eyes of other pagan and Christian writers: Julian himself, Libanius, Eunapius, Zosimus, Gregory Nazianzen, Socrates Scholasticus, Sozomen, and Theodoret.[9]

---

7. "Ut erat inconsummatus et rudis, inter initia [tres versus illos fatidicos] contemnebat, processu vero luctum maximorum abiecte etiam timidus eiusdem sortis recordatione Asiae nomen horrebat," 31.14.8.

8. *Superstitiosus magis quam sacrorum legitimus observator*, 25.4.17.

9. It should be made clear from the beginning that my first object in employing these Christian sources is to reveal pagan rather than Christian activity; a broad interpretation of the conflict that fully encompasses the interests of both parties is not my concern here. Ammianus' presentation of Christianity will be examined in Chapter 5.

. . .

Between 355 and 360 Julian Caesar had fulfilled the duty given him by Constantius: to close Gaul to barbarian raids and to secure the devotion of its army, recently shaken by the usurpations of Magnentius and Silvanus, to his own house. The Alamanni and Franks were repeatedly mastered following Julian's great victory near Strasbourg. Yet these successes in a particular region of the empire could not of course solve every one of Constantius' strategic commitments, and in 359 he demanded many of his Caesar's troops for an impending expedition against Persia. The Gauls responded to this emperor as they often had before by acclaiming another, now Julian, who promised he would never take them from Gaul: "*Redite iam nunc ad sedes nihil visuri transalpinum.*"[10] With the political and dynastic shackles fallen away, there could be no question but that his hidden paganism must soon begin to move out in ever greater sweeps.

Secrecy is the dominant theme of Julian's worship in Gaul: "allowing just a few to join in his secret activities he was thoroughly engaged in soothsaying, auguries, and those other rituals which worshippers of the gods have always practiced."[11] That and every other religious reference for this period redounds to the ex-Caesar's favor and that of the activities mentioned. The prayer to Mercury figures into Ammianus' general praise for the divine inspiration of Julian's intellect and soul.[12] Worship is offered to Bellona at a time when Julian is uncertain about the loyalty of his troops, and their favorable response to the speech that directly follows this ritual is given "as if to some oracle."[13] Thus prayers to two deities are seen to yield specific benefits. If Ammianus elsewhere criticizes Julian's devotion to divination, his first reference to that predilection locates it squarely within what he regards as the legitimate pagan tradition: *et ceteris quae deorum semper facere cultores.* For Gaul, then, we find approval of the Caesar's religious conduct. He may perform his rites in secret, but these, as the historian explicitly points out, are not shadowy forms of cult. By following the reference to traditional worship with notice of Julian's presence at a service of Epiphany "so that these [pagan rites] would be concealed,"[14] Ammianus makes it clear that Christianity,

10. 20.4.16.
11. 21.2.4.
12. *Quasi pabula quaedam animo ad sublimiora scandenti,* 16.5.6.
13. 21.5.9.
14. 21.2.5.

and nothing unseemly in the nature of the *cultus deorum*, was the reason for concealment.[15]

An examination of other pagan sources for this period reveals that they are in general harmony with the account given by Ammianus. Clandestine worship within an intimate circle of *pauci* appears in Julian's *Letter to the Athenians*, where a secret comrade in cult is mentioned among his little retinue of four servants and a physician.[16] Speaking to the need for such secrecy is his jab, reported by Zosimus, at the poor military escort given him by Constantius, which consisted of men who "only knew how to pray," obviously Christians.[17] That the accompanying physician, Oribasius of Pergamum, was himself one of the *pauci* emerges from a congratulatory note sent to him by the Caesar: "I think that you now, if ever, have seen clearly into the future"; Julian too had had a prophetic dream when a new shoot seemed to grow from the base of a great but fallen tree.[18] Eunapius names Oribasius, the Libyan Euhemerus, and the Hierophant of Eleusis as Julian's fellow conspirators, and it was this priest who infused him with the courage to revolt through a secret ceremony.[19] Although such excerpts firmly attest the secrecy of Julian's cultic activity, it should be noted that Libanius' funeral oration does not contain this element but rather avoids suggestions of surreptitious worship to portray the Caesar spending the off-campaign season in harmless symposia among fellow literati from Athens.[20] Nor does the *Letter to the Athenians* return to this matter in Gaul following Julian's initial reference to his pagan confidant.

The need for secrecy in Gaul was created by Christianity—Ammianus makes that clear enough—but Christian coercion at this phase of Julian's career does not appear in any explicit form outside the *Res gestae*.

---

15. A point worth noting when secret rites were often identified with *veneficia* or abhorrent forms of divination. Theodoret in his *Historia ecclesiastica*, ed. L. Parmentier, 3.26–27, speaks of Julian's sacrifice of a woman, concealed within a locked temple at Carrhae, and of human parts later found in the imperial palace at Antioch. Consider the terminology of Ammianus' various magic trials: *secretiora quaedam legibus interdicta*, 26.3.3; *arcanis piacularibus*, 26.3.4; *imprecatoribus carminum secretorum . . . rebus arcanis*, 29.1.29; *artium secretarum*, 30.5.11.

16. Lacombrade, *Works of Julian*, 277b.

17. *Historia nova*, ed. L. Mendelssohn, 3.3. Of this same military escort from Milan, Libanius, *Or.* 18, the *Epitaphios*, 37, states that the troops were the poorest, *phaulotatous*, Constantius could find. We may wonder whether Julian actually knew them to be Christian or was rather employing an idiosyncratic expression for any badly turned out unit of soldiers. Ammianus himself mentions only a *comitatus parvus*, 15.8.18.

18. *Ep.* 17, *Letters of Julian*, ed. J. Bidez.

19. *Vitae sophistarum*, ed. J. Giangrande, 476.

20. *Synanabakcheusas*, 75.

Although one might reasonably argue that the Christian presence was so obvious as to preclude any mention, it is nevertheless of interest that Ammianus, far from being quiet on Christian affairs, wishes to stamp this unmistakably as the chief religious problem in Gaul, an impediment to the expression of traditional, legitimate forms of cult.[21] Neither the historian nor any other pagan source, however, connects the *fides militum* to the problem of Christianity, although Julian was in fact continually worried about Christianity's hold on the ranks.[22]

A question of obvious importance at this stage is the extent to which pagan cult was involved in or, perhaps better, responsible for Julian's revolt. Christian historians such as Socrates and Sozomen immediately proceed to describe his war as one of religion from its very beginning without acknowledging any gap between the announcement of revolt and Julian's public declaration that he was a pagan, nor do they see any gradually diminishing level of secrecy between Gaul and Naissus.[23] In this respect at least, Eunapius' very telescoped description of the event in his *Vitae sophistarum* places him at one with Christian accounts: the Hierophant's ceremony is the explicit prelude to revolt. Our impression from Ammianus, Julian, and Libanius, however, is that although eager to claim the "vote of Heaven"[24] for the revolt, they do not wish to assert that religion was a direct cause.

This desire leads to something of a cat-and-mouse game. Ammianus mixes both precise and general references to omens and secret worship in Gaul. Precisely, the appearance of the Public Genius at Paris, a glowing *imago* at Vienne, and secret invocations of Mercury and Bellona; generally, the many prophetic signs of Constantius' approaching death with notice of Julian's long-standing defection from Christianity and his hidden return to the old gods.[25] In terms of specific incidents, religion

21. See Blockley's assertion (*Fragmentary*, 88) that "Ammianus preferred to ignore things Christian as much as possible." On the other hand, Cameron and Cameron ("Christianity and Tradition," 322) find Ammianus "far less reluctant to deal with things Christian than are the Byzantines [historians of the sixth century]; in their case it is hardly an exaggeration to say that they do not mention anything to do with Christianity unless they have to."

22. See below, p. 45.

23. *Historia ecclesiastica* by Socrates, ed. J.-P. Migne, 3.1.16–18; *Historia ecclesiastica* by Sozomen, ed. by J. Bidez, 5.1–2.

24. *Epitaphios*, 103, *Opera Libanii*, ed. R. Foerster.

25. 16.5.5, 20.5.10, 21.1.6, 5.1. Inasmuch as Ammianus explicitly says *multa* (*praesagia et somnia*), 21.1.6, it is difficult to believe that *all* of these signs were meant to be covered by the two instances that follow his intervening excursus on divination, those of the broken shield and glowing apparition, 21.2.1–2; some must have been left out, hence my designation of this as a general reference.

would not seem to have been an active cause of rebellion. Julian received signs, but we should note that his position at such moments is that of a spectator, not an *instigator* of signs, one who is revealed to have been actively praying for Constantius' destruction. Mention of Julian's divinatory rites, moreover, follows his acclamation at a good, discreet distance from the event. That he was still keeping his paganism a secret in Vienne suggests, as Ammianus undoubtedly intends it to, that the revolt occurred as a result of Constantius' tyranny alone; one who would show his religion to only a small personal retinue even well after the event was obviously not the man to have tried to subvert so great a mass as an army in that way. The timing and extent of Julian's religious disclosure are important, as the historian acknowledges, yet his use of *iam pridem* leaves the door open to serious cultic activities extending as far back into Julian's career as one wishes to go. Such a noticeable blank in the presentation weakens the value of its specifics, and the historian, in sum, cannot be said to have settled reassuringly the question of religion's role at Paris by reference to simply one, cultically detached detail, the appearance of the Public Genius.

Libanius and Julian himself follow this practice of omitting significant references to cultic activity before and, more importantly, on the eve of the acclamation. Both offer an impression of personal worship that is modest or restrained in the aftermath but not explicitly as a response to Christian coercion. In the *Epitaphios*, Julian prays only once, to seek the gods' *psēphos* when told to stand down by those still loyal to Constantius. Here the oath-taking ceremony, which Ammianus joins obliquely to Bellona, occurs without any reference to gods. Mention is made of only one specific god, Apollo, who inspires a soldier to warn Julian of a plot in Paris.[26] The *Letter to the Athenians* is also cultically lean with its two instances of a prayer to Zeus as the soldiers shouted for Julian and a divinatory sacrifice performed upon the eve of his departure for Thrace. Despite Julian's expression of gratitude for the assistance of Athene, Helios, and Selene, they are not linked by him to any particular activities, and we note that he, unlike Libanius, does not bring either Apollo or divine inspiration into his own account of the alleged palace plot.[27] Both Libanius and Julian display no apparent interest in portraying the period in Gaul as a time of substantial religious activity, whether private or public. Personal modesty and passivity, an unpremeditated re-

26. Note how Zosimus, 3.9, uses Helios rather than Ammianus' unnamed *imago splendidior* to prophesy Constantius' death to Julian.
27. *Epitaphios*, 284a–85d, *Opera Libanii*, ed. R. Foerster.

sponse to an unexpected "vote of the gods," would appear to be their desired impression, and Ammianus shares this apologetic spirit: tyranny, not the *cultus deorum*, was responsible for beginning and abetting the revolt.

Following a year of barren negotiations between the rival Augusti, Julian marched on Thrace late in 361 to meet what he expected would be Constantius' imminent arrival in Europe with an army and an open declaration of war. Julian's cultic activity now appears in a doubtful light for the first time when Ammianus depicts him anxious and hesitating, *plura timescens*, in Naissus, his divination yielding no clear responses: "[Julian] was continually searching through entrails and watching the flights of birds as he hurried to foreknow the outcome of events; but he remained unsure about the future, getting no farther than perplexing and dark responses."[28] He could neither believe in the happy prediction of the Gallic orator, Aprunculus, *aruspicinae peritus*, who had found a double-lobed liver—flattery was feared—nor did he have unalloyed faith in an even clearer sign of Constantius' death, the stumbling of his own equerry, although publicly he had shown no reservations about it at the time and immediately pronounced the accident a good omen.[29] The confidence in divination that gave hope to Julian in Gaul lapsed, as apparently also did the memory of the good signs received there.[30] Although one may well believe that his religious crisis at this point serves a dramatic function,[31] Ammianus is nevertheless posing a question about Julian as a *cultor*: was he in sufficient control of his responses to the gods? If inevitable human error prevented divination from attaining perfection,[32] this did not mean that it was any less a science or less worthy of belief, and any science must finally cease to exist as such unless its judgments were accepted at some point. The contrast between events in Gaul and Naissus introduces

---

28. 22.1.1.
29. *Omen, multo praesentius . . . clare monstrabat*, 22.1.2, which, it was later confirmed, had indeed occurred on the day Constantius died.
30. *Animo tranquillo et quieto*, 21.2.3. For example, the *imago splendior*, 21.2.2.
31. Consider, for example, Sapor's halt on the eastern bank of the Tigris while awaiting good signs, 21.13.2; Ammianus has astutely balanced his three rulers: Julian waiting and divining in the West, Sapor doing the same thing in the East, and Constantius holding the central position as a dramatic fulcrum between these other two, himself worried, *relationibus variis anxius, in rationes diducebatur ancipitis*, 21.13.1.
32. "Unde praeclare hoc quoque ut alia Tullius: 'signa ostenduntur' ait 'a dis rerum futurarum in his si qui erraverit, non deorum natura, sed hominum coniectura peccavit,'" 21.1.14 (= *De natura deorum*, 2.4.12).

an element of erratic behavior, an unsettling degree of fluctuation in the responses of one who so respected divination as a *doctrinae genus haud leve*. In Naissus Julian begins to relax his grip on the title of *vir sapiens*.[33]

Whereas Gaul demonstrates close agreement between our various pagan sources, Illyricum divides them. Everywhere but in the *Res gestae* Julian's march east appears as a religious triumph. Christians heard it broadcast in such a laudatory manner by his supporters: Julian designated himself *Pontifex maximus* and immediately began sacrificing, celebrating festivals, and encouraging others to do the same. All this was done to the accompaniment of good omens—grapes that appeared out of season; little crosses in dewdrops that disappeared when they touched clothing; demons that predicted the death of Constantius.[34] Gregory Nazianzen was weary of hearing Julian's partisans continually talk about the divine inspiration of his march—where were those happy demons in Persia?[35] This buoyant spirit is conveyed by Julian, Libanius, and Zosimus. Writing to the philosopher Maximus from Naissus, Julian happily reported that he was sacrificing many hecatombs to the gods in public; more importantly, most of the rank and file among his troops were sacrificing too.[36] It is noticeable that his now unfolding program of public conversion made the army its first object. The *Epitaphios* contains all this frenetic activity and in addition depicts Julian resolving a dispute between the priestly families of Athens.[37] Enlarging this felicitous atmosphere is the prophetic aura surrounding Constantius' death. Zosimus shows Julian confidently divining, awaiting the fatal moment that Helios had predicted in Gaul, and Libanius makes him quiet anxieties within his entourage by producing a book of oracles from which he read the prophecy of a bloodless victory.[38]

We are in a quite different world from that created by the *Res gestae*, where Julian, as far as we know, is bleakly praying in secret and his faith in the *munera divinandi* seems just about to let go. Such a strongly contrasting presentation argues that Ammianus was intentionally seeking a distinctive type of pagan apology, and in fact Julian's image and, more

33. 21.1.7.
34. *Historia ecclesiastica* by Sozomen, ed. J. Bidez, 5.1.8.
35. *Works of Gregory Nazianzen, Or.* IV, ed. J.-P. Migne, 47.76.
36. *Ep.* 26, *Letters of Julian*, ed. J. Bidez.
37. 114–116.
38. *Historia nova*, ed. L. Mendelssohn, 3.11; *Epitaphios*, 118, *Opera Libanii*, ed. R. Foerster. Cf. Ammianus: "somnio enim propius videbatur [note the oracular connotation recalling Julian's *praesagia multa et somnia* in Gaul] . . . principatum denique deferente nutu caelesti absque ulla publicae rei [Iulianum] suscepisse iactura," 22.2.5.

importantly, that of paganism do gather special benefits from his peculiar approach to the Illyrican period. First, the *Res gestae* better preserves the conceit that his was not a war started by and for religion: Julian does not explicitly reveal his personal religion to the public until the end of the civil war when his position is thoroughly legitimate—surely the more dignified moment to introduce the restoration of paganism. Elsewhere it is clear that Julian was already moving in the direction of his later gargantuan sacrifices; but Ammianus postpones his criticism of this doubtful activity until Antioch.[39] The historian well serves the dignity of paganism in another fashion by increasing the distance between Julian's Gallic omens, his continuous divination in Naissus, and Constantius' death. By putting Julian in the dark and making no loud claim for the veracity of the old omens whose *clara fides* was obviously now proven, he tries to allay the not too distant suggestion of *veneficia*, that Julian's rites in Naissus were intimately connected with his cousin's collapse at Mobsucrenae. From this standpoint, surprise was a preferable reaction to confidence.

This service to Julian should, however, be considered secondary to Ammianus' first object, to begin weakening Julian as the perfect, once and future representative of the *cultus deorum* by presenting him as a wavering hero in Naissus. This tragic flaw goes beyond the simple appeal of dramatic zest; we are in the presence of a true technique of religious apology. The historian's perspective is quite different from that of Libanius, the panegyrist who extols Julian as the peerless *cultor*, praises him more loudly as the hecatombs mount, and can find no repair for his loss. But Ammianus replies that paganism was not Julian's personal fief; it did not perish with him, nor could it have perished with him. To hold on to the meaning of a yet dynamic *nomos* independent of and therefore surviving individual *ethos*, the colossal image offered by Libanius needed severe reduction. Here is where Ammianus begins.[40]

---

39. Bowersock (*Julian the Apostate*, 61–62, 79) believes, in my opinion incorrectly, that Ammianus was unaware that Julian and his troops were openly sacrificing in Illyricum; in placing Julian's public profession of paganism in Constantinople, the historian was "proven wrong." Surely this is not a question of Ammianus' ignorance but rather one of the precise apologetic strategy that he has decided to use. As we shall see, information about the murder of Bishop George at Alexandria is also delayed in this apologetically cued fashion.

40. Athanassiadi-Fowden (*Julian and Hellenism*, 196) locates Julian's "first signs of [cultic] extravagance" in Antioch, but I would suggest that Ammianus intends us to have our first questions about his conduct at Naissus. So, too, Conduché ("Ammien Marcellin," 378) places the hinge of his piety-impiety "diptych" at Antioch without mentioning events in Illyricum.

. . .

The perturbation in Naissus is the first in an undulating series of favorable and unfavorable religious events. Now that the seed of Julian's cultic imperfection has been planted following his more estimable behavior in Gaul, Ammianus returns him to favor at Constantinople following the sudden death of Constantius in October 361. This improvement in religious standing is well symbolized by Julian's hurrying to the capital "as if in some chariot of Triptolemus."[41] The emperor thus became like a new founder of the Eleusinian Mysteries, a comparison all the more appropriate to the struggle between Julian and Constantius when we consider that Triptolemus was thought to have received the kingdom of Eleusis from Demeter following an unsuccessful plot against him by its ruler, Celeus.[42] By mentioning Heraclea (Perinthus) as Julian's first stop on his way to Constantinople, the historian of course renews the emperor's contact with Hercules, the founder of the city, and the Argonauts—that is, with paganism's ethic of heroic civilization.[43] As the most important foci of cult and history, great concrete witnesses to the dynamic bond between gods and men, cities such as Perinthus, "which Hercules founded and dedicated to the memory of his companion," are clearly used by Ammianus in this didactic fashion to resonate with his characters: he who encounters a city inevitably provokes it to speak.

Religious activity for the period in Constantinople is limited to two items, announcement of the pagan restoration "by plain and total decrees" and Julian's meeting with dissident Christians.[44] Just as Ammianus presents the religious problem in Gaul as the (unwarranted) constraint of traditional forms of cult by Christianity, so again, through the juxtaposition of decrees and meeting,[45] he proceeds directly to the problem of Christian intolerance, here, of each other. Since Julian has not yet compromised himself in this particular narrative by extravagant public sacrifices, it is fair to say that at the instant of the decrees he and paganism are made to appear in a highly favorable light, particularly when

---

41. 22.2.3. Triptolemus, it should be noted, was regarded as a founder of Antioch, the historian's native city; see Libanius' *Or.* 11, the *Antiochikos*, 45, 51–53, and Strabo's *Geographica*, ed. A. Meineke, 16.1.25–26, 2.5.

42. See Pearson, *Fragments of Sophocles*, 2:241–42.

43. *Civitatem quam Hercules conditam Perinthi comitis sui memoriae dedicavit*, 22.8.5. See pp. 24–25 above.

44. 22.5.1–5.

45. *Utque dispositorum roboraret effectum*.

contrasted to Christian *feritas*. The emperor fills the role of a dignified, general representative of freed paganism.

Such an even, benign mood may again be properly felt in contrast to the *Epitaphios*. Libanius sets the announcement of restoration immediately after Constantius' funeral,[46] in this way showing the end of Christian repression. As I have asserted, however, Ammianus for his own part wishes to avoid a close association between the prosperity of the *cultus deorum* and Constantius' death, or that of anyone: religious restoration— and this is the point of depicting Julian as a modest, virtually self-contained worshipper in Gaul—should not appear as the triumph of vendetta. The historian, therefore, refers the question of toleration less ominously only to the living. For this reason again, nothing is said of Bishop George's murder at its proper point in the narrative, Constantinople; Ammianus secures the event rather to his sad Antiochene section.[47]

Julian's ritual activity in the *Res gestae* is magnified by degrees until its unhappy climax in Antioch. His great sacrifices appear to be peculiar to that stage. But Libanius, we have seen, throws the door open much earlier; in his eulogy, and so too in Christian writings, there is essentially no difference between Naissus, Constantinople, and Antioch. The leitmotif for every period is well put in Libanius' *Monōdia:* Julian would sacrifice herds of victims anywhere at any time.[48] After burying Constantius, announcing the restoration, and rejecting an (overt) attempt to persecute Christianity, the emperor immediately set about his markedly quantitative solution to the difficulties of paganism. Sacrificial smoke was everywhere, and great numbers of wagons carried new and recovered fabric for the temples. All the seers were freed from fear.[49] Julian

---

46. 121.

47. See Bowersock, *Julian,* 80, on George: "Ammianus obscures the significance of this incident [George's murder] in several ways, by dating it a year after it occurred (and thus to a more turbulent season in Julian's short reign)." Again, he has noted an interesting peculiarity of the historian's presentation, but he has not properly seen the apologetic strategy responsible for it. Whatever temporal precision *eisdem diebus,* 22.11.1, *ought* to have, it is in fact a catchall phrase that introduces a whole series of deaths—not just one—from scattered times: Gaudentius, Julianus, Artemius, Marcellus, Romanus, Vincentius, George (*Cumque tempus interstetisset exiguum . . . Artemii comperto interitu,* 22.11.3), Dracontius, and Diodorus. *Eisdem diebus* is, I am sure, only meant to have a broad chronological significance and ultimately provides no ground for thinking that Ammianus has made a fundamental error in dating.

48. *Or.* 17, *Opera Libanii,* ed. R. Foerster.

49. See Ammianus' criticism of the uncontrolled proliferation of diviners, "et quisque cum impraepedite liceret, scientiam vaticinandi professus, iuxta imperitus et docilis sine fine vel praestitutis ordinibus, oraculorum permittebantur scitari responsa et ex-

hurried about to every temple, but as the day was not long enough or frequently interrupted by other business, he constructed within his palace a temple to the God of the Day (a Mithraeum) in which he was initiated and performed initiations. He patronized cities or spurned them as polluted according to the condition of their temples.[50]

To this picture of Julian's religious life in Constantinople we should add, of course, the arrival of his mentor, Maximus, and the subsequent inflation of the imperial entourage by a crowd of "Hellenic" philosophers and sophists—those whom Christians regarded as militant religious imposters.[51] If Ammianus does charge the emperor with *ostentatio* for his ecstatic greeting of Maximus, he actually offers the scene in a less glaring light than Libanius, whose own Julian not only embraces the philosopher but essentially halts further business in the senate by giving a speech in praise of Maximus and then departing with the philosopher on his hand.[52]

For six months the emperor turned himself to trials, municipal and bureaucratic reform, public works, and preparation for war against Persia. Then in June 362, he left Constantinople for Antioch, his strategic base of operations in the approaching campaign. En route Julian made himself accessible to Hellenic pagans and visited temples, making sure to converse with local authorities while standing in close proximity to the cult statue.[53] In this regimen we see him pointed toward several objectives: adding new members to his pagan retinue and thereby amassing a pool of candidates for his projected renewal, or replacement, of the priesthood; winnowing civic leaders by compelling them to do business with him in the *temenē*, where, of course, only those Christians amenable to serious compromising would be willing to go;[54] and importantly, reading for himself the religious sentiments of the community in the good or bad physical state of the shrine.

Ammianus follows Julian to Pessinus and its famous temple of

---

tispicia nonnumquam futura pandentia oscinumque et auguriorum et ominum fides, si reperiri usquam posset, affectata varietate quaerebatur," 22.12.7.

50. *Epitaphios*, 121–27, 129.

51. See Socrates, 3.1.22. Similarly critical, Eunapius (*Vitae sophistarum*, ed. J. Giangrande, 477–78) considered them sycophants.

52. *Epitaphios*, 155–56.

53. Ibid., 161–63.

54. Christians like Pegasius, *Ep.* 79, Bishop of Illium, who carefully maintained the shrine of Hector and later became one of Julian's priests.

Mater. The comparatively large amount of attendant religious detail—this, it should be remembered, in addition to a now lost digression on the goddess' arrival in Italy—signals a special degree of personal interest. I have already noted that the historian uses Julian's career, whatever its failings, as an *indicium* of paganism, a device for religious instruction no different in purpose from the sign that is the story of Venus and Adonis. This becomes clear again at Pessinus. Before arriving there, the emperor had passed through Chalcedon, Libyssa where Hannibal was interred, and Nicomedia. To the last city, recently damaged by an earthquake, he gave generous assistance. At the next halt, Pessinus, we are specifically reminded that from this shrine came the image of Mater, summoned by the Sibylline Books and brought to Rome by Scipio Nasica during the Second Punic War.[55]

We may see then that Julian's route to this point forms a narrative of religion in its own right: two public calamities, Hannibal and the earthquake, followed by two health-giving responses, Julian's aid to Nicomedia and the Scipios' assistance to Rome against Carthage. These saviors come together in reverence for Mater as they inevitably do also for Apollo through his peculiar mark, the Sibylline Books, that god's pledge to the salvation of Rome through prophecy. Ammianus thus brings the emperor to participate in the tradition of Rome's religiously inspired heroes. We should ask as well whether the meeting between Julian and Bishop Eusebius of Nicomedia is not to be set inside such a mosaic. Christians in the *Res gestae* appear with suspicious frequency at moments of disaster, and in this historically interwoven march Eusebius perhaps evokes for Ammianus the infelicitous shadows of Poeni whom he will see at another Cannae, Hadrianople.[56]

But from Julian's own report of his tour of inspection at Pessinus, we learn that in fact he made no rendezvous with heroic religion there. To Arsacius, high-priest of Galatia, the emperor complained generally of the weak pagan response to his overtures and particularly of that shown by the people of Pessinus: they would be cut off from his patronage unless all of them revered Mater.[57] Ammianus and Libanius choose to skirt this disappointment, however, and dwell only upon Julian's piety, al-

---

55. 22.9.2–8; see pp. 23–24, 26–27 above.
56. In that Christian confidant of Fritigern, *conscius arcanorum et fidus*, 31.12.9, whom the Gothic chief sent to Valens before Rome's second Cannae: "[nec ulla] annalibus praeter Cannensem pugnam ita ad internecionem res legitur gesta," 31.13.19.
57. *Ep.* 84, *Letters of Julian*, ed. J. Bidez.

though we should properly judge the *Res gestae* to leave the more thoroughly felicitous impression. If Libanius' mention of another frustrated assassination attempt[58] speaks well for the divine assistance of Mater, it nevertheless recalls that negative correlation between cult and vendetta that Ammianus always seeks to avoid.

58. *Epitaphios*, 161.

· CHAPTER THREE ·

JULIAN *MINAX SIDUS*

The emperor's *adventus* at Antioch during the festival of Adonis in July 362 is the pivotal moment of his religious career. Continuing that benign atmosphere created by Ammianus in Pessinus, the Antiochenes greeted Julian as a god: "and as he approached the city, he was met with open prayers as if he were some deity; and he was amazed at the great cries of the multitude who shouted that a health-giving star shone over the East" (a famine was then threatening the Antiochenes). But to enter Antioch also among the ritual lamentations for Adonis seemed like a bad omen, *visum est triste,* which indeed it was; Julian too would be cut down in his prime, *adulto flore.*[1] These contrasting scenes of joy followed by grief also look forward and backward, Janus-like, to the mixed quality of Julian's religious life: divine inspiration and faith combined with erratic behavior, threatening to separate him from true piety and the gods.

For this period, only the emperor's sacrifice to Zeus Casius can be said to meet with the historian's full approval. Other cultic activity yields *omina mortis,* drunk soldiers, unregulated diviners, and is generally portrayed as unsuccessful. The thorough mixing of divine doom and willful human (cultic) error conveys a not unintended impression that Julian's peculiar brand of paganism must be held blameworthy for his fate in Persia. Ammianus' objections to the pagan restoration in fact directly follow

---

1. 22.9.14–15. Contrast the divine elements of Julian's *adventus* at Antioch, at Vienne, 15.8.21, and Constantinople, 22.2.4–5, with Constantius' ornately hieratic but, to Ammianus, religiously inert entry into Rome, 16.10.1–12. Julian is a true star *demissus de caelo,* his cousin, really, a little presence whose light of earthly jewels is not worth even the height of a single gate in great Rome: "claritudine lapidum variorum, quo micante lux quaedam misceri videbatur alterna. . . . nam et corpus perhumile curvabat portas ingrediens celsas," 16.10.6, 10. The authentic, loftier majesty is obvious. On these *adventus,* see MacCormack, *Art and Ceremony,* 39–50.

his notice of preparations for this expedition. The charges are three: the number of Julian's sacrifices was excessive; their cost an unprecedented burden; diviners proliferated without limit or law.[2]

This is the emperor's third period of extended sacrificing or divination prior to an important event, after those in Gaul and Naissus, and it draws the most severe treatment yet of his religion. Here the sordid murder of George is now described. The implementation of the pagan restoration in Antioch is set in direct contrast to the complimentary presentation of its announcement in the capital, and we find Ammianus carefully separating *ethos* from *nomos*. The restoration moves out of control when Julian is no longer guided as he was in Gaul by "those rituals which the worshippers of the gods [here read, "the pagans of Antioch"] have always practiced." Now he promulgated some sort of distorted and too theatrical version of the *cultus deorum*.[3]

The historian teaches the right and wrong paths to piety through Julian's visits to the two shrines of Zeus Casius and Apollo Daphnaeus.[4] Although holding Apollo himself in the greatest esteem, Ammianus depicts the emperor's particular association with Apollo Daphnaeus in a negative fashion. First, the visit to the oracle is described as the (gratuitous) pursuit of a *nova consilii via*, an extension of that excessive concern with new varieties of divination that Ammianus has just criticized.[5] Ammianus reminds us that Hadrian received an *omen imperii* here, but this is not what Julian received. He addressed the god and then decided—we do not know that Apollo actually said anything in reply—to remove those Christians buried in his *temenos:* had the ritual broken down? The distinctly ominous burning of the temple immediately after

2. "Hostiarum tamen sanguine plurimo aras crebritate nimia perfundebat tauros aliquotiens immolando centenos et innumeros varii pecoris greges avesque candidas terra quaesitas et mari adeo, ut in dies paene singulos milites carnis distentiore sagina victitantes incultius potusque aviditate corrupti umeris imposti transeuntium per plateas ex publicis aedibus, ubi vindicandis potius quam cedendis conviviis indulgebant, ad sua diversoria portarentur, Petulantes ante omnes et Celtae, quorum ea tempestate confidentia creverat ultra modum. Augebantur autem caerimoniarum ritus immodice cum impensarum amplitudine antehac inusitata et gravi et quisque, cum impraepedite liceret, scientiam vaticinandi professus, iuxta imperitus et docilis, sine fine vel praestitutis ordinibus oraculorum permittebantur scitari responsa," 22.12.6–7.

3. E.g., Julian's *ostentatio* in personally carrying sacred implements and surrounding himself with female attendants, 22.14.3. The sort of pagan restoration that Ammianus would have preferred to what Julian offered will be discussed in Chapter 4.

4. 22.12.8–13.5, 14.4–6.

5. "Oraculorum permittebantur scitari responsa et extispicia . . . oscinumque et auguriorum varietate quaerebatur. Haecque dum ita procedunt more pacis multorum curiosior Iulianus novam consilii viam ingressus est," 22.12.8.

the emperor's visit would support such a notion of ruptured communication, harmonizing both with Ammianus' specific disapproval of the consultation as an unnecessary *nova via* and his general censure of Julian's decline from piety into cultic excess, superstition. Beyond its duties as an *omen mortis*[6] and a sign of failing divine contact, this fire teaches several other lessons. One lesson clearly has to do with consuming wrath, the emperor's failure to be guided by *temperantia*. Ammianus significantly begins his account of the disaster by noting that Antiochus Epiphanes, who built the temple, was a king *iracundus et saevus*. Julian too displayed this sort of excess after the fire: "the emperor was so carried away by anger that he ordered tougher investigations than usual [*solito acriores*] and closed the great church of Antioch."[7] His unfair edict against Christian instructors of rhetoric and grammar will naturally come to mind in this context.[8]

The other disasters of that year with which Ammianus concludes the episode, drought and famine at Antioch and now the total destruction of Nicomedia by another earthquake, are similarly suggestive. Famine appropriately portrays the barren fruit of wrath, and drought dramatizes in a very direct fashion the failure of Julian's consultation at the oracular spring of Daphne.[9] The collapse of Nicomedia, a city identified with him through his patronage and one-time residence, adumbrates the emperor's nearing end as a savior. On the other hand, mention of Nicomedia in this important position may be intended to return our attention to Bishop Eusebius and Ammianus' conventional association of Christians with disaster. Of two possible causes recorded for the fire at Daphne, Christian envy and Asclepiades' votive candles, only the latter, we note, is explicitly doubted as a *rumor levissimus*. Inasmuch as the historian identifies himself as a committed pagan but not one in Julian's

---

6. Cf. the burning of the Temple of Palatine Apollo in Rome while Julian was at Carrhae, 23.3.3. Libanius *Or.*, 17, 30, interprets the burning of the temple of Apollo Daphnaeus not only as an *omen mortis* for Julian but as a sign that the god would abandon a then polluted Earth. See above, p. 28, n. 74, and below, p. 60.

7. 22.13.2.

8. *Inclemens*, 22.10.7, repeated, 25.4.20. On this edict and the relationship between pagan and Christian education in Antioch, refer to Festugière, *Antioch païenne*, 211–40, also Boissier, *Fin du paganisme*, 1:199–218.

9. Conversely, Julian once attempted to stay fierce rain storms from the fields of Antioch by standing before an altar; famine and pestilence beset the land when he died (Libanius, 18.177, 293). For the emperor as a giver of rain and harvests (through his justice), see the late third-century rhetorical treatises of Menander Rhetor, ed. D. Russell and N. Wilson (Oxford, 1981), 2.377. Elsewhere in the *Res gestae*, note how the Burgundians are said to make their kings responsible for a healthy crop, 28.5.14. See pp. 91–92 below.

mold, we should properly expect such a complex, intertwining image. The last lesson is a primordial one that carries beyond Julian and his immediate problems: the loss of a temple brings general disaster to a people outside the *temenos*.[10]

If the shrine of Apollo Daphnaeus summarizes what is wrong with the emperor's religious activities, his sacrifice to Zeus Casius reveals the fruit of *temperantia*. In place of *saevitia* there is *clementia*. Theodotus, a virulent enemy now suppliant, received pardon during this ritual; then Julian learned that an Apis Bull had just been found. Fertility, *salus*, here is neatly contrasted with the former scene of sterility, and Julian's continuous association with such religion-bound images of the field in the *Res gestae* prove that they are no accident.[11] This conquest of internal wrath brings a sign of divine approval much as Tertullus' sacrifice to Castor and Pollux quiets the external storm of the sea—and Roman plebs, *iam saeviente immanius*. Grain may at last enter Ostia (Portus), and similarly the creative power of healing is restored to Julian.[12] Again Ammianus avoids a negative correlation between cult and violence as Libanius does not; what he describes as a health-giving exercise in *clementia*, the other treats as *sōtēria*, divine rescue from yet another attempted murder of Julian.[13]

The remainder of the period before the Persian expedition was

10. That the health of the land depends upon that of its temples is a rule which appears prominently in Libanius' *Or.* 30: the *Pro templis*, 9–10, where they are called "souls of the fields" whose rites stir the ground to life at sowing (as the eyes, or souls, of cities, see Section 42 of the same oration). When Christians attack the temples, he states, their acts are in reality no less damaging to the crops than if winter floods ran down upon them. So too, in the *Third Relatio*, 15–17 (*Epistulae*, ed. O. Seeck) Symmachus rests his plea to Valentinian for imperial *clementia* partly upon the observation that famine afflicted every province following Gratian's withdrawal of support from the old religion: "Secuta est hoc factum fames publica et spem provinciarum omnium messis aegra decepit. Non sunt haec vitia terrarum, nihil imputemus austris, nec rubigo segetibus obfuit, nec avena fruges necavit: sacrilegio annus exaruit. . . . commendabat enim terrarum proventum victus antistitum et remedium magis quam largitas erat." Note Constantine's apparent sympathy for traditional divination when this was applied to the relief of natural disasters, *Theodosian Code*, 9.16.3 (A.D. 321–324), 16.10.1 (320–321).

11. Triptolemus, 22.2.3; Fortuna bearing him a *mundanam cornucopiam*, 22.9.1; Adonis, *indicium frugum*, 22.9.15; the temple fire and famine, 22.13.1–4; the Apis Bull, *ubertatem frugum indicans*, 22.14.6; Julian's (Public) *genius* leaving his tent with a veiled cornucopia, *velato capite* as well to signify the sacrifice and bereavement of the State, 25.2.3. Ammianus had personally known that a very real veil was descending upon Julian's cornucopia at that moment, *frugibus exustis*, for his army was starving: "nos destitutos inedia cruciabat iam non ferenda," 25.2.1.

12. Remember that in the *Res gestae*, Apis shares Memphis with another famous divinity, Aesculapius.

13. *Or.* 18.172, *Opera Libanii*, ed. R. Foerster.

marked by a proliferation of bad omens: the destruction of a temple in the making, that of the Jews; the people's malicious chant of two dead grandees and a desired third, "Felix, Julianus, and Augustus" (this worried Julian); the sudden death of a priest at the *Tychaion;* an earthquake at Constantinople; and an unfavorable response from the Sibylline Books when these were consulted about Julian's intended campaign.[14] Whatever advantage there would have been for the emperor's anti-Christian strategy in building a new Jewish Temple, we cannot doubt but that Ammianus interpreted this odd patronage as yet another pursuit of "new ways"—what had Judaism to do with the *cultus deorum?*[15] The alleged extravagance of this scheme, *sumptibus immodicis,* parallels that of Julian's outsized sacrifices, expanded *immodice.*

The various techniques of religious advertisement and persuasion that Julian used in Antioch are thoroughly treated by Libanius, who thereby provides an important opportunity to look more deeply into the sources of Ammianus' censure and to develop further our contrast between the respective apologetic styles of the historian and panegyrist. If Julian's letters describe the establishment of a new corps of pagan priests sworn to follow philosophical precepts and place themselves under the rule of provincial superiors,[16] we do not in fact feel the presence of such a religious bureaucracy operating at Antioch. Pagan restoration in this city becomes totally identified with the immediate presence of the emperor; layers of descending priestly authority simply do not intervene. Libanius' writings convey the impression of a seamless web of ritual activity. No one would probably have been able to do business with the emperor when he was not by some altar in his palace or standing in a temple court.[17] Julian too undoubtedly considered the direct participa-

14. 23.1.5–7.
15. He had a low opinion of the Jews, *faetentes et tumultuantes,* 22.5.5. On Julian and the Jews, refer to du Labriolle, *La réaction païenne,* 399–410; Athanassiadi-Fowden, *Julian and Hellenism,* 164–66; Bowder, *Age of Constantine,* 111–12.
16. In addition to Arsacius, he mentions the high-priest of Asia, Theodorus, *Ep.* 89a (*Letters of Julian,* ed. J. Bidez) and possibly the long fragment, 89b; the priests Pegasius, *Ep.* 79, and Theodora, a correspondent of Maximus, *Ep.* 86. Eunapius offers the philosopher and high-priest of Lydia, Chrysanthius, who built no temples as others did, *thermōs kai perikaōs,* and Julian's comrade, the anonymous Hierophant who eventually departed the court with gifts and a retinue (of prospective priests?) to administer the temples of Greece (*Vitae sophistarum,* ed. J. Giangrande, 476, 510).
17. Cf. Eunapius on the influence of Maximus: "For the ruler and the ruled were in every way under the control of Maximus; night or day made no difference to them, they

tion of the emperor to be one of his program's greatest attractions. Another was magnificence, his unlimited power to enhance the number and scale of such events.

It is no exaggeration to say that Julian surrounded Antioch with a cloud of cult. So in Libanius' oration to Julian on his fourth consulship we find praise of the degree to which cult has taken over the emperor's life: he sacrifices continuously in the manner of an Egyptian of old, not as modern worshippers who are only interested in doing as much as convention requires; his palace is now a temple where the courts are filled with altars so that some even think that it is holier than the temples themselves; great sacrifices raise the soldiers' morale and frighten the Persians; the emperor does not waste time in consultation with his generals, for he simply summons his diviners and knows everything; but best of all he performs all of his sacrifices in person.[18]

This theme of continuous, personally performed—and therefore doubly efficacious—cult runs on in the *Monōdia* and *Epitaphios*. The first contains another reference to the Egyptians but now adds the Libyans; both were always at their temples and never at home when they learned of Julian's magnificent piety.[19] Praises of great sacrificing in the other work have already been mentioned with respect to Julian's residence at Constantinople. Of additional interest are three claims related to the preceding consular oration: Julian outdid Proteus in his multiple identities, *metabolai*, of priest, writer, seer, judge, and warrior—a savior in everything; as a diviner, he himself wielded the knife, surpassing his own seers in knowledge and often making totally unexpected appointments on the strength of these rituals; he demoralized the Persians even before leaving Antioch by using great sacrifices to get the gods on the side of his troops, even paying the men to sacrifice if that were necessary.[20] No doubt Julian viewed his activities in the same light; personal involvement and

---

referred every question to the gods," *Vitae sophistarum*, 477. On the gods as Julian's co-strategists, see Libanius, 15:29–30, where he sets their level of communion beyond that attained through conventional ritual. See below, p. 64.

18. *Or.* 12:79–83. Given Libanius' observations—or those of anyone in Antioch at the time—it is difficult to accept Bowersock's allegation (*Julian the Apostate*, p. 80) that "there was nothing romantic or colorful about the paganism which Julian proposed to establish in the place of the religion of Constantine." See p. 58 below. Similarly, he needs to reconcile Julian's undeniable delight in cultic show with that asceticism which he states was "integral to his practice of paganism."

19. *Monod.*, 18, *Opera Libanii*, ed. R. Foerster.

20. *Epit.*, 167, 176, 180, *Opera Libanii*, ed. R. Foerster. See Athanassiadi-Fowden, *Julian*, 116: massive sacrifices were signs that "betray the state of mind of a man falling increasingly under the domination of one idea, the defeat of Persia."

the proliferation of cult were to bring high returns. In the *Misopogon* he claims that his many rounds of the temples have brought cheering crowds flowing into the holy precincts.[21] The very point of magnificent ritual was to encourage pagan response at a commensurate level, and this is the theory expressed by Julian at the opening of his letter to Arsacius.

Yet even while making this point, Julian admits to Arsacius that he is depressed, for his splendid personal example had not been matched: "Hellenism is not yet working out as I had planned, and it is the fault of we who adhere to it, for the ceremonies of the gods have been made brilliant, great, and stronger than anyone's prayer or expectation." It is to such a question of failed impact that Ammianus' critique of the restoration directly applies. He himself witnessed all the cultic activity described with ecstasy by Libanius and experienced with equal fervor by the emperor, yet his own judgment was tempered by local considerations: were these activities in recognizable harmony with the *nomoi* of Antioch's particular religious tradition, or did they simply constitute an externally imposed dogma, a revolution of one?

The *Res gestae* offers a point-for-point rebuttal of Libanius. Generating particular hostility within Ammianus is the latter's purely quantitative approach to good cult, always the more the better. To Libanius' claim that great sacrifices produced a more formidable army, which, in effect, wounded Persia in Antioch, the historian replies with his own scene of debauched soldiers, a burden rather than a shield to the citizenry—the Gauls in particular, whom the rhetorician rated more highly than Constantius' allegedly enervated eastern men.[22] Whereas the religious appeal of Egypt for Libanius lies in its formerly great passion for sacrifice, Ammianus emphasizes that Egyptian religion consisted of more than sacrifices and would be better appreciated as a highly developed, aboriginal *prudentia*, which had stimulated the minds of Pythagoras, Anaxagoras, Solon, and Plato.[23]

Similarly, Ammianus does not accept the argument that Julian was the best pagan because he was more than pagan—that is, continually going beyond the requirements of conventional religion. What was put forward as an ever greater intensification of the emperor's devotion to the old faith, Ammianus views more soberly as a destructive tendency to override *nomos*: how could Julian have been a *legitimus observator* if as a matter of course he considered himself superior to the priests and di-

21. 346b.
22. *Res gestae*, 22.12.6; *Epit.*, 210–11.
23. 22.16.21–22.

viners of his day? Libanius suggests that the emperor frequently broke away from his advisors whether dispensing with generals to solve the same problem by divination or bypassing his diviners when making appointments. Here was the danger of the rhetorician's Proteus, an emperor whose identity was ever changing and unrestrained, insisting upon his right to enter into or dispense with any role.[24] In this sense Libanius appeared to be praising those very acts by which Julian was both effacing points of definition for traditional paganism and making himself progressively unintelligible to conventional, local pagans.

Libanius fairly concedes this great disparity between imperial example and local impact by frequently stressing the successes of Julian's program within the army. Indeed Libanius seems to prepare the way for such a diversion of attention away from the emperor's failure among the citizens by asserting that Julian would have proceeded directly from the capital to Persia had not his men asked for time to rest in Antioch:[25] so he had originally come for the sake of his troops, not the Antiochenes. Ammianus would probably have agreed with the suggestion that at this stage of Julian's career, the restoration belonged fundamentally to his army, a transient group afloat among the local populace, to whom Julian looked most solicitously for that massive response that was obviously not developing outside the ranks. Certainly the emperor had been anxious to establish religious uniformity among his men since Naissus, and it may be that he always considered the conversion of the armies to be his first religious objective among the mass citizenry, civilians—Antiochenes—coming second.[26]

The contrast between union with his soldiers and isolation from Antioch's pagan community[27] is brought out by Julian's denunciation of the municipal senate for its failure to celebrate the festival of Apollo Daphnaeus. He had gone to the god's shrine expecting to find a great celebration but was shocked to see instead a solitary priest with one fowl to offer.[28] One asks how it happened that he had failed to learn before-

---

24. Ammianus refers to an unstable element in Julian's character, *levioris ingenii*, 25.4.16.
25. *Epit.*, 163.
26. On the religion of Julian's army, refer to Bowder, *Age of Constantine*, 93–95.
27. Listening too long to Julian's loudly voiced disappointments—as if he and his entourage lived alone upon an island of traditional faith—we may forget that such a group did exist. On the size and activities of Antioch's pagan population, see Petit, *Libanius*, 200–203; Mission, *Recherches*, 141–47; Festugière, *Antioch païenne*, 63–89; Liebeschuetz, *Antioch*, 224–32; Browning, *Emperor Julian*, 150.
28. *Misop*, 362a–b.

hand what the *curia* would do; his surprise is itself surprising. That Julian was thus unmindful of what local pagans were doing, or, perhaps better, wanted to do, indicates a failure to fit the tenon of his restoration within its proper mortise among the citizens.

Libanius and Ammianus are separated by the two radically different ways in which their genres and philosophies lead them to use Julian's career as an argument for the vitality of paganism. One turns extraordinary praise on this dazzling young emperor, defying any Christian successor to match him; the other, looking more to the future, a world without Julian, feels compelled to reject his peculiar vision.[29] Ammianus perhaps realized as Libanius did not that to praise Julian without representing his restoration as somehow unrepresentative of paganism was ultimately to leave one's argument for the *cultus deorum* among the debris of Persia.[30] Despite this need for repudiation, however, the historian does not actually deal as harshly with Julian as he might. His account deletes many unhappy episodes we could find elsewhere: for example, the tepid pagan response at Pessinus; the lost festival of Apollo Daphnaeus and Julian's wild rebuke that he knew Apollo had abandoned Antioch from his first visit to the shrine;[31] and his demand—not Libanius' gentle bribe—that soldiers sacrifice when receiving their pay.[32] One act of particular interest, as we consider Ammianus' reverence for the obelisk from Heliopolis, is Julian's questionable decision to bring an obelisk, originally dismounted by Constantius, from Alexandria to Constantinople rather than return the monument in true piety—and in accordance with his edict on the restoration of temple property—to its proper shrine.[33] Clearly the historian wishes to limit the emperor's *heroicum ingenium* but not to destroy it, and in thus composing his narrative for the period in Antioch, he serves both the reputation of Julian and that of paganism whose weaknesses pass unrevealed.

• • •

---

29. Sabbah (*Méthode*, 277) holds, to the contrary, that "Ammianus is far from writing *against* Libanius" whatever their differences.

30. Conduché, "Ammien Marcellin," 378, rightly points out that Christians could easily use Julian to upset the customary pagan argument that Christianity had turned divine favor away from Rome: had not Victory and the other gods utterly abandoned Julian?

31. *Misop.*, 361c.

32. Sozomen, *Historia ecclesiastica*, ed. J. Bidez, 5.17.

33. *Ep.* 59. The text of this edict does not survive, but its existence is known indirectly through a law of Valentinian, *Theod. Code*, 5.13.3 (364).

In March 363, the emperor led his army out of Antioch toward the Euphrates and Persia. At this darkening stage of Ammianus' religious narrative we are well prepared for the bleak campaign that, in spite of the tranquil resignation of Julian's dying speech,[34] witnesses his complete alienation from the gods, the culminating divorce between *ethos* and *nomos*. Although Ammianus once refers to the ineluctable power of fate that compelled the emperor to continue his march, fatalism is not the key to this last episode; it is rather that charge made by Sallustius, *Praefectus Galliarum*, which immediately precedes this reference: "[Julian] courted inevitable destruction if he did not first obtain the blessing of the gods."[35] His doom is to be distinctly referred to his religious policy.

With one exception, the celebration of Mater's festival at Callinicum, religious activity now consists entirely of bad omens and cultic behavior that is defective in some respect: the falling portico and stack of fodder at Hierapolis[36] and Batnae respectively; Julian's depressing dreams in the ominous town of Carrhae, "notorious for the sufferings of the Crassi and the Roman army," and the simultaneous burning in Rome of the Temple of Palatine Apollo; the death of Julian's horse, Babylonius; Sallustius' warning of divine anger; an ominous corpse; the prayer by Gordian's tomb at Zaitha, a pious act *pro ingenita pietate* but another reminiscence of Carrhae, murder, and retreat; the portentous deaths of a lion and the soldier Jovian in the vicinity of Dura; the failed sacrifice to Mars Ultor and the similarly abortive inspection of entrails outside of Ctesiphon; finally, in a single episode, the disappearance of the Public Genius, Julian's frightened *depulsoria*, the appearance of the *minax Martis sidus*, and the emperor's total repudiation of his diviners.[37] It should be obvious that these incidents are but a long projection of Julian's initial failure to achieve the *pax numinum*, a sound pagan restoration, in Antioch.[38]

34. 25.3.15–21.
35. We should remember that, for Ammianus, fate is subordinate to justice. If the divine verdict, or *ordo praescriptus*, cannot be changed, it is nevertheless formed according to the merits of the case: Julian *could* have obtained better *fata* for himself. Cf. Plotinus' statement (*Enneads*, ed. P. Henry and H.-R. Schwyzer, 3.4.3) that a man chooses his particular type of tutelary demon by the kind of life he leads.
36. There was an oracle of Apollo at Hierapolis, see Bouché-Leclerque, *Histoire*, 403–4.
37. 23.2.6–5.14, 24.6.17–8.5, 25.2.3–8.
38. Athanassiadi-Fowden errs in stating that "This failure, as Ammianus gives us to understand, was not so much the work of untoward fortune as the result of bad planning and worse execution" (*Julian and Hellenism*, 193). Conduché ("Ammien Marcellin," 379) rather, hits the mark: "Is it any wonder then [given Julian's "unfolding impiety"] that Victory had abandoned him?"

Their most interesting and, perhaps as Ammianus intended it, most obvious feature is the split between two groups of religious advisors in the imperial entourage whom he distinguishes as diviners and philosophers, the first wanting to abort the expedition given any opportunity,[39] the others urging attack. During the march these groups are twice brought into explicit confrontation on either side of Dura, over the significance of a dead lion, then over the deaths of a common soldier of lofty name, Jovian, and two horses who were all killed by the same bolt of lightning.[40] More will be said about this conflict elsewhere; at present I want to note the clarity with which Ammianus announces his own position on the debate: "But they [the Etruscan *haruspices*] were trodden down by the objections of the philosophers whose authority was then highly respected, but who were frequently in error and very persistent in matters which they did not sufficiently comprehend."[41] He plainly seeks respect for the professional integrity and dignity of diviners—not just anyone could do it—as befits his marked personal interest in formally defined and regulated (that is, legitimate) cult.

Julian had injured the integrity of the *doctrinae genus haud leve* in two ways, before the campaign by allowing the number of diviners to surge randomly and now by adopting the unreasonable position that diviners were somehow less qualified to divine than philosophers. This criticism of the excessive authority wielded by philosophers in Julian's entourage inevitably returns us, as does the original failure to obtain the *pax numinum*, to Antioch, where Maximus is pointedly introduced into the narrative by Julian's ostentatious embrace and the censure of Cicero,

39. Responding to the earthquake at Constantinople and to other bad omens suffered at Carrhae, Dura (twice), and Ctesiphon.

40. The case of the divinatory sacrifice performed in behalf of Jovian, *hostiis pro Ioviano caesis, extisque inspectis*, 25.6.1, is problematic. He was advised thereafter not to remain in his present camp—that is, to continue with the retreat—and retreat had always been advocated by that faction known as the Diviners. Conduché (371) lays the sacrifice in their hands. But given Eunapius' claim (*Vitae sophistarum*, ed. J. Giangrande, 478) that Jovian continued to honor Maximus and Priscus as Julian had done, it is equally possible that the authority of their opponents, the Philosophers, lay behind the ceremony; these too could wield the *machaira* in sacrifice as Julian himself used to do. In passing, we should note that although these two antagonistic groups were unaware of the fact, they had recently been arguing over an *omen* (*mortis*) that perhaps applied even more to Jovian than Julian: the three lightning victims, a humbler Jovian, and two riderless horses that surely stand for the loftier Jovian's two dead imperial predecessors. Jovian, significantly, had driven the wagon bearing Constantius' body to Constantinople and so received an *omen imperii*, although for a reign *cassum et umbratile*, 21.16.21.

41. Continuing in similarly strong language, "et enim ut probabile argumentum ad fidem implendam scientiae, id praetendebant . . . ," 23.5.11.

"Those very philosophers who write books about spurning glory still inscribe their names upon them, so that even when they say they despise public commendation and nobility, they still want themselves to be praised and recognized."[42]

Having finished this tour of Julian's religious life in the *Res gestae* and followed Ammianus' unfolding strategy by which individual *ethos* and public, traditional *nomos* move ever farther apart, we are better able to understand the substance of his charge of superstition in the emperor's necrology. Ammianus is hardly distancing himself from paganism per se. He would have welcomed a legitimate restoration guided by the key principle of *temperantia*, which we may interpret as a truly obedient or modest attitude toward the worship of the gods and a more careful attention to local conventions—each city's *priscae leges et mos antiquitus receptus*[43]—than that displayed by this unusual emperor. For as much as Julian was by no means Ammianus' ideal pagan, it would be incorrect to think that his criticisms must imply a neutral religious position or some latent sympathy with Christianity. He stands between the two adversaries but not as a disinterested umpire; Ammianus desires some type of public paganism, which Julian and his Hellenic *comitatus* were apparently incapable of offering.

The Persian campaign in the *Res gestae* depicts the triumph of divination and Julian's final separation from this invaluable art. As one might expect from the highly individual nature of Ammianus' apology, he is the only pagan writer to make the expedition such a continuous religious event, and a negative one at that. Libanius' narration of religious and divine activity now ceases but for a reference to Julian's worship at Carrhae (which lacks Ammianus' ominous burning of the Temple of Palatine Apollo); another to the emperor's detailed foreknowledge of the precise wound Victor would receive when he led the Roman assault across the Tigris; and lastly to some god's assistance in that victory.[44] That the rhetorician deliberately makes less of the emperor's religious activity than he could have is suggested by Julian's last letter to Libanius from Hierapolis.[45] This contains several references to cult and good omens en route through Beroea and Batnae, surely material enough for further effusions of praise had Libanius been inclined to treat Persia with the

---

42. 22.7.3-4.
43. See Julian's letter to the Roman senate, "Tum et memoriam Constantini, ut novatoris turbatorisque priscarum legum et moris antiquitus recepti, [Iulianum] vexavit," 21.10.8.
44. *Epit.*, 214, 251. [Victor] *ipse umerum sagitta praestrictus, Res gestae*, 24.6.13.
45. *Ep.* 98.

same gloss as Antioch. His silence seems an admission that Julian's cultic activity was better deleted now than driven up against his ultimate failure. The theme of generalship, *virtus,* effectively replaces that of piety, and we can hear Libanius' pride in saying that Julian needed no diviners, no Chalchas or Teiresias, to discover how to unblock the Naarmalcha.[46] Of course the moral of Ammianus' account is that Julian would have been wiser to listen to his diviners. The praising voice of Zosimus similarly dries up; he knows that Julian left Antioch under bad signs but abruptly cuts the matter, stating he will not discuss it.[47]

Ammianus appears to stand alone in his particular rendering of the campaign. Certainly he did not get his bad omens from Julian's correspondence if the letter to Libanius is typical of others that might have followed it out of Persia but are lost; Hierapolis and Batnae should have produced bad signs, not good. There is one man, however, whose interests could have been similar to those of the historian: Oribasius, Julian's physician and comrade from Gaul to Persia. He might well qualify as one of those anonymous diviners who constantly opposed themselves to Julian's philosophers and the expedition. His memoirs, employed by Eunapius for his history, would accordingly be a potential source for the bad omens and bleak religious tenor we find in the *Res gestae* if this physician too had been interested in discrediting the *philosophi*—that is, the circle of Maximus. Details are few but suggestive. In the *Vitae,* Eunapius objects to Maximus' excessive influence at court and that arrogant throng, *ochlos,* of Hellenic pagans who accompanied Julian to Persia. His devotion is instead reserved for Chrysanthius, a more modest philosopher who opposed Maximus' manipulation of divine signs and himself studiously avoided the *comitatus.* Eunapius also had particular feelings of reverence for Oribasius, both as an unsurpassed physician who almost cured his beloved Chrysanthius and as one of Julian's great intimates, a major participant in the Gallic revolt. It was he who demanded that Eunapius apply himself to the task of recording Julian's life as if it would be an act of impiety not to do so.[48] Such strong kinship between the two would also suggest that they shared a common opinion of Maximus:

46. *Epit.,* 245, repeating the sentiment of 15, 29–30, but with a different, secular twist. See above, p. 57, n. 18.
47. *Historia nova,* ed. L. Mendelssohn, 3.12. Conduché (378) thinks there is evidence of Zosimus' embarrassment at the defeat of Julian, and paganism, at 3.30, where blame for the Roman retreat is deliberately misdirected from Julian to Jovian.
48. *Hist.,* f. 8; *Vitae sophistarum,* 476, 498, 501–2, 505.

piety to Julian could well be expressed by shifting blame for the emperor's bad fortune onto the tragic influence of his acknowledged mentor. Eunapius' criticism of the imperial entourage in Persia must, I think, have some roots in the personal experience of Oribasius.

That the physician was not a member of Maximus' circle becomes more plausible as we think about the changes that must have occurred in Julian's retinue as he moved from Gaul to Constantinople. Would those pagans, the *pauci*, who were originally instrumental in helping Julian to power have retained their influence undiminished once he was reunited with Maximus and the latter's own group of pagan courtiers? The western clique could easily have been submerged, and Oribasius with them. At any rate, no one could contest the religious ascendancy of Maximus as every source makes clear. If we have made the physician disaffected in this way, he yet needs to be connected to divination, which is easily done through Julian's letter to him regarding the dream of the young shoot and fallen tree. Oneiromancy is a type of divination that would have been particularly appropriate to an ancient physician.[49] Then too Oribasius has clearly been conferring with Julian about such signs before the sending of this note, and we immediately wonder whether Oribasius was not among those *visorum interpretes* at Carrhae.[50] A triangle, in sum, emerges between Ammianus, Eunapius, and Oribasius, three eastern pagans with a common antipathy to Maximus who were perhaps even acquainted with one another.[51]

In the presence of such possibilities we are at least entitled to con-

---

49. On the oracle of Aesculapius at Pergamum, Oribasius' native city (and that of Galen) see Bouché-Leclerque, *Histoire*, 293–95.

50. Beneath the dubious report in Cedrenus (ed. B. Niebuhr [Bonn, 1838], 304) about Delphi's last oracle, there may lie some actual souvenir of Oribasius' reputation for divining. The story is given that Oribasius, "physician and quaestor," was sent by Julian to restore the temple of Apollo at Delphi. He arrived ready for work only to receive the demon's admission that it was incapable of giving any more oracles. Now Eunapius states that Julian appointed his friend, the Hierophant, to manage the temples of Greece, and such restoration as Julian had in mind for Delphi would logically have been his task, not a concern of Oribasius. If we may nevertheless imagine the emperor sending his other companion on such a mission, there is still the question of its result, the "last oracle," which nods too obviously toward Christian propaganda to be entirely credible; the failure of Julian's or Maximus' oracles was after all a favorite theme of anti-Julian polemic. Yet the oracle given by Cedrenus may capture in distorted fashion the actual division between Julian's religious advisors, some of whom (the Diviners—that is, Oribasius' group) advanced oracles in which the gods in effect turned their backs upon Julian and his expedition. Ammianus of course provides his own instances where Apollo refuses to talk to the emperor.

51. On the possible relationship between Ammianus, Eunapius, and Oribasius, see Thompson, *Historical Work*, 40, 136–37; Thompson, "Ammianus Marcellinus" in *Roman Historians*, 152–54; Blockley, *Fragmentary*, 24–26.

clude that Ammianus' conception of religious events during the Persian expedition has intelligible roots outside of the *Res gestae* and can be nothing so simple as the ancient taste for multiplying divine phenomena as a climax approaches.[52] Despite the intriguing thoughts Oribasius provokes, however, his identification with the apologetic interests of Ammianus should be limited to this one point, rejection of the *philosophi*. Given the physician's intense order to Eunapius that he treat Julian as an object of piety, it is doubtful that Oribasius would in any way have considered the emperor (when Maximus was not in attendance) to be fundamentally *superstitiosus* as Ammianus did, nor would he have intentionally diminished Julian's stature for the sake of defending paganism against Christian arguments.[53]

The historian's purpose in constantly preaching the value of divination, even at the expense of his hero, becomes clearer when we realize the extent to which Christians used Julian's prematurely ruined career as a proof of the failure of divination and its gods. Gregory Nazianzen fills his *Second Invective* against Julian with just such a claim.[54] Philostorgius tells how all the great oracles were consulted when Julianus, Julian's uncle and *Comes Orientis*, lay ill: each predicted his recovery but, for all that, he died in agony.[55] Elsewhere, Maximus gave Julian lying oracles that said he would conquer Persia like an Alexander, and so the emperor stupidly rejected Persian embassies seeking peace—how the Antiochenes laughed! Julian again sent his friends to every oracle. Yes, they promised that the gods would win trophies by the Tigris, but Loxias (Apollo) was a liar. Oribasius looked helplessly upon that same dumb Apollo who had earlier been paralyzed by the relics of Saint Babylas.[56] We see that Ammianus' own presentation of the campaign saves the esteem of divination. Prophecy and the world of traditional deities with which it is in contact continue to flow around the dead emperor and beyond him, *velut ex perpetuis fontibus*.[57] Against those Christians who

52. Note that Sabbah treats these omens in a chapter titled "La persuasion esthetique." See p. 4, n. 12 above.
53. See Conduché, "Ammien Marcellin," 376.
54. *Or.* 4:38–57, 88–91, *Works of Gregory Nazianzen*, ed. J. P. Migne.
55. *Historia ecclesiastica*, ed. J. Bidez, 7.12.
56. Socrates, *Historia ecclesiastica*, ed. J. P. Migne, 3.18, 20–21; Theodoret, *Historia ecclesiastica*, ed. L. Parmentier, 3.21, 25. See Philostorgius, *Historia ecclesiastica*, ed. J. Bidez, 7.35, and above, p. 65, n. 50. For Julian's refusal to negotiate with the Persians, see Libanius, 12, 76–77; 17, 19; 18, 164.
57. 21.1.8.

ridiculed his omens as failed or deceitful, the historian replies that Julian's diviners had been correct but that he had refused to believe them.[58] Yet this willful error held a lesson besides for Libanius who, in his grief, dangerously suggested that the gods themselves had erred and that paganism was totally ruined.[59] In fact the emperor's doom could have been observed long before his death; had he been the perfect *cultor* of Libanius' orations he would not have rejected his diviners in the face of so many proofs of divine displeasure.[60]

I have sought to elucidate Ammianus' ideal of proper cult through the extremely complex figure of Julian, who so often becomes the negative shape of the historian's two desires, restraint and sensitivity to local cus-

58. Gregory (*Or.* 4:93–95) asks why Julian, for all his alleged skill in divination, did not foresee his own death in battle. It is interesting to find Ammianus attributing a statement to Julian that seems to answer this very question: "Nor am I ashamed to confess this: long ago I learned from a truth-singing prophetess that I would die by the sword," 25.3.19. When hearing that he had been wounded near a village named Phrygia, Julian recognized the name from another prophecy, 25.3.9. Cf. his prediction of Victor's wound, above, p. 63.
59. *Monod.*, 6; *Epit.*, 281.
60. On Ammianus and the Christian polemicists, see Sabbah, *La Méthode*, 366–71, also Hahn, "Der ideologische," 225–32. Before quitting this chapter, I would make some final comments upon the interesting thesis of Conduché. He divides Julian's entourage between religiously innovative eastern "neopagans," the *philosophi*, and an alienated group of conservative western (Roman) pagans, the *haruspices*, among whom we are to number the *pauci* of Gaul. The latter eventually became so hostile to Julian that they may even have conspired to kill him. We can certainly accept that geography must have had something to do with significant changes in the religious activity of Julian's retinue. In drawing Julian from the East, stripping him of his old companions, Constantius had, after all, created a social and religious vacuum around his cousin, which another group was bound to fill until reunion with the old was possible. But in my opinion Maximus, not eastern religious ideology per se, was the thorn; considerations of personality should take precedence over those of region. An East-West division would not do justice to the criticism of Maximus expressed by those from his own region (e.g., Eunapius and Chrysanthius). Conduché's suggestion of an alliance between the Diviners and Gallic soldiery is indeed the best way to vent the Gauls' known aversion to service in the East—the very reason for their revolt from Constantius—into Julian's preferred manner of doing business, over the tripod. It would have been prudent to get some kind of representation at these important conclaves. But this must have been an uncertain path to influence, without guarantees, for Libanius reminds us that Julian often "surpassed" his seers and left them out of his divinely inspired decisions. It is possible, though, that the chief internal problem of the Persian campaign can be reckoned without any reference to religion: the desire of the Gallic army to get home, to recall Julian to his old—and broken—pact (see above, p. 40), to make any successor do the same. Note that Julian would appear to have inadvertently reunited the long separated, desperate, and exiled remnants of Magnentius' army, *Res gestae*, 18.9.3; Libanius, 18:104. In these terms, Julian's campaign really ended only when Valentinian divided his army with Valens at Mediana, 26.5.1–3: the Gauls were going home.

tom. It is hardly surprising, of course, that the more conservative and less "Hellenic" Ammianus should have differed with the great radical, reforming pagan of his epoch, the man of *novae viae*.[61] Considering then that the historian was forced to build his apology for a still vital, traditional paganism upon the life of a religious revolutionary, we can only admire the intricate fashion in which he accepts and rejects Julian by turns, directing his arguments both to Christians and to fellow pagans.[62] In recognizing various impediments to the free expression of personal religious beliefs in the *Res gestae*, we must appreciate that Julian, as well as Christian coercion, created a difficult mental environment within which to work.

61. See above, p. 53.
62. On Ammianus' pagan audience, refer above to pp. 10, 34, and my Conclusion.

· CHAPTER FOUR ·

THAT THEY COME TO THE GODS: PHILOSOPHERS IN A NEW RESTORATION

Ammianus stood twice upon the wreckage of the pagan restoration: once in his city, Antioch, again and finally as one of Julian's warriors in Persia. Just as the *Res gestae* embraces more than Julian, however, so a history in its fullest sense is more than an epitaph; it is a guide to the future—*munera divinandi*. Surely that is what the Roman historian wished to believe as he wrote in the Temple of the World twenty years later. And what if there should be a new opportunity for paganism to recapture its old status, or at least to secure its toleration once and for all to an unmovable and ample foundation within the empire by "plain and total decrees"? There would obviously have to be some major change in the way such a program was led, for Ammianus ascribes Julian's difficulties to the faults of bad leadership—an astute tactic, which seems to imply the existence of a mass of frustrated followers standing idle only for want of correct guidance from above. Collaboration, *homonoia*, had broken down within the pagan community. Julian had lost contact with the Antiochenes, and fighting had broken out even within the *comitatus* between his diviners and philosophers. Future leaders must recross that threshold separating moderation from excess, distortion, and division. They would need to regain a sense of community and recover a truer presentation than Julian's odd pagan church, of the diverse, socially benign, and, one might even say, unassuming world of the *cultus deorum*.

Of course Ammianus knew that responsibility for Julian's distortion of what he (Ammianus) himself thought to be the true, that is, moderate nature of paganism lay not only with his emperor but also with that spreading vendetta of religions that had compelled Julian to fight back, and so court the errors of passion. This war of retaliation was bringing on a blackness of misrepresentation. Pagans parting before the Christian wedge were falling into the egocentrism of excessive displays of public devotion or else to aloofness, a proud and silent cultic isolation that was of similarly doubtful help to their threatened community. A way must be found out of the conflict and back through the gate of *temperantia* if in the historian's new city, Rome, he were ever to witness the peaceful victory lost at Antioch.

I would like to bring this problem of cohesion within the pagan community into focus by considering a particularly vital segment of the pagan leadership, philosophers. Ammianus, who makes a bold statement for an age in which philosophers were commonly regarded as masters of ritual, complains that they had too little grasp of such matters when they interfered with Julian's diviners. How should they behave then? To answer that question, and so ultimately learn what message the historian was offering his coreligionists at Rome, we must identify spheres of religious authority in the *Res gestae*, or in other words ask, who is the priest or diviner, who the philosopher? Julian's mentor, Maximus, and the renowned first-century philosopher, Apollonius of Tyana (whom Ammianus explicitly praises[1]) will assist our investigation of roles by making in effect two ends of a conceptual balance laid across the historian's threshold of approval and disapproval. I include Apollonius for what I believe are more interesting reasons than his reputation for miracles or his well-known service to pagan polemic as a rival to Christ,[2] for he also involved himself in political and religious problems throughout the empire in order to raise social concord, *homonoia*. This figure, then, may reveal to us something of the actual inspiration for Ammianus' own idea of a pagan restoration superior to that of Julian: philosophers working temperately alongside of local priests to solidify rather than divide or erode traditional cultic loyalties. Nor should we forget another writer living in Rome while Ammianus was there—Virius Nicomachus Flavianus, author of a life of Apollonius,[3] and the last leader of Rome's pagans following the death of Vettius Agorius Praetextatus in 384.

1. Twice, as a man of manifold virtue in direct contact with his *genius*, 21.14.5 (see p. 20 above), and as *amplissimus ille philosophus*, 23.6.19.
2. See Du Labriolle, *Réaction païenne*, 180–89, 311–14.
3. "Apollonii Pythagorici vitam, non ut Nicomachus senior e Philostrati sed ut Tascius Victorianus e Nicomachi schedio exscripsit, quia iusseras, misi," *Epistulae*, Sidonius Apollinaris, ed. A. Loyen, 8.3.1. For additional evidence of Apollonius' popularity in the

...

Priestly authority cedes nothing to philosophy on the score of venerability. Antique religious figures abound in the *Res gestae* and Ammianus treats them respectfully. Of the legendary diviners, Amphiaraüs, Marcius—both *incliti*—Mobsus, Phineus, and Idmon, Mobsus is particularly notable, for in the historian's own time the sick were still finding cures at his tomb.[4] The special attention given to founders of ritual such as Tages,[5] the Chaldaeans, Zoroaster, Numa, and before all, the Egyptians[6] indicates a recognition of that peculiar virtue that accrues to religion through its connection with the aboriginal history of a people.

Ammianus' priests and diviners, unless they are defendants, are normally anonymous, operating in groups such as the Etruscan *haruspices* or the *visorum interpretes*,[7] while his philosophers enjoy a noticeably greater degree of personal identity. The faceless preservers of the *doctrinae genus haud leve* can scarcely be distinguished from their books of ritual. Quietly they wait to be consulted; rooted to their shrines and secretive, they hold unchanged those divine *res gestae* embodied in ceremony that lay at the source of history and religion.[8] The role of a priest so described appears more tightly bound to an ethic of strict conservation than that of Ammianus' philosopher, whose virtue issues most obviously from personally distinct achievements and characteristics bracketed within a single lifetime. It is the philosopher, not the priest, who displays a dynamic, assertive personality, showing himself to be widely traveled and religiously eclectic.[9] Temporal continuity, antiquity, rises

---

fourth century, see Jones, "Epigram on Apollonius," 190–94. Jones (194) suggests that we might trace some faint path from Apollonius to Nicomachus in the *Historia Augusta, Divus Aurelianus*, 24.2–9, 27.6. Libanius compares Julian to Apollonius, *Or.* 16.56.

4. 14.1.7, 8.3; 22.8.14, 22. "Ex eo caespite punico tecti, manes eius [Mobsi] heroici, dolorum varietati medentur plerumque sospitales," 14.8.3.

5. On Tages and the *Etrusca disciplina*, see P. de Jonge, *Sprachlicher*, 17:246–47; Wissowa, *Religion*, 543–49.

6. 16.7.4; 17.10.2; 21.1.10, 14.5; 22.16.20; 23.6.25. "Sed si intelligendi divini editionem multiplicem et praesensionum originem mente vegeta quisquam voluerit, replicata per mundum omnem inveniet mathemata huiusmodi ab Aegypto circumlata, ubi primum homines longe ante alios ad varia religionum incunabula, ut dicitur, pervenerunt et initia prima sacrorum caute tuentur condita scriptis arcanis," 22.16.19–20.

7. 23.3.3, 5.10; 25.2.7.

8. Note the ambiguous signification of *oraculum* as spoken or written prophecy; e.g., *oracula et auctores docuere*, 21.14.4. Religion as the secret conservation of an unchanging (that is, "written") body of knowledge: *initia prima sacrorum caute tuentur condita scriptis arcanis*, 22.16.20; cf. *secreta librorum mysticorum auctoritas*, 22.14.7.

9. Pythagoras is their archetype, leaving Thales at Miletus to pursue religious studies

before the priest as a guarantor of his ritual, but absorption in the beauty of uninterrupted sequence must also tend to inhibit the idea of individual achievement (excluding the founder's original syntheses[10]). This reduction of the self is nevertheless agreeable to the priest, who regards himself as a holy servant, or to the oracle, who believes that he only relays divine communication.

However great the respect of the historian for his priests, we would not expect to find an entirely favorable presentation of them at every point in the *Res gestae*. The priests of republican Rome habitually misused their right of intercalendration until the Greek calendar was adopted by Augustus.[11] And contemporary diviners were a mixed lot. Certainly the traditional oracles are never criticized, but on leaving the great shrines we can find them ignorant, timorous and flattering, or thoroughly malevolent.[12] Although Ammianus clearly raises the prestige of diviners by pointing out their successes—*vates auguresque praedixere veredice*—in many cases, such as those trials involving the *haruspices* Campensis and Amantius,[13] no praiseworthy achievement or special sign of esteem is apparent.

His philosophers should be the last to devalue the priests' work. That religious wisdom forms the substratum of philosophy is obvious from the numerous connections between these two in the *Res gestae*. When Zoroaster lived among the Brahmins of "towering intellect," he studied natural laws and pure sacrificial rites, which he later combined with Chaldaean learning[14] to form the *scientia*—not *religio*, we note— of the Hagistia, propagated by the Magi and admired by Plato. When dealing with knowledge of this primal sort, Ammianus finds little to choose

---

in Phoenicia, Egypt (there, for twenty-two years), and Babylon: "Furthermore they say that he also made a compound of divine philosophy and worship, learning some ingredients from the Orphics, Egyptian priests, Chaldaeans, and Magi, and adapting other elements from the mysteries of Eleusis, Imbrus, Samothrace, and Lemnos, even taking a bit from the neighboring barbarian lands of the Celts and Iberians," Iamblichus, *De vita Pythagorica*, ed. U. Klein (Stuttgart, 1975), 28.151. In connection with these Celts, note Ammianus' reference to Druidic *sodalicia* formed "as the authority of Pythagoras decreed," 15.9.8.

10. E.g., Zoroaster, 23.6.33.

11. *Licenter gratificantes publicorum vel litigantium commodi*, 26.1.12.

12. E.g., Constantius' diviners, *interpretantes placentia*, 21.14.1; Julian's unregulated *imperiti*, 22.12.7; Heliodorus, the *mathematicus* and informer, *tartareus ille malorum omnium . . . fabricator*, 29.2.6.

13. Of those diviners at Rome who were active in 371–72, Amantius is called *prae ceteris notus*.

14. Called a *philosophia* by Ammianus, although this is scarcely to be distinguished from a religious science or ritual: "his prope Chaldaeorum est regio, altrix philosophiae veteris, ut memorant ipsi, apud quos veridica vaticindandi fides eluxit," 23.6.25.

between philosopher and priest, for at a fundamental level both are active in revealing, to a greater or lesser extent, what is secret, *arcana*, and the result always emerges within some formal intellectual framework or code to which the name "law" might be applied. In this sense the Euhages and Pythagorean Druids[15] are no different from the Magi; all might qualify as *theologi*.[16] The two professions cross again in Alexandria, a center of philosophy whose first inspiration was derived from Egyptian religion. Pythagoras, *colens secretius deos*,[17] Solon, and Plato received the benefits of this archetypal *prudentia*. In the figure of Anaxagoras, whose predictions of natural phenomena are twice mentioned, we see one who effectively combines the roles of diviner and *physicus*: *tremores futuros praedixerat terrae*.[18] Ammianus also cites Aristotle with reference to oneiromancy.[19] Corresponding to such antique associations between philosophy and religion there are, in the contemporary period covered by the narrative, Maximus' prophecy of death for those who attempted to discover the successor of Valens[20] and the habitual sacrifices to Besa performed by the Alexandrian philosopher, Demetrius Cythras.

Despite the frequent bonding between philosophers and priests through divination or the mutual sharing of arcane knowledge, we must yet ask whether each group is important to Ammianus in precisely the same way. I have previously said that priests or diviners do not seem as important to the historian as distinct personalities. Merit accrues to their profession by making correct predictions, *clara fides*—being right; the art, not its practitioner, is the essential point of reference. But philosophers in the *Res gestae* appear on a different footing; *who* they are is distinctly important. Philosophical theories gain their eminence from that of the author—*amplissimi* such as Plato, Aristotle, Anaxagoras, or De-

---

15. "Scrutantes sublimia, leges naturae pandere [Euhages] conabantur. . . . quaestionibus occultarum rerum altarumque [Drysidae] erecti sunt," 15.9.8.

16. Consider the apparent absence of any need to differentiate priestly from philosophical authority in the general phrase, *velut scrutatis veteribus libris*, 15.8.16. The accompanying theory that bodily signs reveal a man's soul, and thus his destiny, could well be ascribed to books of either type or even poetry; cf. Homer's *sempiterna carmina* and theories of the *genius*, 21.14.5.

17. 22.16.21.

18. 22.8.5, 16.22. Philostratus (*Vita Apollonii*, ed. C. Kayser, 1.2) wonders why Anaxagoras' predictions are regarded as evidence of his *sophia* but those of Apollonius, *mageia*.

19. "Quae [somnia] ut Aristoteles affirmat, tum fixa sunt et stabilia, cum animantis altius quiescentis ocularis pupilla neutrubi inclinata rectissime cernit," 21.1.12.

20. "Verum ultro praedixisse consultores ipsos suppliciis poenalibus perituros," 29.1.42. It must be significant that of all the philosophers mentioned by Ammianus, only Maximus gives an oracle.

74 APEX OMNIUM

mocritus—not because Ammianus is convinced that the ideas themselves must be necessarily correct. He habitually groups theories without indicating which he prefers,[21] nor does any resolution seem necessary to him in such contexts; perfect knowledge was, after all, impossible and opinions would vary.[22] Clearly, different expectations are involved. Philosophers need not be right to honor their profession, yet they must, like Plato, be personally eminent.

This particularly important element of individual character, *ethos*, which Ammianus contrasts to the bland identities of his priests submerged in *nomos*, suggests a connection between the historian's reliance upon past philosophers for their theories and his tendency to portray their modern counterparts as men of courage in the face of imperial tyranny.[23] Professional authority ultimately becomes an affair of the individual; he validates his doctrines within the confines of his own person. For as many times as Ammianus mentions philosophers, there are but three references to philosophical schools: the Academy (abandoned by Demosthenes), Zeno "that ancient Stoic," and the Druidic Pythagorean brotherhoods.[24] Types of philosophers do not exist for him as do types of diviners, and so the philosopher of the *Res gestae* is not permitted to drop into priestly anonymity; rather his self-demonstration is expected and valued.[25] Here and in the philosopher's more aggressive commitment to synthesizing and disseminating various kinds of knowledge, using conserved rituals as tools for disputation outside the *temenē*, lay obvious tensions between him and priest. Despite Pythagoras' twenty-two years in Egyptian temples, philosophy—and this is Ammianus' point—can only speak for religion in a particular way. That professional philosophers are not the only interested spokesmen is shown by the list of those in special contact with their *genii*, where Pythagoras, Socrates, Apollonius of Tyana, and Plotinus are balanced by Numa, Scipio, Marius, and Augustus.

21. See the excursus on earthquakes, 17.7.9–14.
22. "Ad ipsius enim veritatis arcana, non modo haec nostra vulgaris inscitia, sed ne sempiterna quidem lucubrationibus longis nondum exhausta, physicorum iurgia penetrarunt," 17.7.9. "Suppetunt aliae multae opiniones et variae," 20.11.30.
23. With the exception of the weak Epigonus, *quidam amictu tenus philosophus*, 14.9.5; otherwise, Demetrius Cythras, *corpore durus et animo. . . . fiducia gravi fundatus . . . intrepidus*, 19.12.12; Pasiphilus, *robustae mentis*, 29.1.36; Simonides, *verum nostra memoria severissimus . . . firmitate animi. . . . constantiam gravem*, 29.1.37, 9; Coeranius, *haut exili meriti virum . . . tormentorum immanitate invictum*, 29.2.25.
24. 14.9.6, 15.9.9, 30.4.5.
25. See Fowden's "virtuosi of the spiritual life" in "Platonist Philosopher," 381. There he speaks of the tendency of pagan philosophers toward "self-constitutionalization" in the difficult period after Julian's death.

When considering whether one of these two distinct schemes of professional (self-) validation carries greater authority or power of proof within Ammianus' mind, we should note that his arguments generally rest with a diverse mixture of authorities. Eminent statesmen and poets contribute to the excursus on *genii*, and the latter have a definite bearing upon religious discussions: if Anaxagoras may be considered a diviner, so may Virgil, the *Mantuanus vates*.[26] As our circle of participation in theological proof is drawn ever larger, the position of Ammianus' philosophers relative to his priests must appear less domineering. He is neither exalting the former as religion's sole spokesmen nor implying, through the exclusion of other sources of authority, that they would be superior replacements for the conventional, non-"Hellenic" priesthood. Although philosophers might be better suited than others to comprehend the priests' ritual ministrations—both groups begin at the temple—religion in the *Res gestae* shows itself historically prior to philosophy, thus in Alexandria, and must remain entitled to its distinctive professional base. A threshold exists beyond which even philosophers will become *perseverantes in parum cognitis*. For Ammianus, it is the function of the priest to conserve ritual, both in its secret and social forms of expression, while the philosopher is to absorb learning from every source, making it plastic in the form of new *logoi*, and to display his virtue through *ethos* rather than *nomos*. Personal courage, we note, is not an obvious attribute of his pagan priest. Although there was every reason and need for cooperation between the two groups, particularly when members of both found themselves responsible for guiding the emperor to his *sidus*, one could not replace the other or be its proof.

We leave the preceding section with two contrasting images of priest-diviners and philosophers, drawn on the rule that distinctive methods of presentation proceed from different expectations and concepts of function. From suggesting that code of professional relations that Ammianus brings to the religious conflict within Julian's entourage, I shall turn more particularly to the implicit cause of this trouble, Maximus.

Although the historian could not have disowned Julian's restoration without treating this philosopher similarly, his criticism is in reality oblique, and the three references to Maximus in the *Res gestae* do not record explicit opposition: the philosopher is embraced by Julian in the *curia* at Constantinople; with Priscus and the dying Julian he discusses

26. 15.9.1; cf. *poetae veteres et theologi nuncuparunt*, 17.7.12.

the soul; he is executed for failing to reveal what he has learned of the oracle naming Theodorus as Valens's successor.[27] The last reference carries a notable compliment: "that widely known philosopher, a man with a great reputation for learning, through whose rich discourses Julian stood out as an emperor abounding in knowledge." There, however, Maximus is praised only in a rather conventional capacity as a man of learned discourse, *sermones*; his cultic activities—and whether or not the historian considered him pious, a *legitimus observator*—are omitted from the compliment. Nor does Ammianus take advantage of Maximus' correct prediction of death for those trapped by the oracle to note his acute perception of *fata*.

Our closest approximation to overt criticism of the philosopher concerns the *ostentatio* of Julian's reunion with him at the capital, which, interestingly, foreshadows a fault to come in the pagan restoration: "At the same time, he [Julian] was called cow-killer instead of priest by many who ridiculed the great number of his sacrifices. And to this extent he was fittingly criticized, for he took improper delight in carrying the holy tools in place of the priests and in being dogged by a troupe of female attendants, all for the sake of empty show [*ostentationis gratia*]."[28] It is particularly significant that Ammianus explicitly links *ostentatio* to interference in those religious duties conventionally performed by others, *pro sacerdotibus*, for he indicts Julian's philosophers on the same charge of encroachment during the Persian expedition. If Julian is the one of the embracing pair called unmindful of Cicero's remark against the vanity of philosophers, we cannot ignore Maximus who is, after all, the only professional philosopher on the scene; he more obviously evokes the category of *ipsi illi philosophi*.[29] Similarly, Ammianus may not take a straight lunge at the philosopher during those interpretive arguments on either side of Dura, but in identifying Maximus and Priscus at the emperor's deathbed—the only philosophers named in the entire expedition—he inevitably lays the frustration of Julian's diviners at their feet.

Why the historian did not simply criticize the religious abuses of Maximus openly as he did those of Julian is difficult to say. Perhaps he spared Maximus out of respect for his martyrdom at the hands of Valens, or he may have wished to avoid diminishing his lofty theme of imperial (heroic) religion by suggesting that Julian's restoration was to some undue extent the creation of another. If paganism might ever guide the conduct of future emperors, it would be better displayed as an organic out-

27. 22.7.3, 25.8.23, 29.1.42.
28. 22.14.3.
29. And is himself later called *ille philosophus*, 29.1.42.

growth of the imperial office itself—seen to have whole *maiestas*—untouched by courtiers. Moreover, if Ammianus made much of the philosopher's influence at court, he would be indicating all too plainly that Julian shared a vice with Constantius, *palatinis quibusdam nimium quantum addictus*.[30] In sum, there was nothing to gain by explicitly blaming Julian's faults on Maximus, for this would only raise another damaging question: how had the emperor permitted this philosopher to attain such a dominating position? Julian would only appear dangerously dependent and less heroic, falling unacceptably below even that mark drawn purposely low for apologetic purposes.

If Ammianus did say less than he wanted to on the unhappy subject of Maximus, we are still capable of summoning up a probable facsimile of that lost voice from Eunapius. Egotism is the dominating theme of his sketch in the *Vitae*, manifest in its religious guise as an independence of cultic restraints and a lack of true obedience to the gods. Eunapius hints at this outgrown religious self-sufficiency in his first remark about the philosopher, who, he states, entranced his listeners as if he were an oracle. Granted, this is a familiar enough description of a riveting philosopher,[31] yet it is also one peculiarly suited to Maximus, who was executed as a direct consequence of his reputation for giving oracles. It was to find him that Julian left the company of Eusebius and Chrysanthius when he learned how Maximus once brought a statue of Hecate to life. By relating this *theatrikon* to Julian, Eusebius had intended to make more obvious the reason why he himself chose to pursue the gods through conventional dialectic, *katharsis dia tōn logōn*, but in the event made it appear less attractive. Nor did Julian judge Chrysanthius' work sufficiently engaging to detain him in Pergamum, although this philosopher, like Maximus, was particularly interested in divination.[32]

After Julian became emperor one decade later, Maximus triumphed, arriving at Constantinople with a great retinue and immediately lording it over everyone: "for the ruler and the ruled were in every way under the control of Maximus. Night or day made no difference to them; they referred every question to the gods."[33] But the philosopher paid for this exalted station by choosing to ignore unfavorable omens that he had received before his journey to the capital; to go, he deliberately twisted bad signs into good. Chrysanthius, on the other hand, had respected the

30. 21.16.16.
31. *Vita Pyth.*, 6.30.
32. *Vitae sophistarum*, ed. J. Giangrande, 474–75.
33. *Vitae sophistarum*, 477. Contrast Libanius' praise for the same incessant ritual activity, p. 57 above.

dark signs of his own divining and never would join the *comitatus*. In time, the arrogance of Maximus thoroughly infected the court, even if this was partially mitigated by the more restrained behavior of his colleague, Priscus. Nor did the Persian expedition relieve this oppressive scene, for Julian departed with a mob, *ochlos*, of inflated savants who gloried in his close association with them. Maximus survived Julian's fall but was seriously implicated in the alleged conspiracy of Theodorus, whose members had apparently sought to gain enhanced prestige for their oracle by tricking Maximus, generally reputed to be the best judge of divine intents, into putting his name on it. But when they asked him to interpret "THEOD . . . ," pretending it to have been one of his own utterances, the philosopher saw the ruse and instead predicted that now their own deaths were imminent.[34] That these men believed he would not have been able to recall all his oracles will perhaps strike us as some indication of the frequency with which Maximus was accustomed to give them.

Eunapius' sketch is consonant both with the harsh mode of rendering events in Antioch used by Ammianus and with the historian's tendency to incline his philosophers toward personal display. Not surprisingly, the faults of Maximus parallel those of his imperial devotee, for neither adhered sufficiently to a religious mean. Chrysanthius, Eunapius' own model of piety, knew not only how to prophesy, but, more importantly, how best to use what he revealed. Right comprehension of the gods depended upon having the correct spirit of humility before them; obedience was everything: "When a man obeys the gods, then truly they listen to him."[35] To obey was to perceive more fully through a willingness to be instructed, yet such cautionary moderation characterized neither Maximus nor Julian. By distorting omens, the former had really done no less than lay force on the gods: "The foremost Hellenes," said Maximus to Chrysanthius, "and especially those who have been trained in ritual art, should not just fly from the field when they first encounter their opponents, but rather they should push their way through [*ekbiazesthai*] those ranks into the very nature of the Divinity until it kneels to him who kneels before it."[36] He talks of ritual warfare as if he were some Julian wanting to loose himself upon an invisible Persia. Even if only a portion of what the *Vitae* contains were true, Maximus would hardly have been one to foster self-restraint in the emperor, and

34. *Vitae sophistarum*, 477–78, 480, 501.
35. *Vitae sophistarum*, 477. This is a verse from the *Iliad*, 1.218, which a god spoke to Chrysanthius in a dream, warning him not to go to Constantinople (with Maximus).
36. *Vitae sophistarum*, 477.

accordingly we can appreciate how little chance of success those diviners who opposed the Persian expedition would have had when competing against such an advisor. His career suggests a problem of the first importance to any proposed renovation of paganism, the philosopher's often transcending ego. Would so many *imperatores*, accustomed to ruling private campaigns of the soul by the light of their own rituals and religious priorities, be capable of collective effort within a broader community of less extraordinary pagans such as Ammianus?[37]

Maximus emerges then as the antithesis of benign collaboration between philosophers and priests—between, so to speak, the creative and conservative aspects of sacred wisdom, *ethos* and *nomos*. Ammianus believed that the two groups, together with their laity, must find a way back to the temple again in *homonoia*. There had once been a dynamic breath between philosophers and those *temenē* where they had learned so much; this must be revived: follow Pythagoras, Solon, and Plato to Egypts' priests—the Serapeum that was temple and library[38]—but do not say with Plotinus, "Let the gods come to me."[39] It was, after all, by just such a predilection for "fleeing the temples" that a *goēs* was thought to reveal himself.[40] To draw a philosopher away from his private Persia and back to the concerns of civic religion in the right spirit of cooperation would be to reintegrate him with pagan society at large, rendering him more sensitive to the needs of place, a superior leader at one with his public.[41]

---

37. For other assessments of Maximus, see Athanassiadi-Fowden, *Julian and Hellenism*, 33–36; Du Labriolle, *Réaction païenne*, 364. Assessing paganism's loss in the death of Praetextatus, Cameron ("Paganism and Literature," 17) states, "He was their one intellectual. He was a philosopher. The importance of philosophy, or rather its absence, in the collapse of western paganism has not (I think) been fully appreciated." So too, Browning (*Emperor Julian*, 167) assumes that the cause of paganism was necessarily strengthened by philosophy: Iamblichus and his successors formulated a pagan credo to remedy the lack of coherent doctrine, "one of the weaknesses of traditional paganism." I have indicated in this and the previous chapters that Ammianus, for his part, did not find the participation of philosophers to be so unquestionably advantageous; they were rather a mixed blessing. Philosophical paganism, Hellenism, had surely had its hour in the light with Julian, but it revealed serious flaws and must have always seemed socially adrift. By choosing to come to Rome, Ammianus may actually have been turning his back on that particular path to religious restoration.

38. 22.16.13.

39. *Vita Plotini*, 10, *Enneads*, ed. P. Henry and H.-R. Schwyzer.

40. Philostratus, *Vita Apollonii*, ed. C. Kayser, 8.7.

41. Consider the aloofness to conventional, public forms of worship expressed in Porphyry's *Epistula ad Marcellam*, ed. A. Nauck (Leipzig, 1896), 17, where Marcella is said to commit no impiety by refusing to trouble herself over the statues of the gods like a commoner. For an excellent discussion of the philosopher's (increasing) isolation from society, *philosophia akoinōnētos*, see Fowden's "Pagan Holy Man," especially sec. 4, "The Drift to-

. . .

A positive reply to the faults of Maximus and Julian appears in Apollonius of Tyana, a philosopher always interested in questions of religious reform and social integration. Ammianus mentions him in a favorable light as one of those great men visibly assisted by their *genii* and as *amplissimus ille philosophus* in connection with the Cappadocian temple of Zeus Asbamaeus.[42] Such compliments place him within the first rank of Ammianus' philosophers, among whom only Plato is similarly titled *amplissimus*;[43] he is distinctly above Maximus. We should then consider what specific, personal impact the life of this philosopher might have had upon the historian.

Although during his life Apollonius experienced every exotic and supernatural phenomenon known to Late Antiquity, the purpose of Philostratus in writing his famous *Vita Apollonii* was to defend his subject against charges of *goēteia*, much as Ammianus himself wished to deny that divination belonged among the *pravae artes*.[44] He twice breaks the narrative to contrast Apollonius' pious, socially benign conduct with the sterile marvels of others, which were empty of virtue. For example, the philosopher only admired some Indian automatons out of courtesy without having any desire to work similar effects.[45] The interrogation of Apollonius by Domitian stands at the climax of the *Vita*, and there the philosopher totally refutes the charge of wizardry.[46] Philostratus' work demonstrates a socially interested, apologetic thrust, which would have held a new relevancy for those fourth-century pagans who found their religion shoved increasingly out of the imperial light into a private, magic-tinged blackness.[47] For Philostratus at least, the miracles that collected about Apollonius were secondary to his mastery of conventional virtue, and however transcendent the possession of this power made him, the philosopher remained quite socially intelligible and appealing.

---

wards Marginality," and sec. 5, "The Holy Man beyond Society," 51–59. "It is important to realize that the holy man's ideal view of his relationship with his fellow men was one of essential *non*-involvement," 54.

42. 21.14.5; 23.6.19.

43. 23.6.32.

44. *Vita Apollonii*, 1.2; *Res gestae*, 21.1.7.

45. *Vita Apollonii*, 5.12, 7.39. Contrast this reaction to Maximus' pride in activating the statue of Hecate.

46. *Vita Apollonii*, 8.7.

47. To convert imperial, civic paganism into private acts of worship, *arcana* really, through continually tightening legislation was, of course, to encourage such a self-fulfilling definition. Legitimacy and publicity were interdependent. Cf. Julian's secret ritual life in Gaul, pp. 40–41 above.

When Apollonius entered a city, it was his custom to meet with local priests to learn what rites they used, and if there were any that he thought deviated from the correct, traditional forms of Greek worship, he would learn who had devised them and their purpose, and suggest improvements. In the day's work, religious concerns always preceded philosophical discourse.[48] This sketch is sufficient by itself to indicate that mixture of tendencies toward religious conservation, innovation, and tolerance that we observe in Apollonius' specific acts. He illustrates the principle of toleration through his reply, made twice, to the King of Persia, who asked that Apollonius join him in a sacrifice, "You, King, sacrifice as you normally do, but grant that I may sacrifice in my own manner."[49] Although the philosopher followed Pythagorean precepts, this personal enthusiasm did not render him immovably dogmatic. In a modest spirit he considered his public discussions first as a means of making himself more wise.[50]

The impulse to conserve rises in his attention to neglected rites and monuments such as the graves of the Eretreans near Babylon, those of Achilles and the Achaeans, and (in obedience to the command of Achilles himself) the statue of Palamedes.[51] His habit of living in temples, whether that of Aesculapius at Aegae or those in Rome, must obviously have drawn attention to their state of repair.[52] To the extent that Apollonius regarded himself as struggling for Hellenic *nomima* against religious barbarism, we may rightly judge him a conservator. It was in this respect that he was disappointed by the shrine of Apollo Daphnaeus, for Greek custom had established that its priests show the gleam of intelligence, but there the priests seemed coarse and unaccomplished; there was no spark.[53] Generally, though, he was firmly attached to the

---

48. This regimen, which can stand, I think, as a general representation of his conduct anywhere, has been abstracted from Apollonius' particular *adventus* at Antioch (1.16)—the battleground of Julian.

49. *Vita Apollonii*, 1.31.

50. Ibid., 4.19.

51. Ibid., 1.24; 4.11, 13, 16. Cf. Pegasius' care for the shrine of Hector, p. 49, n. 54, above.

52. *Vita Apollonii*, 1.8, 4.41. Cf. Julian's tours of inspection, pp. 49, 50 above. In Antioch, Apollonius lived in such shrines as were not closed, *mē kleista*, 1.16. Philostratus gathered information about Apollonius from the various temples he had revived, 1.2.

53. *Vita Apollonii*, 1.16. Julian, of course, had his own unhappy experiences at this shrine. We may now feel ourselves slipping away from religious considerations strictly speaking and into the world of the sophist or *mousikos anēr*. On the (mobile) distinction between philosopher and sophist during the Second Sophistic, see Bowersock, *Greek Sophists*, 11. He thinks Apollonius' temple of Aesculapius at Aegae a probable "breeding ground of sophists," p. 19. It is interesting to note that Maximus' native Ephesus had been, along with Athens and Smyrna, one of the three great centers of sophistic training, p. 17.

traditional Greek oracles and visited them all, the oracle of Colophon in fact claiming a special kinship with him.[54] When Apollonius and the Brahmin Iarchas discussed divination, both agreed that this art, the greatest gift conferred by the gods, made men divine and through its devotees contributed to the salvation of all mankind.[55]

In raising religious interest, *spoudē*, to what he thought it had been, the philosopher was conservative. But this respectful attitude, a sensitivity to the several turns and values of a complex tradition, which drew him into discussions with local priests about their particular rituals, was also joined to a spirit of innovation. That he turned the temple of Aesculapius at Aegae into a Lyceum and Academy[56] is more than a stylistic flourish containing the thought of an enlightened priesthood; it also contains the notion that dialectic might properly be applied to tradition. When Thespesion, head of the Egyptian Gymnosophists, advised Apollonius not to probe ancient rites such as those of Dionysus or the ones practiced at Eleusis and Samothrace, the philosopher agreed but added that if they were seriously discussed, he and Thespesion would to the contrary find many good arguments in their defense.[57] This rejoinder indicates that the philosopher envisioned a temple-Academy shaped along relatively moderate lines, insisting on the right to examine traditional rituals yet having every good hope of finding them soundly based. Such a program of productive and, it should be added, cooperative inquiry was clearly meant to heighten zeal through encouraging intellectual curiosity.

Accordingly, the Apollonian priest becomes more socially docile, less *amousos;* and perhaps it is in this way that we should understand the more belligerent of his corrective confrontations with those priests who tried to keep him from Epidaurus, Eleusis, and the oracle of Trophonius at Lebadea, or with that complacent Alexandrian priest who wondered what anyone could tell an Egyptian about cult.[58] The *Vita* conveys the impression, however, that confrontation was not the rule, for priests and eminent men continually attended him during his tour of Greek shrines.[59] As I have noted, Apollonius habitually sought opportunities for consultation, yet this impulse would have been of little advantage to him without some fundamental regard for compromise, the values of others. It is

54. *Vita Apollonii,* 4.1, 24.
55. Ibid., 3.42–44.
56. Ibid., 1.13. See above, p. 81, n. 53.
57. Ibid., 6.20.   58. Ibid., 4.18, 5.25, 8.19.   59. Ibid., 4.24.

difficult to believe that he could have provoked a religious revival in Rome without showing great tact to its aristocratic priesthood.[60]

One important reason for the philosopher's broad appeal must have lain in his principle of the cultic mean.[61] Apollonius discouraged what he considered excessive ritual: occasionally there was *spoudē* enough but of the wrong sort. Early in his career he rejected a particularly rich offering to Aesculapius—as he suspected, it concealed a crime—and subsequently lectured on proper sacrifices: "He would tell those who sacrificed or made votive gifts not to exceed the mean."[62] Apollonius found the citizens of Athens and Gades lacking in cultic restraint.[63] We should perhaps not think that he wanted to narrow the rich, inherited spectrum of classical piety in any way so much as he wanted to conserve its ultimately finite resources. Offerings should be measured out prudently like money, for many gods and temples required support. Thus when earthquakes damaged the cities of the Hellespont and their citizens enlisted the help of certain Egyptian and Chaldaean diviners who unscrupulously demanded ten talents to perform the requisite expiations, Apollonius drove them out, arranging sacrifices in each city for a fraction of the cost.[64] Honoring the gods with a less consuming form of cult had certainly been one of Ammianus' concerns as he watched Julian perform his restoration, and we can, of course, through the *Third Relatio* follow the problem of religion and money in another important guise, parsimony, to Rome—the historian's Rome.[65]

60. Ibid., 4.41. The consul Caius Lucius Telesinus was impressed by Apollonius' religious principles and accordingly cleared his way to visit, and inhabit, the temples of Rome.

61. An example of this spirit of the Mean, which is particularly appropriate to our examination of the *Res gestae*, appears in Apollonius' advice to the Indian ruler that he not adopt, as he had wanted, every feature of the philosopher's life, for his subjects would consider him vulgar or mean, *Vita Apollonii*, 2.37. Compare Ammianus' criticisms of the ostentation shown by Julian in embracing Maximus; his participating too intimately in priestly processions; and his proceeding on foot to the consular ceremonies of Nevitta and Mamertinus, a thing *affectatum et vile*, 22.7.1.

62. *Vita Apollonii*, 1.11.

63. *Philothutai*, 4.19; *perittoi de eisi ta theia*, 5.4.

64. *Vita Apollonii*, 6.41.

65. Whether or not Symmachus and his fellow pagan senators might easily have sustained the old civic cults on their private resources alone, the Prefect is still pitching as strongly as he can for imperial money; after toleration, money for cult is his most important issue: "quanto commodo sacri aerarii vestri Vestalium virginum praerogativa detracta est?" 11; "honori urbis delata conpendia desinunt esse tribuentium, et quod a principio beneficium fuit, usu atque aetate fit debitum," 18. Naturally we are talking in this case about the "face" value of money as that barometer of imperial commitment to a social activity that inevitably determined its prestige.

Whatever tension his sharp examinations of Greco-Roman and barbarian cults might provoke, Apollonius wished to be understood as a champion of *homonoia*. We find him lecturing the Smyrnaeans on creative rivalry, *philotimia*, their best hope for social concord.[66] He ended a famine in Aspendus and saved the Roman governor from a mob by reconciling the people with those magnates who had been holding back their grain from the local market in order to export it. This incident will immediately bring to mind, by way of contrast, the failure of Gallus and Julian to resolve so happily their own encounters with impending famine at Antioch; unlike Apollonius, Gallus delivered his governor, Theophilus, to the mob.[67] Once an earthquake at Antioch helped frustrate an attempt by the governor of Syria to divide the citizens against each other inasmuch as everyone suddenly turned to prayer; and this, the philosopher asserted, was God's attempt to reconcile the Antiochenes through a common fear.[68]

Considering the life of Apollonius not as a parade of miracles but rather as an impressive series of well-navigated relationships between priests and nations of every sort, we have in Philostratus a guide to religious harmony and reform that is surprisingly appropriate to Ammianus: when Apollonius entered Antioch, there had been a different story to tell. He employed a cultic mean, as Julian and Maximus did not, to create harmony, restrain sacrifices, reduce expenditure, and revive interest in religion.[69] His ego was carefully bound by the obligation of philanthropy and by the incentive of *philotimia*.[70] Rather than glorify the spiritual temple or "tripod" within himself,[71] he rejected such a temptation to cultic solitude and actively sought out local priests. Their temples became his bases of operation. Unlike those many later philosophers who stood aloof from the conventional concerns of civic religion, Apollonius had chosen to "come to the gods" in that social sense that Ammianus thought particularly crucial to his own time and place. Fourth-century Rome, until the massacre at Thessalonica made Theodosius a suppliant before Ambrose, still offered Ammianus the prospect of traditional cults that even yet might avoid being turned into *ar-*

---

66. *Vita Apollonii*, 4.8. On Apollonius and *philotimia*, see Brown, *The Making of Late Antiquity*, 30–31.
67. *Vita Apollonii*, 1.15; *Res gestae*, 14.7.5–6; 22.14.1–2.
68. *Vita Apollonii*, 6.38.
69. In the opinion of Ensslin, *Ammianus Marcellinus*, 55, both Julian and Constantius transgressed against the teachings of Apollonius.
70. However, Mazza, "L'Intelletuale," 93–121, stresses the confrontational, as opposed to the mediating, tendency in Apollonius' character.
71. *Vita Apollonii*, 3.42.

cana. But that task would require the help of more gregarious, socially adept philosophers on the model of Apollonius, who would assist the priests, not deny them.

The ideal philosopher of Ammianus could throw off the tyranny of a Nero or Domitian and rally men of any rank around him in piety: he stood in the middle of all. To Eunapius, Apollonius was some *meson* between men and gods[72]—that is, a body apart and tensely suspended between the "many" of two worlds—a more complicated sense of mean. And it is through his *Vitae*, finally, that we are able to observe this multifaceted tension, which of itself must have seriously hindered philosophers from following Ammianus back to the temples as he wished, even had there been no such thing as Christianity.[73]

For the Eunapian philosopher, religious instruction—mysteries—could begin at childhood within the immediate, visible presence of specially dispatched divinities, who endowed their pupil with the power to give oracles. Later, when choosing a master in some metropolis of the empire, he expected to learn upon admission that peculiar set of rituals by which his group paced off a territory of invisible dimensions for itself and to combine the examination of Greek philosophical doctrine with that of *theiasmos*.[74] If the disciple respected his master's desire to treat privately with the gods, he would at times also demand from the master some open demonstration of that divine authority that must ultimately support the endless search for causes; then a miracle would result. This challenge might issue as well from another philosopher who was attempting to work a spell—defeated—on the master, or from without his profession in the shape of conventional priests and diviners matching their *sophia* against his own. Great magistrates who were yet openly and enthusiastically devoted to the old religion also demanded that his master come forth as an act of public ritual to exhibit his power to reach the gods. Religion was an *agōn*.[75]

When ready to leave the circle as a master in his own right, the phi-

---

72. *Vitae sophistarum*, ed. J. Giangrande, 454.

73. On Eunapius, see Momigliano, "Popular Religious Beliefs," 148–49; Brown, *Making of Late Antiquity*, 61–62. Brown observes (p. 60) that pagan literature of the fourth and fifth centuries was preoccupied with "the delicate balance between 'heavenly' and 'earthly' forms of supernatural power."

74. See Wallis, *Neoplatonism*, 120–23.

75. The foregoing sketch is a composite image drawn from the following *vitae*: Iamblichus, 459–60, 473; Eustathius, 466; Sosipatra, 467–69; Maximus, 470, 474; and Chrysanthius, 500, 503.

losopher inevitably looked back upon much of his religious experience then as a series of demands, centrifugal forces riving his power of interior concentration upon the gods—depending upon how much of his religious life he thought it right to reveal. Maximus would scarcely have agreed that he felt any spiritual diminution by going to Julian's court. At the other extreme stood Eusebius, who was totally opposed to theurgy and advocated the pursuit of unmixed, conventional dialectic.[76] There were others between these two, representing different combinations of ritual and dialectic such as Antoninus who, although lecturing from the Serapeum, could hardly bring himself to discuss anything that pertained to the gods. He too opposed theurgy. Chrysanthius was *homopsychos* with Maximus in his eagerness to probe divination, but he refused either to proceed to the next step of aggressively manipulating the gods or to lay such momentous rituals before the notice of a wider public, palace courtiers included. The Christians of Lydia in fact scarcely knew that he was among them when he served as one of Julian's high-priests.[77] In his case, particularly, we must have a fair approximation of that ritually engaged but restrained philosopher to whom Ammianus was calling. Still, the decision faced our emerging Eunapian philosopher: would he become a Eusebius, Antoninus, Chrysanthius, or Maximus;[78] was piety silent or voiced; who should know the gods who visited him: no one, fellow masters, disciples, local priests, magistrates, the emperor? Answers became murky when even the great theurgist Iamblichus could call it impiety for his followers to request visions from him.[79] Those philosophers who joined Julian's *comitatus* were obviously not men who suffered such dilemmas, nor, we should note, did they succeed at what they attempted. Those like the reluctant Chrysanthius who experienced the greatest tension and stayed away, would perhaps in their doubt have become the most effective pagan leaders in Antioch. Now they were the quarry of Ammianus.

76. *Vitae sophistarum*, ed. J. Giangrande, 474.
77. *Vitae sophistarum*, 471, 474, 501.
78. Or even the wild and mysterious Olympius, "somebody dressed like a philosopher," who bodily defended the Serapeum in 391, shouting that pagans must risk death for their ancestral faith, Sozomen, *Historia ecclesiastica*, ed. J. Bidez, 7.15. When Theodosius decreed absolutely that Egypt's shrines must be destroyed, Olympius secretly left the Serapeum and took ship for Italy—a good choice for a pagan, as Ammianus would have agreed. One wonders whether a combative man, or philosopher (if he were such), of this type would not have reemerged at Rome during the pagan revival led by the Flaviani in 393.
79. *Vitae sophistarum*, 459.

· CHAPTER FIVE ·

COMPARISON OF RELIGIONS

The ethnographic cosmos set in motion by Ammianus turns through a mass of references to native and foreign religions, which we may draw into a superior, highly articulated vision of his religious attitudes. The Mediterranean world of the fourth century A.D. was filled with religions, yet the impact of this diversity has been lost in earlier critiques through their too exclusive concentration upon the relationship between the Greco-Roman *cultus deorum* and Christianity. These two competed not only with each other but under the gaze of those religions evolving simultaneously among the Huns, Tauricans, Gauls, Persians, and Egyptians. Surely the religious beliefs of one as well traveled as Ammianus were formed against a variety of ethnic encounters. All the more then should we suspect any interpretation that dismisses his ethnographic excursuses as bare "learned relief"; they are, to the contrary, parallel reservoirs of ideology. And it is by drawing together all of the religions from every area of the *Res gestae* that we most clearly see why Ammianus, far from being neutral, held Christianity to be an inferior religion. Yet paganism itself does not appear everywhere equal as, for example, between Persia and Egypt. Guided by his hands we will now climb a ladder of simple and complex ethnic religions toward the critical pair, Christianity and the Greco-Roman *cultus deorum*.

This ascent should begin with Ammianus' Huns, Quadi, and Alans, the first of whom show no religious development at all: "Like thoughtless animals, they are entirely ignorant of what is honorable or dishonorable, word-twisting and unintelligible, never distracted by any regard for religion or superstition."[1] Those whom he judges the most savage people[2] are also those—the only nation so described by him—who lack any sign of religion. His remark not only offers us the most natural starting point for a study of progressive states of religious development in the *Res gestae* but also reveals his belief in the necessary relationship between religion and civilization: the one cannot develop without the social discipline of the other.[3] Religion in its most basic form is restraint, and the Huns have none of this.[4] A step beyond them are the Quadi, who do practice sacred oaths, raising divinized swords to their throats in the presence of Constantius.[5] They have deities, even if these are only gods of violence and primitively enclosed within weapons *quos pro numinibus colunt*. This sword cult is also practiced by the nomadic Alans: "There is no temple or other shrine to be seen among them, not even a grass-covered hut can be picked out, but a bare sword is stuck in the ground, as barbarians customarily do, and they reverently worship it as Mars, leader of the sacred dance about those lands which they circle."[6] However, they also possess a distinctive, and accurate, method of divining with sticks.[7] Here the religious focus widens from oaths, *reverentia*, to describe a slightly more complex state of cult. Although the Alans' god bears witness to their adoration of violence, the development of a not contemptible practice of divination speaks for the stirring of *doctrina*. And they are, in fact, rated less savage than the Huns.[8] Nevertheless their lives have, from the historian's point of view, no constructive pur-

1. 31.2.11.
2. *Omnium acerrimos facile dixeris bellatores*, 31.2.9.
3. "Aguntur autem nulla severitate regali, sed tumultuario primatum ductu contenti perrumpunt, quidquid inciderit," 31.2.7.
4. See Ensslin, *Ammianus Marcellinus*, 57.
5. 17.12.21.
6. 31.2.23. See Momigliano, "Popular Religious Beliefs," 148. As an historian whose values are fully those of a long-settled people, Ammianus has a particular aversion to nomadic barbarians, whom he regards quite literally as fugitives from reality—that is, temporally fixed, historically intelligible bases. They live in two dimensions and are somehow not fully alive—as, for example, the *natio perniciosa* of the Saracens: "sed errant semper per spatia longe lateque distenta sine lare sine sedibus fixis aut legibus [lacking then, in Ammianus' view, fixed points of social definition]. . . . vita est illis semper in fuga . . . ita autem, quoad vixerint, late palantur, ut alibi mulier nubat, in loco pariat alio liberosque procul educat," 14.4.3–5. These sentiments are repeated in connection with the Huns: "Omnes enim sine sedibus fixis absque lare vel lege aut ritu stabili dispalantur semper fugientum similes. . . . nullusque apud eos interrogatus respondere, unde oritur, potest alibi conceptus natusque procul et longius educatus," 31.2.10.
7. "Miro praesagiunt modo. . . . aperte quid portenditur norunt," 31.2.24.
8. *Verum victu mitioris et cultu*, 31.2.21.

pose, and religion for them must be judged a stimulus to violence rather than a deterrent: "Just as quiet and peaceful men take their pleasure in repose, so danger and war soothes those barbarians."

To none of these nations does Ammianus attach any past, an omission worth noting when examining the degrees by which his religious descriptions expand before us. For within a history, a subject accorded no past misses the vitality that necessarily grows from our perception of a retreating series of events, or change over time. The subject sits two-dimensionally within a continually vanishing present, *fugiens* like a nomad. When Ammianus describes a religion or people without adding this most basic historiographical dimension in however simple a form—*quondam*, for example—we may suspect that it holds a weaker conceptual value for him. The Thracian Scordisci are the most primitive people in the *Res gestae* accorded this historical dynamic: "And the Scordisci inhabited part of these lands, although they are now far separated from them; once cruel and wild, as antiquity teaches us, they make offerings of their captives to Bellona and Mars, greedily drinking the blood from hollowed out skulls."[9] Their rites of human sacrifice are clearly related to the habit of several nations in the *Res gestae:* the Alans who hang human skulls from their horses; the Anthropophagi; and particularly the Tauricans who offer human beings to Orsiloche.[10]

If the religion of the Scordisci is in substance no improvement over the others so far discussed, its manner of treatment does represent a significant expansion over their own. Here Ammianus describes a particular rite for two named gods; by contrast he provides no divinity for the Huns and no specifically named gods for the Quadi. *Antiquitas* and an advance in descriptive complexity thus appear simultaneously. Moreover, a distinct if oblique connection is suggested between the ancient Scordisci and the modern Tauricans: the former have been dispersed long ago, and the latter still practice human sacrifice, both using human heads in their cult. One religion moves naturally over time to the other, enhancing the conceptual depth and vitality of both.

The still more complex description of Taurica contains three religious items, which appear as discrete stages of development coexisting with one another. Their order of presentation indeed harmonizes well with the proclivity of Ammianus to work from a nation's savage past

9. 27.4.4.
10. 22.8.34; 31.2.15, 22.

(vice) to its civilized present (virtue).[11] The most crude or violent reference is here clearly set first and the civilized last. The savage Tauricans[12] make human sacrifice to Orsiloche and place the heads on her temple. Nevertheless they do surpass the nomadic Huns and Alans by having a permanent building for their worship[13] and by honoring a deity who is not only a war god, a sword stuck in the ground. Ammianus' second item, the Island of Leuce consecrated to Achilles, shares the threatening nature of the first—no one could spend the night there without endangering his life—and is connected with the cult of the warrior that seems to typify barbarian religions for Ammianus.[14] Nevertheless Leuce's dark aura has a vague and abstract quality, for the temple there is not explicitly associated with human sacrifice. Finally there are the cities of Taurica, "undefiled by human victims":[15] the most civilized areas and the least menacing cult have now come together. This complex description of ethnic religion both spans a broad temporal range that reaches back to Achilles (antedating the republican *antiquitas* of the Scordisci) and makes civilized cult appear. At the same time, since Ammianus describes Taurica as he thinks it is, not only as it was, dynamically tensed savage and civilized religious elements yet divide this frontier region.[16]

The detailed treatment of those funeral rites given the prince of the Chionitae at Amida[17] fits well within our evolving hierarchy of religions. Ammianus values a cult more highly as it draws away from violence—in this case, human sacrifice or an exclusive concentration upon war gods. Although the Chionitae were among the fiercest tribes confronting Sapor,[18] they nevertheless substituted human images for real victims in their ceremony. The only other suggestion of human sacrifice appears in the not unconventional vow of the prince's father, Grumbates—himself worthy of particular notice[19]—to propitiate his shade by destroying Amida.[20] The elaborateness of the rites, their explicit connection with the Greco-Roman *cultus deorum* at two points,[21] the inclusion of a Homeric

11. See the Gauls, 15.9.1–8, and Alans, 31.2.17–25.
12. "Immani diritate terribiles . . . intendente savitiam licentia diuturna," 22.8.33.
13. *Fani parietibus*, 22.8.33.   14. *Barbarico ritu*, 31.2.23.
15. 22.8.36.
16. On the somewhat involved question of the civilized (Greco-Roman) status of this particular region, see below, p. 108, n. 108.
17. 19.1.7–11.
18. With the Gelani, *omnium acerrimi bellatores*, 17.5.1; *ferae gentes*, 18.4.1.
19. "Mente quadam grandifica, multisque victoriarum insignibus nobilis," 18.6.22.
20. 19.2.1.
21. "Ut lacrimare cultrices Veneris saepe spectantur, in sollemnibus Adonidis sacris,"

(heroic) element,[22] and the unusually high regard shown a barbarian king—all suggest that we are now meant to see some more estimable ethnic religion in the hands of a previously unencountered type of heroic barbarian. The Chionitae are savage but worthy, more complex human beings, *"mente quadam grandifica,"* possessing a certain sensibility. They are certainly not *animalia* like the Huns.[23]

A better, perhaps more secure candidate for a barbarian people freed from savage religion are the Burgundians, who stand in a favorable light without the customary references to lawlessness, rootlessness, ignorance, and perfidy. Oddly enough, it was Roman *reverentia* that vanished when Valentinian failed to honor his alliance with the Burgundians against the Alamanni.[24] (This was the second incident of Roman perfidy that year: the generals Nannienus and Severus had previously annihilated a Saxon army withdrawing under truce.[25]) The special status of this nation among other barbarians is indicated by their Roman lineage: "The Burgundians know that they are Roman by ancient descent."[26]

Such positive traits of honorable behavior, or faith dishonored by Valentinian, and common ancestry must make Ammianus more intellectually responsive to the Burgundians, for they provoke from him this singular comment on a barbarian religion: "Among them, a king is called by the general title of Hendinos, and by ancient custom he is deposed if under his rule the fortune of war should falter or the earth deny its fold of wheat, just as the Egyptians are accustomed to attribute calamities of this sort to their own leaders. And in fact the high-priest of all among the

---

19.1.11; "hastam infectam sanguine ritu patrio nostrique more coniecerat fetialis [Grumbates]," 19.2.6.

22. "Apud Troiam quondam super comite Thessali ducis exanimo socii Marte acerrimo conflixerunt," 19.1.9.

23. Contrast the reliability of Grumbates, *fidenter domino suam operam navaturus,* 19.1.7, with the alleged faithlessness of the Huns, *per indutias infidi et inconstantes,* 31.2.11. That the Chionitae possess a cult so refined, without the usual human sacrifices and dangling heads, and display none of the bad habits Ammianus normally associates with the most savage tribes, as these are said to be, is suspicious. He may be purposely romanticizing this primitive religion to set the siege of Amida in a more thoroughly heroic atmosphere. He explicitly points us to the *comes Thessali ducis,* Patroclus. Homer, of course, mentions a human sacrifice of twelve Trojan nobles at this hero's funeral (*Il.* 23.175, 180–82); Patroclus had been the death of Troy as Grumbates' son was now fatal to Amida: *funestus nobis ceciderat adulescens.* As for the presence of facsimiles on this pyre instead of some Roman equivalent to the Trojan victims, we could lay this to one particular difficulty Ammianus would have had in following his Homeric model: *primates* from the town were not available for such a sacrifice so early in the siege.

24. 28.5.10.   25. 28.5.4–7.   26. 28.5.11.

Burgundians is called a Sinistus and holds his power for life without being subject to those dangers which beset the kings."[27] This is the only time that he mentions a barbarian priesthood. The explicitly antique mooring of the observation signals some degree of positive mental engagement, as does the reference to Egypt, whose *prudentia* Ammianus reveres.[28] To be compared with Egypt honored the religion of any nation; even the Chionitae are deficient in this respect. But his allusion to Egypt is most interesting, because the persistence of religious authority amid the vagaries of royal power—here Sinistus against Hendinos—echoes what we shall find to be the main point of the Egyptian excursus, that Egypt's sacred wisdom would endure all disasters, natural and man-made.

By this stage I think I have adequately demonstrated that Ammianus tends to correlate religious progress with social refinement (or pedigree), and in this regard, Burgundian cult may properly finish the evolution of those specifically barbarian religions that he describes. It can hardly be an accident that the only barbarians to find any explicit connection with one of the historian's important religious paradigms are also those who were Roman by race.

The creation of *doctrinae*, intellectual activity at its most refined level, where religious and secular speculations become integrated, occurs only within a civilized society. In Gaul, where the esteemed Bards, Euhages, and Druids arose, we encounter a settled society as ancient as the labors of Hercules. The Gauls themselves believed that Hercules had once taken wives in their land after defeating the tyrants Geryon and Tauriscus. The socially productive activities of their chosen progenitor—destroying tyrants, laying a road through the Alps, and founding the port of Monaco[29]—stand in contrast to the elevation of violence for its own sake, which Ammianus observes in the barbarian warrior cults. The history of Gaul begins with a creative, not destructive, ethic. It was less surprising that those possessing such an origin should have developed learning long before the historian's contemporary barbarians who had yet to produce anything of the kind:

27. 28.5.14.
28. *Ritu veteri; ut solent Aegypti*. Egypt is always synonymous with great antiquity; see below, pp. 96–100. Ammianus also attributes an Egyptian origin to the Chaldaeans, 22.8.24, keepers, we will note, of the Golden Fleece.
29. 15.9.6. [*Monoecum*] *ad perennem sui memoriam consecravit*, 15.10.9.

Throughout these areas, after their people had gradually become civilized, study of praiseworthy branches of learning flourished, begun by the Bards, Euhages, and Druids. And the Bards of course sang in verse about the brave deeds of illustrious men to the harp's sweet rhythms; the Euhages truly, studying the sublime, tried to reveal the secrets of nature. The Druids, possessing loftier intellects than the others, drew themselves together in brotherhoods according to the rule of Pythagoras and intently pursued investigations of hidden and profound subjects; looking down upon the things of this world, they pronounced souls to be immortal.[30]

The order of these three groups is suggestive, for each marks a more refined form of intellectual activity, much as our three religious items from the Taurican passage settle into a neatly graduated scheme: the Bards sing, a skill embodying the chief artistic production of heroic society; the Euhages as *physici* probe natural phenomena; but the Druids rise above heroes and nature to what appear to be primarily theological subjects—*despectantes humana*. Again, the loftiest role comes last. An Egyptian connection asserts itself through the *sodalicia* of the Druids, whose Pythagorean *auctoritas* was directly descended from Egyptian religion.[31] If the Gauls thus enjoy an Egyptian bond as do the Burgundians, their own contact is nevertheless more firm as one would expect from the representation of Gaul as fully civilized. The Burgundian Sinistus and Hendinos prompt Ammianus to recognize an essentially loose ethnic analogy, but through Pythagoras we meet the suggestion of actual ideological contact between Egypt and Gaul.

The Persian Hagistia is one of the most favorably presented civilized religions in the *Res gestae*. Ammianus regards the Persians, whatever their vices, as a nation of undeniable cultural achievements; if bandits, they are never called barbarians. One manifestation of this respect is a comparatively thorough discussion of the Magi within his Persian excursus.[32] If the more recent cultic activities of the rulers of Persia are added to this,[33] we enter a new area of extended presentation, where ancient and modern religious dimensions are fully realized. Yet the historian also shows the Hagistia to have become a marred faith, one whose vir-

---

30. Note that this description of *doctrinae* in Gaul follows directly upon a reference to its many towns, "dein secutis aetatibus oppida, aucta virium copia, instituere non pauca," 15.9.7: learning is contingent upon the existence of settled, urban life.

31. "Hac institutus prudentia [Aegypti sacerdotum] Pythagoras colens secretius deos, quicquid dixit aut voluit, auctoritatem esse instituit ratam," 22.16.21. See above, p. 71, n. 9.

32. 23.6.32–36.

33. Their deification, 23.6.4–6, and Sapor's divining, 18.4.1, 7.1; 21.13.2.

tues had either not survived the accession of Arsaces or had perhaps simply run their limit in a society that never escaped its barbarian inheritance.[34]

Long ago, Ammianus writes, Zoroaster of Bactria learned astronomy and pure sacrificial rites from the lofty Brahmins; and these principles, together with Chaldaean teaching, he gave to the Magi. Excepting the later contribution of Darius' father, Hystaspes, *rex prudentissimus*, this became the finished form of the Hagistia. The Magi grew in honor and power[35] as the only lawful priests of the Persian Empire until Darius overthrew those who took the throne following the death of Cambyses in Egypt. Ammianus' presentation is quite friendly, taking its tone from an opinion attributed to Plato that the Hagistia was the "purest worship of the gods."[36] Far advanced over savage religions, the Hagistia was born of a fusion of rites and *doctrinae* from several enlightened sources. Evidence for the power of its Chaldaean element appears to us both in those obviously potent *arcana Chaldaeorum* that guarded the temple of Apollo Comaeus at Seleucia and the historian's praise of Chaldaea as an ancient center of philosophy and divination.[37] No primitive stage of human sacrifice or its recollection stained this "purest" of religions.[38] Neither do the Magi look bad when Darius arrives, for Cambyses, whom they had attempted to replace, was demonstrably impious, greedy, and cruel.[39] There is a reminiscence of the Burgundians, who ensured religious continuity by elevating their high-priest above the *casus* of the king. Although Darius replaced the Magi, his father had ostensibly been one of their own theologians; turning them out did not imply, then, any return to the *immanitas* of Cambyses, and king and priesthood appear poised for a well-balanced relationship.

That harmony was broken, however, by Arsaces. Far from being the advent of an enlightened patron of the venerable Hagistia, the rise of this king is represented as a clear rupturing of religious continuity.[40] The deification of Arsaces—carried by popular acclaim, not any religious authority[41]—and the consecration of his arrogant successors, *praetumidi*, as

34. Perfidy, 21.13.4; war lust, 22.12.1, 23.6.83; cruelty, 23.6.80.
35. "Legibus suis uti permissi, religionis respectu sunt honorati," 23.6.35.
36. 23.6.32. Bidez and Cumont, *Les Mages Héllenisés*, 2:33, n. 1, were unable to find this opinion in any of Plato's dialogues.
37. 23.6.24–25.
38. Cf. the *imagines* used by the Chionitae.
39. "Quoad vixerat cupidus et immanis . . . ne deorum quidem donariis parcens," 17.4.3. See above, p. 28, n. 74.
40. "Obscuro geniti loco, latronum inter adulescentiae rudimenta ductoris," 23.6.2.
41. "Certatimque summatum et vulgi sententiis concinentibus," 23.6.4.

Brothers of the Sun and Moon apparently have nothing to do with the Magi. The cultic activities of these later rulers should properly be divorced from the original Hagistia, which Ammianus explicitly endorses. Sapor is a study in arrogance, proclaiming his divine kingship to Constantius and raging at the impious citizens of Amida who assaulted him, a temple in their midst.[42] Nor does he receive any positive recognition for his repeated acts of divination, a science that the historian readily praises elsewhere, but Sapor is even charged with descending into necromancy.[43] Thus, with Arsaces, Ammianus sends a formerly great religion into decline. Judged by its contributions to civilized life, the sort of creative impulses that yielded *doctrinae*, contemporary Persian religion could be described only negatively. The king resorted to necromancy like a *veneficus*, or, if his subjects were well bent to the prohibitory aspect of religion in their fear of enchantment and the laws,[44] they displayed none of its positive inspiration toward intellectual creativity. No Persian *philosophi* are mentioned now. To Ammianus, Persians are congenitally warlike, and the unrelievedly military character of Sapor's divination suggests that their religion has fallen to serving this violent impulse, reverting to the warrior cults of the Alans, Quadi, or Scordisci.

42. *Genuino fastu*, 17.5.2; *quasi in sacrilegos violati saeviens templi*, 19.1.6.

43. "Consilia tartareis manibus miscens et superstitiones omnes consulens de futuris," 18.4.1. Compare Ammianus' criticism of Julian's unregulated diviners, 22.12.7. In both cases the simultaneous pursuit of many forms of divination is regarded not as evidence of manifold piety but rather gratuitous experimentation, in effect a cultic promiscuity that rendered both rulers superstitious. As with the Chionitae, however, I would not exclude the influence of dramatic enhancement. All of Sapor's ceremonies occur in identical contexts: the bandit king about to cross a river to create havoc in Roman territory, *caedum et direptionum monumenta saevissima*, 22.12.1. And I suspect that the historian may be using divination simply as a dramatic prop to emphasize Sapor's evil, mysterious character. Divination deals with unknown, yet to be revealed, divine will; adding this characteristically mysterious activity to the Persians' general reputation in the *Res gestae* for perfidy, *occulta fallacissimae gentis*, 21.13.4, and secrecy, *apud quos Silentii quoque colitur numen*, ibid., intensifies the sum of inscrutability and, obviously, dramatic tension: the unknowable Persian meditating evil, waiting on the divine unknown. Compare the triangular tension between Julian, Constantius, and Sapor (see above, p. 44, n. 31). Considering Sapor's notable military successes during the reign of Constantius and Constantius' own bad fortune in foreign wars (14.10.16, 21.16.15), we might be tempted to believe that Ammianus is even promoting the Persian as some guide to the right path for Roman victory through a similar attention to divination, now neglected, 19.12.20. From his fiercely critical handling of Sapor, however, it must be clear that the historian never intended the conduct of this king to serve as a model for any activity whatever. Note, though, Ammianus' approval of good King Cyrus, *ille superior rex amabilis*, 23.6.40; *egregium illud Cyri veteris dictum*, 21.9.2.

44. *Venenorum et secretarum artium metu*, 23.6.78; *leges apud eos impendio formidatae*, 23.6.81.

. . .

A more durable religion that still retains its civilizing virtues is that of Egypt, a land conventionally held to be synonymous with great antiquity, fertility, wisdom, preservation, and eternity—in short, *miracula*.[45] Here, especially, religion and city are one: where Peleus once purified himself as the gods had ordered, there he founded Pelusium[46]—*ritus* brings *civitas*; or, see civilization as a prolonged ritual starting from that moment. The Egyptians expressed a plain message with monuments of unparalleled dimensions. "Beyond any height attainable by the human hand"[47]—what could be farther from the nomads' houseless worship?—stretched a plain message: Egyptian *prudentia* would survive any disaster. What was cut would grow back like those rites once protected down in her caverns from a great flood; Thebes had stopped the impiety of Cambyses.[48] To understand why Egypt has such great ideological significance for Ammianus—why, in essence, Alexandria stands as the *vertex omnium civitatum*[49]—we must take to ourselves his own penetrating vision of the interdependent genesis of religion, monument, and city. As the pagan *indicium* of Julian's career has already shown, cities in the *Res gestae* are meant to speak of religion. For Egypt, we shall find Memphis, Alexandria, and Heliopolis very audible.

His Memphis brings together the Apis Bull, Aesculapius, and the Festival of the Nile[50]—elements bespeaking fertility and *salus*. Julian, whom Ammianus regularly endows with images of conferred fertility, effectively joins Apis in Memphis by forgiving the suppliant Theodotus; through *clementia* he has become a harbinger of *bona* in his own right.[51] Echoing the search for a new sacred bull, *alter cum publico quaeritur luctu*, and the law that he die at a fixed time are the bad omens of this emperor's entry into Antioch amid ritual mourning and the withdrawal of the Public Genius with its veiled cornucopia—*nec enim ultra eum trahere licet aetatem*.[52] The meaning of Memphis as fertility and *salus* is underscored by Aesculapius, who made her *clara* by frequently appearing there. Like

---

45. Iamblichus (*De mysteriis*, ed. E. Des Places) 7.5, states that Egyptians were the first to speak with the gods. Moreover, they retained this sacred language unchanged, unlike the Greeks who were infected with the love of novelty.
46. 22.16.3.   47. 22.15.28.   48. 17.4.4, 22.15.30.
49. 22.16.7.   50. 22.14.6–8, 15, 17.
51. "Faustum, et ubertatem frugum diversaque indicans bona," 22.14.6. See above, pp. 54–55, nn. 9–11.
52. As for the question of how completely Julian should be identified with Tacitus' Germanicus, it may be worth noting that Apis rejected Germanicus, as Ammianus states,

Tertullus calming natural *saevitia* through cult, the priests of Memphis could even render crocodiles placid during the Festival of the Nile: "And these same beasts are ever enraged; but for the seven days during which priests celebrate the birthday of the Nile they grow mild, just as if they were soldiers agreeing to a truce, forsaking any violence."

Holding such essential themes in mind, we turn to the Crown of Cities, Alexandria, where they are heard proportionately louder. This Greek city is the heir to Egyptian fecundity in both its material and intellectual forms: great monuments surrounded by intense mental activity. An omen of fertility occurred at her very birth, when the architect Deinocrates drew Alexandria's boundary in flour instead of lime. That the city achieved her full growth immediately mimes this special generative power—more than a little, surely, the way that divinities themselves were born full-grown.[53] There Greek philosophical studies grew from the *religionum incunabula* preserved by Egyptian priests.[54]

But if Alexandria was the home of great achievements issuing from divinely based wisdom, these had also been forced to maintain themselves through several crises. Together, the magnificent Serapeum and philosophy survived Caesar's attack, despite the loss in books—a lesson to Valens.[55] Ammianus' enumeration of the valuable studies that were yet alive in the city proceeds significantly from a reference to those insurrections during the reign of Aurelian that nearly destroyed the Bruchion Quarter. Whatever any emperor might do, whether Aurelian or Caesar, this vitality would not be stopped; the statues of the Serapeum were still breathing.[56] Such rescues of religion and *doctrinae* will recall us to the ancient priests' protection of their rites from the flood or, as we turn to Rome, the saving of the Sibylline Books—barely—from the burning Temple of Palatine Apollo.[57] Holding a similarly recognizable story of sal-

---

but the bull obviously accepted Julian (even if from a distance). Kennedy (*Literary Work of Ammianus*) fully identified the two heroes. She did not, however, discuss this particular passage in her work. On the relationship, or lack of one, between Ammianus and Tacitus, see Sabbah, *La Méthode*, 101–10; Blockley, "Tacitean Influence," 63–78; Matthews, "Ammianus Marcellinus," 1131–33.

53. "Quod civitatem post haec alimentorum uberi copia circumfluere fortuito monstravit," 22.16.7; "sed Alexandria ipsa non sensim ut aliae urbes, sed inter initia prima aucta per spatiosos ambitus," 22.16.15.

54. 22.16.19–22.

55. Cf. his burning of *innumeri codices et acervi voluminum multi* during the trials of 371–72, 29.1.41.

56. *Diuturnum praestantium hominum domicilium*, 22.16.15. *Spirantibus signorum figmentis*, 22.16.12.

57. 23.3.3.

vation is the Pharos, the beacon that lit the way for ships that otherwise would have wrecked themselves on the sandbars outside of Alexandria's harbor. In building a causeway, the Heptastadium, out to the Pharos, Cleopatra outwitted the Rhodians in their attempt to tax the island.[58] With the force of so many correlations behind us, knowing that throughout the *Res gestae* Ammianus creates a past that speaks to his present, we must not suddenly go blind: there is another saving torch—on top the obelisk of Sol in Rome; another nautical image of salvation and fertility— the worship of Tertullus that filled the granaries of Ostia (with Alexandrian wheat); another tax to frustrate—that on Alexandria's temples suggested to Constantius by Bishop George; and a more general threat— Sol (paganism)—is beset by this emperor's looting *palatini*.[59] But Constantius, Aurelian, Caesar, so too Cambyses and Constantine, were gone while Alexandria remained. Ammianus has written, in sum, a tribute to achievement and survival under the aegis of religion: the beacon shines.[60]

A further articulation of these broad expectations of Egyptian religion exists in the form of an obvious religious *documentum*—the inscription on the obelisk from Heliopolis, which is, as other Egyptian monuments, presented in the context of potency and *piaculum*.[61] Constantine

58. 22.16.9–11.
59. 22.4.3, 22.11.6.
60. The Hermetic *Asclepius*, ed. W. Scott, 3.24b–26a, similarly concerns itself with crisis and regeneration. Hermes praises Egypt as the image of Heaven and Temple of the World, but he warns that Egyptian religion will one day be destroyed, "nihil sanctum, nihil religiosum, nec caelo nec caelestibus dignum audietur aut mente credetur." The shrines of this sacred land will be filled with corpses in a decadent world of *inreligio, inordinatio*, and *inrationabilitas*. There are several points of resonance between this document and the *Res gestae*: Rome, as the *Templum totius mundi*, 17.4.13; the corpse-filled basilica of Sicininus, 27.3.13; the unhappy truth that unexpiated portents now passed *inaudita* and *incognita*, 19.12.20. See the prediction of Eunapius' Antoninus that Egyptian religion would be destroyed (*Vitae sophistarum*, ed. J. Giangrande, 471, 473). Libanius makes Rome and Egypt comrades in degeneration because of Julian's death, 18.298.
61. There is confusion over which of our surviving obelisks is the one actually raised by Constantius and described by Ammianus. Those who have an opinion on the matter, moreover, seem to assume that the inscription itself comes from some other obelisk. See de Jonge, *Sprachlicher und historischer*, 17:92–95, 118–19; Roullet, *Egyptian and Egyptianizing*, 69–70. It should perhaps be considered that in our present state of knowledge we are in less danger of confusing ourselves about obelisks than was Ammianus. At any rate, we are given a set of obelisks and their locations: Constantius' in the Circus Maximus, 17.4.12–15; one on the Vatican Hill; another in the gardens of Sallust; and two before the mausoleum of Augustus, 16. Then Ammianus offers the inscription from that *quem videmus in Circo*, 17. He has just pointed us back to the first obelisk in his series of five, thus stitching Hermapion's translation back to section 15 after the intervening section 16: for Ammianus—if not for us—the inscription is one with the great obelisk he describes.

had been a despoiler of temples, a modern Cambyses, when he took it from its shrine; nor was that crime forgotten when Constantius raised the monument in Rome, for a lightning bolt clearly signified divine anger by striking the acroterial orb, symbol of his *imperium*. In its place arose a torch whose victory, so to speak, over the orb restates in a different way how Cleopatra, and her beacon, frustrated the Rhodian tax collectors. That Ammianus honors the obelisk as the *apex omnium*[62] will similarly return us to Alexandria, the *vertex omnium civitatum*. Prepared now for the important inscription, we should note as a preliminary matter that although the historian is otensibly presenting only an irregular portion of Hermapion's translation,[63] the material is surprisingly continuous. If the rubrics are ignored, there is really no sense of gaps or disturbed order at all; if spoken, the lines would sound like some unbroken reading from a book of ritual. I suspect in fact that the true function of the inscription in the *Res gestae* is to communicate a personal religious message, to be a mass of flame—a Sibyl. The lightning, if wrath, has suddenly made this object *sacer*, striking its words into divine animation.[64] Rameses may have dedicated the monument, but the direction of address in the inscription is rather from Helios to Rameses, and so takes the form of an oracle.

The god speaks of Heliopolis, not simply that city in Egypt where Sol is particularly revered, but also that divine city of the gods gathered about him and those other earthly cities transformed into "Heliopolis" by their reverence for him.[65] Rome, the *Templum totius mundi*, will of course be one of these, possessing its own great Pharos now like Alexandria. This bond is firmer for the piety of Augustus, who revered Apollo Palatinus and left this same object to remain in its shrine: he had truly been a "child of the Sun." In return for worship, Sol offers *imperium*, for this is the lesson of Rameses' life; he retained his power

---

62. "Deo Soli speciali munere dedicatus, fixusque intra ambitiosi templi delubra, quae contingi non poterant, tamquam apex omnium eminebat," 17.4.12.

63. South face, lines one through three; west, two and three; east, one. See above, pp. 29–30 and p. 30, n. 87.

64. Note the acroterial torch, *velut abundanti flamma candens*, 17.4.15. This is the act of consecration foreshadowed by Constantine's deed: *miraculum Romae sacraret. . . . vi ignis divini contacta* [*sphaera*], 13, 15.

65. Again, refer to *Asclepius*, ed. W. Scott, 3.24b: "Do you not know, Asclepius, that Egypt is the image of Heaven and, a thing that is fully as true, that it represents the translation, or descent, of everything decided or done in Heaven?" If on one hand, Ammianus makes a city, Rome, into a temple, he can also turn a temple into a city: the Pantheon's coffered ceiling, a reticulated pattern, which might have suggested to him an urban vision of intersecting streets or *insulae*, is called a *regio*, 16.10.14.

through valor and protected Egypt by conquering other nations. An obviously militant theology reveals itself to us: Ammianus seeks emperors for Rome who will be "mighty Apollo, all radiant child of Helios."[66] He looks for ones like Julian who will—if ultimately with better fortune—aggressively defend the empire by carrying war outside its boundaries to *alloëthneis*, such as the Persians. He scorns men like Constantius or his weak replacement for Ursicinus, Sabinianus,[67] who let the cities of the empire be passively ground away in sieges and razzias. Emperors are to be Apollo and Ares: philosopher, judge,[68] and warrior. It is through this inscription then that the historian shares a personal vision of imperial, heroic religion, which sees Rameses' Helios—Egyptian *prudentia*—coming to the Apollo of Augustus.[69]

This epitome of a civilizing religion is one standard at least against which we should properly assess Ammianus' presentation of Christianity.[70]

66. 17.4.20.   67. *Imbellis et ignavus*, 18.5.5.
68. *Ho hestōs ep' alētheias*, 17.4.19.
69. Egypt was an education not only to Rome but also to Constantinople, whose own Circus received a great obelisk at the command of Theodosius; see above, p. 38, n. 6. Sabbah provides a good discussion of "cette assimilation implicite" between Constantius and Theodosius, Rome in 357 and 389 (*La Méthode*, 327–32). De Jonge (*Sprachlicher und historischer*, 17:98) accused Ammianus of making "no effort to understand the mentality of this completely different and old [Egyptian] civilization." While it is true that Ammianus does not like every Egyptian (e.g., 22.6.1–5, 22.16.23), he is thoroughly absorbed in Egypt's seemingly ever-fresh ability to grow *bona* within men's minds. Another devotee of her spiritual crop is the anonymous fourth-century author of the *Expositio totius mundi et gentium*, ed. J. Rougé (Paris, 1966), 34–36: "[Nilus fert] viros similiter nobiles, deos colentes eminenter: nusquam enim deorum mysteria sic perficitur quomodo ibi ab antiquo et usque modo, et paene ipsa omni orbi terrarum tradidit deos colere. Dicunt autem Chaldaeos melius colere, tamen quos vidimus miramur et in omniprimos esse dicimus. Etenim ibi deos habitasse aut et habitare scimus. . . . Et dii coluntur eminenter et templum Serapis ibi est, unum et solum spectaculum novum in omni mundo: nusquam enim terra aut aedificium ⟨tale⟩ aut dispositio templi ⟨talis⟩ aut religio talis invenitur. . . . [divinam Aegyptum] quam et nominans a diis plus esse puto, ubi deos, uti praediximus, colentes bene historias maxime ⟨eis⟩ offerunt. Et sunt sacra omnia et templa omnibus ornata; aeditimi enim et sacerdotes et ministri et aruspices et adoratores et divini optimi abundant; et fit omnia ordine: aras itaque invenies semper igne splendentes et sacrificiorum et ture plenas, vittas simul et turibula plena aromatibus divinorum odorem spira⟨ntia in⟩venies." The *Res gestae* contains all of these sentiments, although we should note that the *Expositio* does not make the Serapeum bend its knee to the reverend Capitolium. For a less engaged contemporary pagan, and an Alexandrian as well, see Cameron, *Claudian*, 200–208; L. Homo, *De Rome païenne*, 255.
70. Scholarly opinions about Ammianus' presentation of Christianity have been most clearly dominated by a belief in his liberality, which is, of course, fully in keeping with the prevailing tendency to stress his objectivity, neutrality, indifference, or confusion in reli-

Would it contribute as much to the *salus* of the empire? The reply from the surviving books of the *Res gestae* is clear enough: Christianity, if to Ammianus a *religio licita* and plainly superior to barbarian cults, was no serious competitor for virtue with the great civilized religions. Rather these would have to show it how to occupy a socially productive place among the *diversitates religionum*.[71] The most persistent feature of his presentation is the raw state of Christianity. Rawness conveys itself through the absence of a glorious past, or any past at all, and none materializes for this religion. Unless the missing books of the *Res gestae* contained substantially different material, there is nothing to indicate that Ammianus' historical perspective of Christianity was different from the one that he ascribes to Julian—that is, Jewish dissidence in a new form thrusting itself into the light through Constantine the *novator*, Christianity's real founder and first truly historical, imperial moment.[72] By comparison with the enlightened origins of the Hagistia and Greek philosophy, which he finds in the Brahmins and Egyptian priesthood, respectively, the few bits constituting Ammianus' "history" of Christianity show only some "innovator and disturber of the laws and custom handed down by antiquity" and a people indistinguishable from those Jews, "disgusting and seditious," whom Marcus had judged to be as violent as barbarians.[73] Any reference to the pre-Constantinian persecution

---

gious matters. In this group are Witte, "Ammianus Marcellinus," 12, 15; MacKail, *The Last Great*, 110–11; Ensslin, *Ammianus Marcellinus*, 99; Momigliano, "Pagan and Christian Historiography," 95; Camus, *Ammien Marcellin*, 264; and Solari, "Particolarismo," 502–3. Others seem more attached to a hesitation that whispers imperial repression: Heyne, cxxxiii in *Res gestae*, ed. J. Wagner and C. Erfurdt; Yonge, *Res gestae*, v; Thompson, *Ammianus*, 114–15, and Cameron, "Paganism and Literature," 8. Very few have directly asserted that he opposed Christianity. To Blockley (*Ammianus Marcellinus*, 128), passages displaying hostility are more numerous and of greater importance. A. Selem ("Considerazioni," 260–61) attributes to him an anti-Christian bias but leavens this with a "generous impulse." D'Elia ("Ammiano Marcellino," 380) makes the strongest statement of opposition by focusing upon Ammianus' praise for the leaders of the Pagan Reaction and his censure of Christian emperors; even then he believes that the historian would have endorsed Christianity if it kept to the margins of political and social life. Neri ("Ammiano," 25–70) provides a good summary of views. To my knowledge no one has gauged the meaning of Christianity for Ammianus by setting the problem within its most obvious analytic environment, the *total* set of religious presentations in the *Res gestae*.

71. 30.9.5.

72. 21.10.8. This statement should be qualified. Although the extant books of the history reveal an undeniable tendency to ignore, cut, or confine the new imperial religion, naturally we cannot know what Ammianus may have said in the lost books. Tacitus regards the Jews as a *taeterrima gens* (Ammianus, *faetentes et tumultuantes*), but this disgust does not prevent him from devoting an excursus to them in the *Histories*, 5.3–10.

73. 22.5.5.

of this religion is omitted with obvious consequences for the valuation of martyrdom; the period of suffering previously withstood is not there to lend greater intelligibility to the reprisals now inflicted upon pagans.[74] At any rate, his temporally stripped version of the Christian past firmly defines this religion as a child of strife, culturally raw and unaccomplished.

Just as the ascent of the low *ductor latronum* Arsaces thereafter divided Persia's kings from the worthy Hagistia, coarsening the imperial succession, so in Constantine we are meant to recognize another *latro*, whose greed and thievery[75] similarly infected religious concord within his own empire. These impulses were inherited by his son Constantius, who abetted the temple robberies of his officials and the "pagan tax" of George.[76] By raising the obelisk, he completed the *piaculum* his father had set in motion. Such cultural banditry, added to their Jewish love of sedition, inevitably set Christians in the same category as Sapor's predators. Ammianus' opinion of this unequal relationship between Christianity and the *cultus deorum* is most suitably expressed by a single denunciation: *latrocinium*.

Egyptian religion had survived threats from nature and man to render considerable service in the war of civilization against savagery. As for the Christian *agōnistēs*, Ammianus offers numerous domestic and foreign struggles where he is involved. A disturbing scene emerges: within the metropolitan interior of the empire a Christian was, as Julian said, ferocious,[77] but on the frontier he was quiescent before Rome's enemies. Great urban bishops such as George, Damasus, and Ursinus provoked serious *seditiones;* even the more worthy Liberius had his faction.[78] For Ammianus, Christianity was a popular religion in this ominous sense, and the humble were always close at hand such as that *plebs dis-*

---

74. There is an exception, "qui deviare a religione compulsi pertulere cruciabiles poenas ad usque gloriosam mortem intemerata fide progressi et nunc martyres appellantur," 22.11.10. This, of course, refers to the Persecutions, but only implicitly so without having any specific, textually grounding detail apart from George's murder.

75. *Metrodori mendaciis avidius acquiescit*, 25.4.23; his theft of the obelisk. Constantine is the sinning rich man of Julian's myth; see above, p. 35.

76. Note the alleged greed of Strategius Musonianus, *lucrandi aviditate sordescens*, 15.13.2, who assisted Constantius' sectarian investigations; so too the extravagance of metropolitan bishops, 27.3.14. Insofar as the old shrines were actual *thesauri* of (disturbingly) portable wealth, pagans like Ammianus and Symmachus (see above, p. 83, n. 65) were concerned that the *cultus deorum* could, somewhere far below the abstract contest of ideas, literally vanish in a greedy moment.

77. 22.5.4.

78. 22.11.3–11; 27.3.11–13, 9.9. *Populi metu, qui eius amore flagrabat*, 15.7.10.

cissa who listened to Julian in the company of their bishops, or the *humiles* and presbyter sent by Fritigern to Valens.[79] It is this inflammable popular devotion that sets the cult of the martyrs in a doubtful light. Although Ammianus compliments the unshaken faith of those who would not renounce their religion and represents the honor given the "Innocents" of Milan as merited, he also suggests that the title might be debased to extol simply anyone killed in a riot. The pagans of Alexandria evidently feared that even someone so universally hated as George was by both Christian and pagan would find his way to this honor.[80] Eupraxius' salutary warning to Valentinian that he avoid making martyrs[81] proceeded from the apparent assumption that to pardon guilty men would be less injurious to public order than to make martyrs and thereby inevitably provoke something worse, *seditiones*. The appeal of the quaestor hardly flattered the cult of the martyrs, which as a deification, in effect, of the smoldering *amor populi* appeared socially menacing.

Christianity in the shape of its contentious metropolitan bishops and unsettled plebs was obviously in no position to offer peace to the cities, nor does Ammianus bring forward any eminent Christian philosophers to contribute the luster of *doctrinae*. But what of those other bishops who receive his well-known praise for pursuing modest lives worthy of the Eternal Spirit?[82] The provincial hinterlands where this mild spirit presumably throve were also witnessing Rome's endless, now worsening, struggle against the barbarian nations, and his portrayal of Christian activities on the frontier raises the doubt whether their two characteristically violent and mild temperaments were not turned about. Would Christians not contribute more to the *salus* of the empire by demonstrating mildness in the metropolis and directing their ferocity out to the edge against Rome's enemies? Their religion hardly seemed an impenetrable bulwark; Sapor had hoped to use it to soften opposition in Mesopotamia:

> Yet when he also found other maidens [at Reman and Busan] who were consecrated to holy service in the Christian rite, he commanded that

---
79. 22.5.3, 31.12.8.
80. 22.11.10, 27.7.5.
81. "Interpellavit Eupraxius tunc quaestor et 'Parcius' inquit 'agito, piissime principum; hos enim, quos interfici tamquam noxios iubes, ut martyras, id est divinitati acceptos, colet religio Christiana,'" 27.7.6.
82. "Qui esse poterant beati re vera, si magnitudine urbis despecta, quam vitiis opponunt, ad imitationem antistitum quorundam provincialium viverent, quos tenuitas edendi potandique parcissime, vilitas etiam indumentorum et supercilia humum spectantia perpetuo Numini verisque eius cultoribus ut puros commendant et verecundos," 27.3.15.

they be left unmolested; they were to practice their religion as usual without any man impeding them. He was only pretending to be gentle for the time, really, so that those who before had been terrified of his awfulness and cruelty would freely put aside their fear and come to him, convinced by new proofs that he controlled his rising fortune with humanity and gentle habits.[83]

As Ammianus suggests, the frontier was a hard region where such *humanitas, lenitudo,* and *placidi mores,* if highly desirable in their own right, were a dangerous illusion, a provincial Sirens' Song of peace, capable of delivering the individual Roman or his town to barbarian cruelty. That this mildness was actually a fiction emerges from the siege of Bezabde; the *placidus sermo* of its bishop counted for nothing against Sapor's rage: "But it was useless to argue these and similar points when confronted by the wild craziness of the king who stubbornly swore that he would not depart until he had destroyed the fortress."[84] It was even suspected, with some appearance of truth, that the bishop had betrayed to him knowledge of the weakest parts of the wall. The historian's moral is clear: it would have been better if the Christian had never gone to Sapor in the first place. But Christians continued to listen to the barbarian song like those who later parleyed on behalf of the African rebel Firmus and the Goths.[85] Ammianus regards the one Gothic mission as deceitful, the other, contemptible.

Far from appearing as a heroic religion and shield of the empire, Christianity was actually a distraction from the task of *imperium.* It was incredible that the Alamannic war band of Rando could simply walk into Mainz, *praesidiis vacua,* during a Christian festival.[86] A small but distinct reminder of this sort of martial disarray occurs in the account of Palladius' suicide; his guards were off at a vigil.[87] No markedly Christian emperor is a hero in the *Res gestae.* It was Jovian, *Christianae legis itidem studiosus et non numquam honorificus,* who struck a shameful treaty with the Persians of unparalleled concessions.[88] Constantius, the most Christian emperor of the surviving *Res gestae,* was of course famous for his bad luck in foreign campaigns; he provided the timid defensive strategy for his martyr-clinging appointee Sabinianus.[89] Christianity, according to

---

83. 18.10.4.
84. 20.7.8.
85. 29.5.15, 31.12.8, 31.15.6. On the equivocal role of Christians at such moments, and their imperfect identification with *Romanitas,* see Angliviel de la Beaumelle, "Remarques," 19–23.
86. 27.10.1–2.   87. 28.6.27.   88. 25.7.13, 25.9.9, 25.10.15.
89. "Dum haec celerantur, Sabinianus, inter rapienda momenta periculorum communium lectissimus moderator belli internecivi, per Edessena sepulchra, quasi fundata

Ammianus, was in no better condition to master external conflict than it was sedition in the cities. These faults are embodied in Constantius, who, on one hand, excited violence within the empire through his sectarian investigations and, on the other, was unable to subdue it without.

The primitiveness or barbarity of Christianity, when compared with the great achievements of other religions, posed a hard social problem: the Serapeum was filled with the beauty of almost living statues; the basilica of Sicininus, with the 137 corpses of a *plebs efferata*.[90] To engender the right elements of civil concord and heroic endeavor within Christianity, it must be drawn up—that is, brought into a happy relationship with the *cultus deorum*—by its best qualities: courage, justice, and simplicity.[91] In the matter of a specifically religious liaison, Ammianus offers evidence that Christianity could well be considered theologically permeable. Athanasius, Constantius, Jovian, and Valentinian are all found associating with divination, theoretically abhorrent to Christians.[92] Constantine and Constantius had both admired the obelisk of Sol; the father had been mindful of Rome's position as the Temple of the World, and his son had stood in awe of the city's great shrines.[93] Given Ammianus' demonstrably low opinion of Christianity, it would be reasonable for him to have thought with some confidence that in any fair interplay of religions, the inferior one could not help but bend to the superior.[94] A studiously observed policy of imperial toleration recreating Valentinian's pragmatic spirit of neutrality[95]—not Julian's blighted liberal-

cum mortuis pace, nihil formidans, more vitae remissioris fluxius agens," 18.7.7; "Sabinianum etiam tum sepulcris haerentem," 19.3.1.

90. 27.3.13.

91. Courage: the deacon Maras, "nihil fateri compulsus," 14.9.7; the martyrs, "ad usque gloriosam mortem intemerata fide progressi," 22.11.10. Justice: Pope Liberius, "nec visum hominem nec auditum damnare nefas ultimum saepe exclamans," 15.7.9; the "Innocents" who died attempting to bring a count to justice *ex lege*, 27.7.5. Simplicity: the provincial bishops, 27.3.15.

92. 15.7.7–8, 21.14.1, 25.6.1, 26.1.7.

93. "Quicquid viderat primum, id eminere inter alia cuncta sperabat: Iovis Tarpei delubra, quantum terrenis divina praecellunt; lavacra in modum provinciarum exstructa; amphitheatri molem solidatam lapidis Tiburtini compage, ad cuius summitatem aegre visio humana conscendit; Pantheum velut regionem teretem speciosa celsitudine fornicatam; elatosque vertices scansili suggestu consurgunt priorum principum imitamenta portantes, et Urbis templum forumque Pacis et Pompei theatrum et Odeum et Stadium aliaque inter haec decora urbis aeternae," 16.10.14.

94. On the interpenetration of pagan and Christian religion, see M. Nilsson, "Pagan Divine Service," 63–71.

95. "Postremo hoc moderamine principatus inclaruit, quod inter religionum diversitates medius stetit nec quemquam inquietavit neque ut hoc coleretur, imperavit aut illud; nec interdictis minacibus subiectorum cervicem ad id, quod ipse voluit, inclinabat, sed intemeratas reliquit has partes ut repperit," 30.9.5.

ism—which would control all extremists, should permit this natural process to do its civilizing work, all to the advantage of paganism.[96]

We can clearly state once and for all, I think, that Ammianus does not endorse Christianity. It had contributed no *doctrinae* and was clearly *infelix* for the empire in its present state, hardly an imperial religion. It was attractive as a small-town phenomenon but incapable of living peacefully in the great cities. Before approaching that high level of inspired creativity that yields wisdom, Christians must first make their way to that salubrious, prohibitory aspect of religion, fear of the laws, which was necessary for social restraint and its concomitant *homonoia*; then they should at least be on a par with the God-fearing Persians. We should furthermore distinguish between Christianity's ethical and doctrinal virtues. Although a provincial bishop commended himself to God by his simple mode of life, Ammianus says nothing about specific theology here; the man could just as easily be leading the life of an abstemious pagan philosopher.[97] So too the martyr's "glorious and unshaken faith" should be compared with the identical behavior of Ammianus' pagan philosophers such as Demetrius Cythras.[98]

With a finer awareness of this faith's comparatively low rank within the *Res gestae*, we may better unravel Ammianus' famous definition of Christianity as a *religio absoluta et simplex*.[99] Although this highly visible phrase is assumed to be a compliment,[100] precisely what kind of theological endorsement does it amount to? *Absoluta* and *simplex* are not elsewhere part of Ammianus' theological vocabulary. They occur in none of the digressions, and such isolation from his most important funds of theology suggests rather that this phrase probably does not house a personal ideal of religion. The historian's obvious delight in religious influences ramifying themselves throughout the world would be difficult to characterize as an attraction toward the virtue of simplicity;[101] and what

---

96. Many have alleged (e.g., Ensslin, *Ammianus Marcellinus*, 99–101) that Ammianus was moved by a Neoplatonic principle of toleration. At best, this must be an incomplete definition of what he sought from the continued coexistence of Christianity and the *cultus deorum*: toleration yes, but preparatory to tipping, peaceably, the flow of conversion back upon his Christian competitors—that is, reconversion.

97. This distinction has been observed by Syme, *Ammianus*, 138: "That phrase [*perpetuo numini . . . verisque eius cultoribus*] conveys a distinction: Christianity is not the true faith."

98. 19.12.12.

99. "Christianam religionem absolutam et simplicem anili superstitione confundens, in qua scrutanda perplexius quam componenda gravius excitavit discidia plurima," 21.16.18.

100. Gimazaine, *Ammien Marcellin*, 69; Solari, "Particolarismo," 502; Momigliano, "Pagan and Christian," 95; Camus, *Ammien Marcellin*, 249; Selem, "Considerazioni," 256.

101. E.g., the spread of Egyptian religion *per mundum omnem*, 22.16.19.

value would the concept of absoluteness have in connection with his desired interplay of *diversitates religionum*?

Rather than refer *absoluta et simplex* to a lofty philosophical notion such as the indivisible Platonic Godhead, it would be more correct in my opinion to ascribe it to the historian's more mundane realm of religious law where, in fact, the search for parallel usage bears more fruit, most obviously in Julian's restoration of paganism *planis absolutisque decretis*. While Ammianus does not refer to any other religion as a *lex*, it is often used of Christianity, probably revealing the mentality with which he approaches this religion.[102] For him, Christianity is first a legal reality or given: straight, motionless, and simple, it confronts one; it is there. There is nothing—yet—to operate at that greater, speculative level of religious activity whose concern is the complex *arcana veritatis*.

Christianity appears undeniably *infelix* then and unsuited to the elevated role of an imperial religion; this must be truly heroic. On the other hand, heroes had always been the distinctive creation of the Greco-Roman *cultus deorum*. In contrast to the apparent poorness of Christianity in social contributions, the record of paganism in this history, generally comprising references to foundation stories, temples, and the ancient activities of gods, heroes, and seers, speaks importantly to the ultimate foundations of civilized life. By identifying numerous scenes of struggle, achievement, and cult, Ammianus is not performing some antiquarian exercise. He is rather laying out the boundaries of a precinct: here is the geography of paganism and a reminder of its heroic capability, where *temenē* stood as trophies upon the *cosmos*. Physical proof of this strength existed, as in Egypt, in the *miracula* of shrines and cities all about one, the very criteria of reality by which Roman citizens such as Ammianus distinguished imperial from barbarian life. He conceives of heroic paganism as a cycle of struggle and accomplishment, the necessary cooperation of gods and men in continually renewing the divine promise of civilization: *Romam perpetuamque fore spopondit [divinum Numen]*.[103] The specific instance of this pledge is, significantly, connected with Tertullus' sacrifice in the heroes' shrine of Castor and Pollux. The resulting portrayal of salvation, shiploads of grain coming safely into harbor after the subsiding storm, distinctly evokes the saving mission of

---

102. *Coetus . . . eiusdem legis cultorum*, 15.7.7; *a proposito legis abhorrentia*, 15.7.8; *Christianae legis antistes*, 20.7.7; *Christianae legis itidem studiosus*, 25.10.15. Contrast Egyptian religion as a *prudentia* or *mathemata*.
103. 19.10.4.

the Pharos. The Black Sea excursus essentially projects this marine image of salvation, interleaving cities, shrines, gods, heroes, seers, and philosophers within a world where cult and history stand identified with one another. This time the stormy sea about Ostia is replaced by the Pontus "Euxinus," an area of savagery where civilization tenses itself against surrounding barbarism. In place of the threatened boats of the corn fleet we see the *Argo*.[104]

It is a journey of many types. Set between the spreading of Julian's fame even to India and his first preparations for the Persian expedition, this excursus must be understood as an imperial mandate to civilize, to enter the *Argo* and take the Golden Fleece in Persia[105]—just as Julian receives his other heroic mandate when Caesar to be a Hercules battling tyranny in the West. Inasmuch as Hercules had also been an Argonaut, the Black Sea excursus continues Julian's association with this god's labors. First Ammianus introduces the urban praefecture of Tertullus following the destruction of Amida, a siege both disastrous and symbolic; then by concluding his description of the Black Sea with the happy news of Aquileia's surrender to Julian, he offers a benign contrast to this loss of Amida amid eastern *turbines*.[106] In a greater sense, of course, the journey of the *Argo*, *prima omnium navis*, a ship of heroes and seers, expresses Ammianus' concept of a dynamic civilization and its religion.[107] The idea of journey is paramount, for he describes a frontier where Greco-Roman society remains in a posture of confrontation. Taurica is a land where unpolluted cities and human sacrifice still coexist.[108] This can hardly be

104. 22.8.15.

105. Ammianus thought he saw Sapor wearing a golden ram's-head helmet at the (expressly symbolic) siege of Amida, 19.1.3. In the *Argonautica* of Apollonius Rhodius (ed. by H. Fränkel [Oxford, 1961]), Jason seems, like Julian, to be a torchbearer of Helios, a radiant child of the Sun: he appeared like Apollo walking from a temple, 1.307–11; to stare into the sun was an easier task than to look upon him, 1.725; a picture of Apollo shooting Tityus adorned the purple mantle given him by Athene, 1.759–62; he resembled Ares and Apollo Crysaöros, 3.1283. Note the opening words of the epic: *Archomenos seo, Phoibe*. See above, p. 100.

106. "Dum haec per varios turbines in Orientis extimo festinantur," 19.10.1. "Verum caeleste Numen ut Romanae rei totius aerumnas intra unius regionis concluderet ambitum," 19.1.4. "Accesserat aliud ad gaudiorum praesentium cumulum," 22.8.49.

107. Before Jason's battle with the Colchians, 4.203–5, he reminded his men that Hellas depended upon their victory.

108. Ammianus' description of the Black Sea combines things seen and read: "visa vel lecta quaedam perspicua fide monstrare," 22.8.1. It is a conceptual mortar poured from the real eye and the mind's eye; hardened, it becomes the reality set before us. Of course, we know that someone traveling to the Taurican Chersonesus in A.D. 380 would not have seen a land full of Greek colonies whose quiet inhabitants lived peaceably from the soil and defended their "unpolluted" cities from man-sacrificing barbarians (22.8.32, 36). He or she

an antiquarian's hymn to perfect Hellenic civilization, an accomplished cultural ideal. The *Res gestae* is replete with challenge and response: Tauriscus, Amycus, the Trojans, Persians, or Constantius meet their Hercules, Pollux, Achilles, or Julian.[109] The Goths had again penetrated the empire along the shore of the Black Sea, and the Huns were behind them. To the historian's best knowledge, this civilizing journey must go on to eternity. New heroes, and seers to guide them, would always be needed, and these must come if the promise of the divine Numen to Rome were true.

The creation of such cultural and religious mediators was for Ammianus the greatest virtue of paganism and its characteristic achievement. Julian stands directly in this heroic tradition.[110] Like the Black Sea excursus advancing through scenes of piety, combat, and philosophy, his career parallels these—another voyage of the *Argo*. He shows himself to be the *articulus* between the past and present of the *cultus deorum*, joining the progress of his *imperium* to a steadily accumulating flow of religious events. Journeying, he holds *reparatio*, the life-giving power of gods: the cities of Gaul and Thrace thrive again and barbarism is pacified.[111] But none of this could be accomplished without a fully developed awareness of *prisca mos*. *Reparatio* demands an active desire to remain in

---

would have found a country that had been thoroughly absorbed by the Sarmatians and Goths many decades before, no longer a client of Rome, or Hellenism for that matter, but dissolved in the *Scythicum litus* (22.8.44). Is Ammianus merely being careless? A hint of something might be gathered from what he says about Trajan and Aurelian in Book 31, where we have the former's winning of Dacia but *not* the latter's abandoning of it, only Aurelian's victorious expulsion of the Goths from Thrace (31.5.16–17). I think Ammianus himself does not want to give up Rome's claims north of the Danube but rather let them play within a lively personal vision of imperial, Hellenic, power yet to be wrested from the Black Sea: Taurica is still *coloniarum plena Graecarum*, waiting for that new Trajan—it might even be Theodosius—who will drive the *limes* ever eastward and northward (note the Bosporani who pledged tribute to Julian, 22.7.10). If this seems too fantastic, it is no more so than his belief in Rome's universal dominion: "per omnes tamen quot orae sunt partesque terrarum, ut domina suscipitur et regina," 14.6.6. In sum, we may as well accept that Hellenic Taurica exists for him in just such a psychological present, that quite real land of Someday.

109. Note the heroicized battles at Amida and Ctesiphon: the Gauls were like the Achaeans slaying Rhesus (a Thracian king), 19.6.11; Julian used a *Homerica dispositio* outside the Persian capital, 24.6.9; of the same battle, *sonent Hectoreas poetae veteres pugnas*, 14.

110. He is, for example, called a Trajan, *bellorum gloriosis cursibus Traiani simillimus*, 16.1.4. As Caesar, Julian regarrisoned one of Trajan's forts among the Alamanni, 17.1.11. Cf. Valentinian, *si reliqua temperasset, vixerat ut Traianus et Marcus*, 30.9.1.

111. "Urbes quin etiam per Thracias omnes cum munimentis reparans extimis curansque sollicite, ne arma vel indumenta aut stipendium vel alimenta deessent, 22.7.7; cf. his repair of Nicomedia, 22.9.3–5. See above, p. 24, n. 54.

contact with the past, and for the Greco-Roman hero this impulse can only direct him to the great cultural achievements memorialized in the temples. Historical re-creation in such a world cannot occur without piety—paganism. Accordingly, when Julian enters Vienne, its citizens see a *genius salutaris* about to shine on their catastrophes, while at the same time a blind woman shouts that he will repair the temples of the gods.[112] By joining the gods to men, uniting men to each other, and guaranteeing the continued existence of material and intellectual vigor within his cities, the heroic emperor's concern with restoration becomes indistinguishable from an attempt to achieve total social integration—civilization—through himself. In this progressive sense of being directed toward an ideally integrated society, the *reparatio* to which the pagan *agōnistēs* of Ammianus commits himself is not antiquarianism but a dynamic awareness of history, which insists that an emperor determined to preserve and extend his *imperium,* the civilized world, assume as Julian did the role of *articulus* mediating past and present through himself.

In performing this duty, as the historian of course realizes, even a Christian emperor must in some sense become pagan, and it is noticeable that his heroic scheme will allow for Christian participation. If Christians will not fight on behalf of paganism itself, let them see the necessary struggle for Greco-Roman civilization, which Ammianus shows in his several excursuses to be coextensive with the achievements of the *cultus deorum.* Taking that inducement, the temples should still be left intact. What he seeks is a confession of historical obligation. To stand in his succession of heroes an emperor must acknowledge the cultural foundation of the world for which he is fighting. This is the challenge with which Ammianus confronts the Theodosian house, certainly capable of great deeds for Rome, through the pointedly unfinished oracle, "THEOD . . . ", cast by Patricius and Hilarius.[113]

112. 15.8.21–22.
113. The success of the elder in Britain, "officiis Martiis felicissime cognitus," 27.8.3, and Africa, "Domitii Corbulonis et Lusii simillimus veterum," 29.5.4; "triumphanti similis redit, aetatum ordinumque omnium celebrabili favore susceptus," 29.5.55. The outstanding victory of the younger Theodosius, "princeps postea perspicissimus," over the Free Sarmatians, 29.6.15. Given what I read to be signs of pride, hope, and unresolved suspense, I would accept the suggestion of Cameron ("Review," 261–62) that Ammianus had already "laid down his pen" before Faltonius Probus Alypius became Prefect of Rome in June 391 (see also Gimazaine, *Ammien Marcellin,* 124–25). The consulship of Neoterius, 26.5.14, is the last fixed date in the *Res gestae.* "But suppose Ammian was writing in 390/1," Cameron states, "Throughout 389/390 Theodosius pursued a remarkably conciliatory policy towards the pagan aristocracy of the West. . . . Theodosius had passed through phases

Pagan cults father heroes, but there will be no last hero and no last evil; Romans must continue to strive for *heroica ingenia* in the gods' Circus through circles of light and darkness. A victor in this endless series of races is, like Rameses, rendered *aiōnobios*. The most important illustration of this dynamic ideal of religion appears in those gods and emperors gathered by Ammianus about the obelisk of Sol, *quem videmus in Circo*, for a new Pharos has been erected whose beacon radiates glory on men like Augustus and Julian who will follow its inscription toward piety. This symbol rises in the history, *tamquam apex omnium eminebat*. In its cosmos the historian firmly moves us to the center of an ideological confluence, the intersection of religions where he himself wants to stand.

---

of persecution before, but to a western observer in 390 it might well have seemed that he had finally settled down into the ways of Valentinian. Ammianus' praise of Valentinian might have been intended rather as implicit praise of Theodosius' new found tolerance." There can be little doubt but that Ammianus would ideally have liked to convert one of the new Christian emperors just as the Christians had laid hold of Constantine. He is at once both more and less truculent than the Ammianus portrayed by Sabbah and the Neoplatonist Synesius described by Bregman (*Synesius of Cyrene*). In Sabbah's opinion (*La Méthode*, 332) Ammianus uses the *adventus* of Constantius, implicitly that of Theodosius in 389, to condemn New Rome's pretensions: Theodosius was embarking upon an "orgueilleuse entreprise architecturale" at Constantinople, his new forum; but mortals would never be able to make another Rome. If one *adventus* does actually subsist in the other, I yet do not believe that Ammianus wants to make Theodosius odious by such a comparison. His goal, rather, is positive: to encourage the emperor always to revere and emulate man's greatest city; Rome—but pagan Rome—should be a *paideia* for (imperially) young Christianity. A *Forum Theodosii* inspired by Trajan and a Hippodrome bearing a great obelisk are good beginnings. However, the Synesius of Bregman (58–59) has given up such pagan *paideia* for a more fatalistic *entente;* Christianity becomes "a new form of expression for Hellenism," the sole shieldbearer for *Romanitas:* "The battle to save Hellenism from barbarism, to save *Romania* and its civilized institutions from the barbarization of its population, was more important to him than the battle between paganism and Christianity." To Ammianus, however, if the *cultus deorum* were irretrievably lost, there could be no final victory for Rome.

· CHAPTER SIX ·

THE SHIELD OF ACHILLES

Around the *Res gestae* are other late pagan histories and breviaries whose strong or weak voices will mold our finished design in relief. Religion is most abbreviated in the shortest of these works, the breviary of Rufius Festus (about 370), which holds simply a handful of generally vague allusions.[1] These references do make contact, however, with that important, widely disseminated theme of the emperor's celestial *felicitas*, for Festus is eager to set his own patron, Valens, among those divinely gifted leaders like Alexander and Pompey who had conquered in the East: "Let only that felicity endure, granted by God and that friendly spirit in whom you trust and to whom you are entrusted, so that to this huge victory over the Goths may be added the laurel of a Persian peace." Heavenly favor would descend to Valens through a subordinate *numen amicum*, that is—Christian overtones or no—a tutelary *genius*. Of course Ammianus himself uses this theological scheme to articulate the divine promise of Rome's eternity, Jupiter's perennial transmission of *heroica ingenia* to the empire. The characterization of Severus Alexander by Festus similarly suggests the cyclical nature of the heroes' struggle against barbarism: "Aurelius Alexander was, so to speak, [Alexander] reborn by a certain fate for the destruction of the Persians."[2] The supreme Numen had given the soul of Alexander of Macedon to another and so made one more link in the eternal chain of heroes. In its own tiny fashion this bre-

---

1. *Breviarium*, ed. J. Eadie (London, 1967), the sacrifice of captives by the Scordisci (cf. *Res gestae*, 27.4.4), 9; Pompey's dedication of a sacred grove at Daphne near Antioch, 16; *fato quodam*, 22; *superno numini . . . invidiam caelestis indignationis*, 24; *infesta insigna*, 28; *dei nutu . . . amico numine*, 30.
2. 22. Cf. Maximus' claim that Julian had inherited the soul of Alexander, above, p. 66.

viary captures Ammianus' encouragement of Christian emperors to identify their *imperia* with the traditional, heroic appeal of paganism. Festus' particular manner of knitting the bond between empire and divinity seems, however, to depend precariously on the character, *heroicum ingenium*, of the emperor alone, for he presents us with no other agents of divine *salus* such as priests. As a result, religion here misses the sense of a preexisting *nomos*, a broad and fixed cultic background against which passing emperors play out their *res gestae*. By not grounding imperial *felicitas* within a general environment of religious activities, Festus essentially reduces the idea of Roman religion to some ad hoc pact, only valid until the next reign and new imperial personality—precisely that subordination of *nomos* to *ethos* that Ammianus shuns.

The longer breviary of Eutropius (after 364) produces a similar effect of personally confined religion but adds a perceptible tug from *nomos*. This is felt not through rhythmic allusion to Rome's splendid religious past—that is all over by Tarquin[3]—nor through omens trailing diviners, signs that a second zone of religious power exists apart from the emperor's *pactus* (the portentous comet announcing Constantine's death passes without any allusion to seers or divination).[4] Rather Eutropius uses *consecratio* to show the emperor in tension with some other, earthly source of religious authority; for deification was the senate's award and one not always free of debate.[5] His reigns regularly close with these notices whose constantly varying forms betoken some particular interest in the topic. He varies his basic phrase, *inter divos relatus est*, with the addition of a form of *merere*.[6] Augustus and Trajan receive ornate versions, Trajan's divinity even arriving in advance of his *consecratio*;[7] but a bad emperor finishes like Domitian, *ignobiliter est sepultus*.[8]

Merit is the obvious key to such stylistic variation—through his acts an emperor attains divinity in the eyes of men. Again, though, religion seems made to kneel before *ethos*, for piety, attention to cult for its own (the gods') sake, is not actually stated or shown to be a requirement for

3. *Breviarium*, ed. J. Ruehl (Leipzig, 1919), 1.1.1, 3.1–2, 8.1.
4. 10.8.2.
5. E.g., "Senatus ei [Hadriano] tribuere noluit divinos honores," 8.7.3.
6. E.g., Antoninus Pius, "atque inter divos relatus est, et merito consecratus," 8.8.4; Aurelian, "meruit quoque inter divos referri," 9.15.2; Constantine, "atque inter divos meruit referri," 10.8.3.
7. "[Augustus] vir qui non inmerito ex maxima parte deo similis est putatus," 7.8.4; "ob haec per orbem terrarum deo proximus nihil non venerationis meruit [Traianus] et vivus et mortuus," 8.4.1. Boer (*Some Minor*, 150–58) was the first to comment upon Eutropius' special use of *consecratio*.
8. 7.23.6.

divine status. Jovian's consecration embraces nothing more "sacred" than a good disposition.[9] Only once does *consecratio* show its particularly cultic side when the senate decides to place a golden statue of Claudius Gothicus at the Capitolium, *ingenti honore*.[10] Eutropius, like Festus, allows his presentation of religion to fall deeply within the hands of personal *ethos*. There is equal disparity between Eutropius and Ammianus—the natural result of virtually eliminating *nomos* for *ethos*—in the breviary's support for Constantine, "a man to be compared with the best emperors when he first reigned, with ordinary ones at the end. Innumerable virtues shone in his mind and body. . . . And he deserved to be placed among the deified emperors."[11] Ammianus thought of Constantine as a *latro* and could never have been so appeasing, at least to *his* Christian dynasty. In sum, Eutropius is a soft pagan, and when he criticizes Julian for his excessively harsh treatment of Christians[12]—his only opinion on imperial religious policy—the point holds nothing of Ammianus' commitment to a better, more enduring form of paganism.

Sextus Aurelius Victor (after 360) surpasses Eutropius in the depth of his religious presentation as Eutropius does Festus. For example, the *De Caesaribus* contains some reflection on *consecratio:* "Emperors and the best among mortals whose fame has been judged worthy of a virtuous life, so it is thought, go to Heaven, or at least they are honored as gods by men."[13] Deification is described in truly cultic terms: *templa, columna, sacerdotes*.[14] Victor names more temples than Eutropius[15] and generally offers a more rounded world of religious activity exterior and anterior to the emperors. Among the details that contribute to this fullness are Hadrian's initiation into the Eleusinian Mysteries, Caracalla's introduction of Egyptian rites, and the mob cursing Gallienus by Mother Earth and the *Dii inferni*.[16]

Although Victor, like Eutropius, uses *consecratio* to tag the emperors,[17] he gives his paganism firmer grip through the addition of several references to divination. Among the historians and epitomators we

9. "Nam et civilitati propior et natura admodum liberalis fuit," 10.18.2.
10. 9.11.2.
11. 10.7.1–2.
12. *Nimius religionis Christianae insectator*, 10.16.3.
13. *De Caesaribus*, ed. R. Greundel (Leipzig, 1970), 33.30.
14. Marcus Aurelius, 16.15.
15. The Capitolium, 9.7, together with the shrines of Pax, 9.7, Minerva, 12.2, and Constantine's Gens Flavia, 40.26.
16. 14.3, 21.4, 30.31. 21.4 is Victor's only reference to ethnic religion, and it reveals no particular enthusiasm for Egypt.
17. Augustus, for example, receives an elaborate form, "hincque uti deo Romae

shall encounter, Victor alone suggests that Carus' death by divine lightning was attributable to oracles known and spurned: "For although he had learned from oracles that he should encounter victory only so far as this city [Ctesiphon], by going beyond it he paid with his life. Thus Fate is hard to turn, and knowledge of the future was wasted upon him."[18] Claudius Gothicus attained unexcelled glory by obeying the voice of traditional prophecy:

> It was declared by the Sibylline Books that the first man of the most eminent order must devote himself to Victory. As for who should be the one to offer himself, it became clear that the task belonged rather to him who was in truth leader of the senate and everyone. Without any setback to our army the barbarians were thus shattered and driven off, and thereafter the emperor made an offering of his own life in behalf of the State. His memory and his deliverance of the citizens are still cherished by good men, things which contribute not only to his personal glory but, in some very real sense, to the felicity of his descendants as well. This is indeed the case as we look from Constantius and Constantine up to our present emperors.[19]

Considering the rewards, prophecy—piety—had proven its worth to Claudius. Without subtlety Victor draws the prosperity of the Constantinian house from this famous act of obedience to Rome's great oracle and the ancient religion it represents.

Divination most blatantly promotes the old faith in Victor's treatment of the Millennial Games celebrated by Philip in 248. He adds that in his own time, a century later, the year passed with none of the customary festivities (for the Secular Games), "thus was negligence [sc. of the old rites] continually gaining ground in Rome"[20]—a decay, moreover, that had been prophesied by several omens. When pigs were sacrificed *lege pontificum* during the reign of Philip, the officiating *haruspices* found that each pig had the genitals of both sexes, signs foretelling an increase in vice and the corruption of youth; so Philip outlawed male prostitutes. Other diviners, however, saw something different—that effeminacy would prosper now that virtue was universally neglected. Victor himself

---

provinciis omnibus per urbes celeberrimas vivo mortuoque templa, sacerdotes et collegia sacravere," 1.6; Marcus Aurelius, something less, "patres ac vulgus soli omnia decrevere templa, columnas, sacerdotes," 16.15; and Caracalla, nothing, "corporis reliqua luctu publica relata Romam atque in Antoninis funerata sunt," 21.6.

18. 38.4–6.
19. 34.3–7.
20. 28.2. Refer to the edict of Constantius and Constans dated 346, *Theodosian Code*, 16.10.4, closing temples and banning sacrifice.

believes that all of these observers were mistaken: the omen meant in truth that no one could reckon himself fortunate if *pudor* were lost, while any hardship could be borne if it were kept.[21] Given the line of thought in this section of the *De Caesaribus*—neglected *solemnia, minima cura* at Rome, and prophecies to that effect—we cannot do otherwise than take Victor's concluding invocation of *pudor* as a call to maintain the *leges pontificum*.[22] *Pudor*, in this sense, should suggest *reverentia (deorum)*, and a later reference to Diocletian's having conserved the old religion *castissime* supports such an interpretation.[23]

If I have read him correctly, Victor will then leave the bland company of Festus and Eutropius for the more deeply engaged paganism of Ammianus, another who actively deploys divination in defense of his religion. To any fourth-century pagan apologist, the Millennial Games of Philip must have appeared one of the most symbolically replete moments to shine ritual *pudor* over the bleaker religious waters of his own time. But Victor must part with Ammianus over Constantine, whom he freely praises in the manner of his fellow epitomators: "But to my recollection Constantine manifested the other virtues as well and rose even to the stars amid the prayers of everyone. Indeed, had he but moderated his liberality and desire for popularity . . . he would have been scarcely less than a god."[24] For Ammianus, Constantine was not this good Cyrus seen by Victor but rather an Arsaces: he declines to lay such flattering lures to religious reconciliation before the Constantinian house.

Nevertheless Victor does attempt to wrap or, perhaps better, restrain the new Flavians in the mantle of pagan *nomos*. Their explicit tie to Claudius, whose glory rose from the Sibylline Books, has already been mentioned. It is noticeable that churches are omitted from his enumeration of Constantine's *opera*; most prominent are those to the glory of the imperial *gens*.[25] By directing our attention to the clan, Victor seems to ask

21. 28.3–10.

22. Cf. the monstrous birth at Daphne, *Res gestae*, 19.12.20, which Ammianus similarly refers to the problem of ignored rites, "non expiantur [portenta] ut apud veteres publice, inaudita praetereunt et incognita."

23. *Veterrimae religiones curatae*, 39.45. Boer (70–73) understands the omen differently as a "political commentary with moral overtones": the senatorial *boni* were depraved and indifferent to military glory. Nor does he make the connection (91) between Diocletian's "chaste" behavior in protecting ancestral religion and Victor's earlier call for *pudor*. But to some very important degree I think we must be dealing with the morality of maintaining ritual observance.

24. 40.15–16. A reference to the virtue of Cyrus immediately precedes this praise, "ea Persarum regi Cyro aeternam gloriam paraverint," 40.14.

25. "Urbis fanum atque basilicam Flaviis meritis patres sacravere. . . . tum per Af-

that we disregard Christianity and choose another road to the divine source of Constantine's authority. It is one that leads not only to the pious Claudius but also, of course, to Constantius Chlorus, who had himself been raised by a greater lord than he, Diocletian, as Jovius, founder of a divine family of emperors modeled on Heaven: "Thereafter Maximian received the name Herculius together with this god's cult, just as Valerius [Diocletian] titled himself Jovius. . . . In sum, his fellow lords looked upon Diocletian as a parent or great god, a comparison whose aptness, as we consider the history of Rome even unto our own time, has clearly been shown by the great deeds of these kinsmen."[26] *Gens* carries this certain message and obligation: for as much as Constantius had honored his patron Diocletian, a great conservator of religion, so should Constantine (one to be reckoned in the line of Diocletian's divine *propinqui*) and Constantine's Christ ultimately give homage to Diocletian's Jupiter.[27]

Anyone who compares historiographical modes of religious presentation in this era, and is willing to put aside the question of historicity, will find that the *Historia Augusta* (about 390) falls nearer the *Res gestae* than any other work. Only the Scriptor offers religion in comparable bulk, and he repeatedly presses home the ideal of heroic paganism found in Ammianus. Of course this moves on an airy mass of verbiage, a raw delight in generating details—*sum enim unus ex curiosis*.[28] He freely absorbs any view or story while pretending critical restraint.[29] Whatever the charade, though, religious references in the *Historia Augusta* do coalesce into a pagan position quite similar to that of the *Res gestae*, an affinity we

---

ricam sacerdotium decretum Flaviae genti," 40.26–28. Note that Ammianus himself offers no church in his list of the Roman *decora* admired by Constantius, 16.10.14–17.

26. 39.18, 29. See Boer, 91.

27. Although Victor praises Diocletian for strengthening the old cults, he would nevertheless appear to reject any persecution of the Christians if his assertion that Constantine, unlike Licinius, behaved charitably toward his enemies may stand for some general opinion on the subject: "eo pius [Constantinus], ut etiam vetus teterrimumque supplicium patibulorum et cruribus suffringendis primus removerit. Hinc pro conditore seu deo habitus," 41.4.

28. *Scriptores Historiae Augustae*, ed. H. Peter (Leipzig, 1884), *Probus*, 2.8.

29. The criticisms of Cordus, "qui haec omnia usque ad fabellam scripsit," *Maximini Duo*, 31.4, and of Marius Maximus, "homo verbosissimus qui et mythohistoricis se voluminibus implicavit," *Firmus*, 1.2. Cf. Ammianus' rebuke to Roman nobles who read only Juvenal and Marius Maximus, *detestantes ut venena doctrinas*, 28.4.14. On the fictive nature of this work, see Syme, *Ammianus*, 102, 205; Syme, *Emperors and Biography*, 263–80; Barnes, *Sources*, 13–22.

can best judge by resorting to our familiar topical scheme of theology, cult, religious authority, and comparative religion.

Theology compares weakly—although this would be true for any other late pagan history we could produce. There is no well-developed excursus in the *Historia Augusta* to set with Ammianus' description of Adrasteia, and the Scriptor contents himself with short explanatory phrases or thin digressions like those on the name of Luna/Lunus, Nemesis as a certain power of Fortuna, Fate's governing the empire by revolutions, or Fortuna as the enemy of Iustitia.[30] The last two appear in a discussion of Rome's long history of crises, *varietates*, which resembles the yoked digressions on Adrasteia and *fortuna mutabilis* in the *Res gestae*;[31] but in this case there is none of Adrasteia's accompanying theology. That he makes Nemesis a power of Fortuna and Fortuna hostile to Iustitia halts further comparison with Ammianus, who clearly allies Nemesis to *aequitas*.[32] If those bits of theology render Iustitia the diminished captive of Fortuna, the *Historia Augusta* nevertheless counterbalances their suggestion of human helplessness with a great deal of attention to omens and divination, an art that assumes the value of attempting to influence and grapple with divine *fata*. Aurelian's happy consultation of the Sibylline Books, *noti beneficiis publicis*,[33] when he needed help against the Marcomanni prominently advertises the value of divination. These same holy books stayed a universal wave of earthquakes.[34] Another sign of the Scriptor's resistance to fatalism is his reply to those who would invoke that *vis fati* which forbade Rome from ever advancing beyond Ctesiphon: they behaved cowardly, for the Persian victory of Galerius proved what men might yet accomplish if they did not spurn the promised favor of the gods.[35] This demand for unrelenting

---

30. *Antoninus Caracallus*, 7.3–5 (see *Res gestae* 23.3.1–3 on Carrhaes' Luna); *Maximus et Balbinus*, 8.5; *Carus*, 1.1–2, 3.7.

31. 14.11.25–26, 29–34.   32. 14.11.24.

33. *Aurelianus*, 18.5.

34. *Mundanum malum esse sedatum*, *Gordiani Tres*, 26.2.

35. *Carus*, 9.3. Of course Julian's philosophers also used this same victory of Galerius as a rallying cry: "Et enim ut probabile argumentum ad fidem implendam scientiae suae, id praetendebatur quod et Maximiano antehac Caesari [Galerius Valerius Maximianus], cum Narseo Persarum rege enim congressuro, itidem leo et aper ingens trucidati simul oblati sunt, et superata gente discessit incolumis, illo minime contemplato, quod aliena petenti portendebatur exitium, et Narseus primus Armeniam Romano iuri obnoxiam occuparat," *Res gestae*, 23.5.11. "*Aper*" also becomes an omen for Diocletian in the *Historia Augusta*, for a Druidess tells him, "Diocletiane, iocari noli, nam eris imperator, cum Aprum occideris," *Numerianus*, 14.3. Compare the Scriptor's *promissus numinum favor* with that pledge made to Rome by Ammianus' *divinum numen*, 19.10.4.

strength, *virtus*,[36] in drawing down heavenly favor grows naturally from the central belief of divination, that men should use the gift of divine communication to advance their own labors.

Whom specifically should they supplicate for the *favor numinum?* There can be little confusion here, for the Scriptor does not refer to an anonymous, supreme Numen, and a similarly nondescript Deus appears only three times.[37] The choice for first place within his divine hierarchy ought to fall instead to one of two far more pervasive deities, Fortuna-Fatum or Jupiter, and we will take the Father of the Gods after considering those occasions in the *Historia Augusta* where religion is made to appear most attractive, meetings of the Roman senate. That is the Scriptor's paradigm of ideal cult; he obviously wishes us to begin our hierarchy at the Capitolium. Sacrifices there are frequently mentioned, and Jupiter Optimus Maximus blesses the most esteemed emperors.[38] The senate also looks to Apollo, Juno, Minerva, Castor and Pollux, and Concord. Deities profaned by Elagabalus, such as Vesta or Mater, are also strongly vouched for by the Scriptor.[39] There is nothing unconventional then about his pantheon, nor does he show any explicit enthusiasm for markedly exotic or ethnic gods like Ammianus' Egyptian Sol, although these often appear.

While the *Historia Augusta* loudly supports paganism[40]—its god-filled senate meetings easily recall those imperial speeches in the *Res gestae* that evoke Numen and Deus—the Scriptor is more silent than Ammianus about divinities coexisting with men upon the earth. Despite his numerous omens and taste for sensation, he offers only three instances of divine *imagines:* a human form bearing Severus to Heaven in a dream; the ghost of Apollonius warning Aurelian to spare Tyana; and the god

---

36. *Timiditas calcanda virtutibus.*

37. *Severus Alexander,* 49.6; *Aurelianus,* 1.5; *Tacitus,* 4.2.

38. E.g., *Severus Alexander,* 43.5; *Maximus et Balbinus,* 3.2–3. "Iovis Optimi Maximi et deorum inmortalium senatusque iudicio et consensu generis humani suscepisse vos rem publicam," *Maximus et Balbinus,* 17.2; "dis inmortalibus gratias et prae ceteris, patres conscripti, Iovi Optimo, qui nobis principem talem qualem optabamus dederunt," *Probus,* 12.1.

39. *Severus Alexander,* 6.2; *Maximini Duo,* 16.1; *Valeriani Duo,* 5.4; *Claudius,* 3.4; *Aurelianus,* 19.4; *Probus,* 11.5, 12.7. "Sacra populi Romani sublatis penetralibus profanavit," *Antoninus Heliogabalus,* 6.7

40. "Di te praestent!" appears frequently, e.g., *Claudianus,* 4.3. Note how repellent the Scriptor finds Elagabalus' strict monotheism: "omnia Romanis veneranda in illud transferre et id agens, ne quis Romae deus nisi Heliogabalus coleretur," 3.4; "nec Romanas tantum exstinguere voluit religiones, sed per orbem terrae, unum studens, ut Heliogabalus deus ubique coleretur," 6.7.

Elagabalus, *ea forma*, assisting the same emperor at Emesa.[41] He is apparently not as reluctant as Ammianus to let a god "mix with mortals," nor does he regard the arrival of a *species* with any comparable degree of awe or dread, only stating quite happily that Apollonius' appearance to Aurelian increased the fame of a venerable philosopher.[42] Then why does the more casual *Historia Augusta* lack that populous world of terrestrial divinities so prominently displayed in the *Res gestae*? It may be possible, beyond stylistic considerations, that we are witnessing some true variation in the degree to which *numina* impinge upon two minds, Ammianus feeling the greater penetration and immanence as he walks in his particular world.

Cultic activity in the *Historia Augusta* generally belongs to one of two spheres, the senatorial or the imperial. The former represents the continued maintenance of Rome's traditional rites—Ammianus' *quae deorum semper fecere cultores*—while the other assumes the more plastic shape of individual preference. Good emperors find harmony with the conservative, senatorial sphere, but the bad seem to turn into unreal, socially unintelligible characters, actors, in effect, who are isolated by their extreme idiosyncracies from the conventional religious practices of the *populus Romanus*. Commodus must be regarded as such an infelicitous ritual actor. At sacrifices, it is alleged, he appeared not in the costume of an emperor but that of a *victimarius*.[43] He defiled the rites of Isis, Bellona, and Mithras by bringing their symbolic expressions of pain to full and violent realization.[44] The emperor paradoxically turned actor to bring greater realism to religious ceremonies—that is, incidents of ritual acting—but in the event he perverted their identities and his own. Didius Julianus also departed from acceptable patterns of worship after the senate rejected his request that they, together with the priests and Vestals, go to Severus as suppliants *praetentis infulis*.[45] Failing to secure his *imperium* to the saving power of Rome's ancient religion in this way, Julianus crazily attempted to fix the soldiers and people with weird rites.[46] This

---

41. *Severus*, 22.1; *Aurelianus*, 24.2–9, 25.3–6.
42. *Aurelianus*, 24.2. Cf. Mars' aid to Fabricius, *Res gestae*, 24.4.24.
43. *Commodus Antoninus*, 5.5. Cf. the Antiochenes' joke that Julian was a *victimarius*, *Res gestae*, 22.14.3; also see Libanius' praise of Julian for performing his own sacrifices, *Opera Libanii*, ed. J. Foerster, *Or*. 12.82.
44. 9.4–6.
45. *Didius Julianus*, 6.5–6.
46. "Fuit praeterea in Iuliano haec amentia, ut per magos pleraque faceret, quibus putaret vel odium populi deleniri vel militum arma compesci. Nam et quasdam non convenientes Romanis sacris hostias immolaverunt et carmina profana incantaverunt, et ea quae

brought on *amentia*, cultic isolation and a loss of identity. But the worst of these emperors was Elagabalus, who would have destroyed the integrity of every god by bending him to the worship of his own Elagabalus. Yet Roman religion survived his leveling: the Vestals successfully deceived him by surrendering only replicas of their sacred emblems. He was again kept away from the sources of divine *favor* when he failed to discover that ritual by which Marcus Aurelius had turned away the Marcomanni.[47] In Elagabalus' frustrated attempts to control *sacra* we can recognize the story told by Ammianus of how Egyptian *prudentia* would survive Christian threats.[48]

If, on the one hand, there appears an unrestrained imperial idiosyncracy that wants to destroy cultic identities, a personal *ethos* rising up against public or ancestral *nomos*, on the other hand, we see Antoninus Pius, *princeps* of those emperors who pursued a correct religious policy: "He deserved the flamen, games, temple, and holy Antonine brotherhood. He was nearly the only emperor to pass his life without shedding the blood either of a fellow citizen or a barbarian (if the choice were ever his to make). And he was rightly compared to Numa whose good fortune, piety, serenity, and religious rites he ever maintained."[49] Keeping faith with Rome's original *caerimoniae* is essential to the Scriptor, and the senate must be allowed to negotiate the pact. This is why he always regards a senatorial emperor (whatever his ultimate fate) as particularly good for *felicitas*.[50] Traditional ceremonies are especially noticeable in the joint reign of Maximus and Balbinus.[51] Those soldier emperors who worked well with the senate, Claudius and Aurelian, are also favorably associated with the *sacra Romana*.

Here, as elsewhere, the *vita* of Claudius is intended to be a mirror for the new Flavians (and their Christian successors): "We come now to the

---

ad speculum dicunt fieri, in quo pueri praeligatis oculis incantato vertice respicere dicuntur Iulianus fecit," 7.9–10.

47. 6.8, 9.1.

48. See above, pp. 97–98. Straub (*Heidnische*, 189–90) believes that the Scriptor is using the fall of Elagabalus to warn away those Christians who were attacking polytheism in his own day.

49. 13.4. Eutropius, 8.8.1, also compares Pius to Numa but does not allude to the preservation of traditional rites.

50. "Di praestent praestabuntque hanc orbi Romano felicitatem," *Maximus et Balbinus*, 17.8; "quod bonum, faustum, felix, salutareque sit rei publicae orbique Romano," *Tacitus*, 18.2.

51. Sacrifices at the Capitolium, 3.2, 8.2, 4; their joint assumption of the office of *Pontifex maximus*, 8.1; *sacra celebrata* after Gordian's elevation, 8.4; Balbinus' offering of a hecatomb after the defeat of Maximinus, 11.4–5.

emperor Claudius whom we must describe with care, out of respect for Constantius Caesar."[52] In its reflection they were to see several images of the old religion: the senate convening at the Temple of Mater during her festival, joyfully learning of Claudius' elevation, and adjourning to the Temple of Palatine Apollo to read his letter; Claudius himself consulting oracles that prophesied *imperium* for his descendants; and the senate rewarding his final devotion of himself to the Goths with a colossal golden statue set before the Capitolium.[53]

If fear dominated the relationship between Aurelian and his senators,[54] yet he is the emperor, rather than Claudius, around whom the Scriptor casts that gilt scene of senate and emperor drawing together in concord and victory over the Sibylline Books: "We lay before you, Conscript Fathers, the advice of the priests and a letter from our emperor Aurelian, requesting that we consult those Books of Fate, blessed by the inviolable authority of the gods, which embrace our hope of ending the war."[55] Aurelian's subsequent defeat of the Marcomanni through religion represents a perfect combination of senatorial and imperial religious authority, the *pontificum suggestio* and *principis litterae*.[56] By contrast, Didius Julianus and Elagabalus, both estranged from the senate, had been thoroughly unable to move religion against their enemies. The presence of two balancing, mutually hortatory *documenta*, the *senatus consultum* followed by Aurelian's enthusiastic order that the consultation now be performed, literally concretizes the idea of harmony before us.[57] Such an intensely benign scene would suggest that we must be near the Scriptor's personal ideal of cult; and his documents do instruct the pious in a similar fashion to Ammianus' own pair of *documenta*, the obelisk and the confession of Hilarius, themselves bespeaking the *Apollinis beneficia*. In our

52. *Claudianus*, 1.1. "Pollio" names Constantius again at 3.1, 9.9, 10.7, 13.2.
53. 3.4, 4.2–3, 10.1–7.
54. "Populus eum Romanus amavit, senatus et timavit," 50.5.
55. 19.1. See Syme, *Ammianus*, 141. I am puzzled why, for all the other oracles he recites in his *Divus Claudius*, the Scriptor does not tell how Claudius rode forward to his illustrious *devotio* after consulting the Sibylline Books. As Victor demonstrates, that *kairos* was a fine opportunity to stick paganism deeply into the imperial Christian *gens*.
56. "Denique nisi divina ope post inspectionem Librorum sacrificiorumque curas monstris quibusdam speciebusque divinis impliciti essent barbari, Romana victoria non fuisset," 21.4. See my comment on Synesius, above, p. 111, n. 12. Cf. Marcus Aurelius' defeat of the same barbarian nation through ritual.
57. 19.1–6, 20.4–8. "Libet ipsius senatus consulti formam exponere, quo libros inspici clarissimi ordinis iussit auctoritas," 18.7. Contrast this episode with Julian's unsuccessful consultation of the Sibylline Books, *Res gestae*, 23.1.7, and his disharmonious relationship with divination generally.

alleged decree of the senate, it is argued that no imperial crisis could be solved without consulting the Sibylline Books, and those who denied that an emperor needed this assistance were either fooling or flattering him: great men cultivated the gods and sought their favor. These books were *fata rei publicae aeterna*—that is, prophecies eternally valid for Rome. To this message, the opening of Aurelian's letter adds an important warning. Christians would ignore those prophecies and cripple Rome at her worst moment: "I am amazed, revered Fathers, that you have hesitated so long to open the Sibylline Books, as though you were deliberating in a Christian church and not the Temple of all the Gods."[58]

Apart from his successful consultation there are other signs of Aurelian's solicitude for religious harmony. He filled the Capitolium and every other temple at Rome with offerings. When restoring the looted temple of Sol in Palmyra, he requested that the senate appoint a *pontifex* to rededicate it; the spirit of the Sibylline consultation is still warm.[59] This act of deference prefigures the benign manner in which Aurelian, unlike Elagabalus, raised his personal veneration of Sol peaceably to the side of Rome's other cults. It is noticeable that the foundation of the temple and college of Sol Invictus follows the statement that he strengthened the city's priesthoods in general, *sacerdotia composuit*.[60]

While the *Divus Aurelianus* reveals without question its author's determination not to surrender belief in Rome's traditional religion, he explains himself at greater length in, as we might expect, the *vita* of his ideal emperor, Severus Alexander—a sketch that is, most importantly, intended for Christian emperors.[61] Alexander is most favored by, and favoring to, the senate, and their fields of cultic activity appear coterminous with the exception of the emperor's unusual *lararia*.[62] Those fig-

---

58. 20.5. See my remarks on Christian military disarray, above, p. 104. Cf. Victor's charge of *minima cura* for rites, 28.2; also, the Scriptor's *Templo deorum omnium* and Ammianus' *Templo mundi totius*, 17.4.13. The last similarly appears within an anti-Christian context, the stealing of the obelisk by Constantine.

59. 31.9–10, 41.11.

60. 35.3. For the religious program of Aurelian, see Halsberghe, *Cult*, 135–48. "It [the reintroduced Sol Invictus] had to be subservient to the emperor's policies and it must in no sense be in conflict, or even cause the least friction with, the religious ideas of the Romans of the time," 135.

61. "Soles quaerere, Constantine maxime, quid sit quod hominem Syrum et alienigenam talem principem fecerit," 65.1.

62. "Felices nos imperio tuo, felicem rem publicam," 6.5; "vos ipsi [patres conscripti] magnifici unum me de vobis esse censete," 11.5. The greater *lararium* of *divi principes, optimi electi*, and *animae sanctiores* housed images of Alexander the Great, Apollonius of Tyana, Christ, Abraham, Orpheus and Severus Alexander's ancestors; the lesser, Virgil, Cicero, Achilles, and other *magni viri*, 29.2, 31.4–5.

ures whom he placed within his two private chapels he venerated, we note, as *optimi, divi,* and *sancti*—most obviously then as outstanding and blessed mortals. They are called neither *dii* nor *numina* which, if an indication of their subordinate rank, suggests that the *lararia* should not be regarded strictly speaking as any substitute for the regular Roman pantheon. At any rate, the word to keep in mind is *lararium*—*lares familiares*—the cult one practiced at home over his own hearth as distinguished from that which he brought before the city and people.[63]

Let us borrow the religious theme of this biography from Aurelian, *sacerdotia composuit:* Alexander placed divination on a regular, professional footing in Rome by offering salaries and lecture-rooms to diviners; he sacrificed in the Capitolium every week and went frequently to the city's other temples; he adorned the double shrine of Isis and Serapis but usually liked to confine his offerings to four or five pounds of silver; he treated the Roman priesthood with deference and allowed the senate to accept or reject his pontifical appointees.[64] While Elagabalus had wished to gather Rome's several cults in his hands to destroy them, his cousin studied gods rather to assist them and support plurality of worship. Accordingly he tolerated both Judaism and Christianity; after all, to take the Scriptor's odd case, it was better for a building to become a church than a cookhouse if in some way, no matter how, the worship of God would increase.[65] Yet Alexander's benign supervision descended upon cults in a distinctly hierarchical manner. Christ, for example, might thrust out a low *popina* or stand darkly within a private *lararium* of holy spirits, but the emperor did not raise him higher, for he knew what diviners had said: if Christ received a *templum*—that is, imperial status equal to the other cults of Rome—all shrines but his would be deserted.[66]

Victory came to those who were obedient to traditional religion, and one of this emperor's *omina imperii* in fact presaged his future triumph

63. See MacMullen, *Paganism,* 92–93.
64. 22.5, 26.8, 27.5, 43.5, 44.4, 44.9, 49.2.
65. "Iudaeis privilegia reservavit. Christianos esse passus est," 22.4. "Cum Christiani quendam locum, qui publicus fuerat, occupassent, contra popinarii dicerent sibi eum deberi, rescripsit melius esse, ut quemadmodumcumque illic deus colatur, quam popinariis dedatur," 49.6. Straub (*Heidnische,* 106–24) discusses Severus Alexander's adherence to the Golden Rule.
66. "Christo templum facere voluit eumque inter deos recipere. Quod et Hadrianus cogitasse fertur, qui templa in omnibus civitatibus sine simulacris iusserat fieri, quae hodieque idcirco quia non habent numina, dicuntur Hadriani, quae ille ad hoc paresse dicebatur. Sed prohibitus est ab iis, qui consulentes sacra reppererant omnes Christianos futuros, si id fecisset, et templa reliqua deserenda," 43.6–7.

over the Persians.⁶⁷ The Scriptor sets this campaign, however mediocre to real history, at the apex of his *vita*, and there the senate acclaims him as high-priest and victor: "Iuveni imperatori, patri patriae, pontifici maximo. per te victoriam undique praesumimus."⁶⁸ Happier than Julian, Alexander returned to dedicate Persian trophies in the Capitolium.⁶⁹ When we finish with this emperor, it is difficult to avoid thinking that the Scriptor has just offered us Julian but in a more successful form. The replacement of Elagabalus, an intolerant, theologically divisive monotheist, with his philosophical or "Hellenic" cousin repeats the change from Constantius to Julian portrayed by Ammianus. But Alexander, one no less committed to the *cultus deorum* than Julian,⁷⁰ shows himself more truly temperate, tolerant, and deferential to civic *nomos;* his diviners are regulated. He obeys the command of Apollonius to modest offerings; but this rule of the Mean does not shorten the reach of his piety, for all of Rome's temples receive imperial support and prayers.⁷¹ In sum, Severus Alexander avoids Julian's faults and receives a different reward, to face Persia, as Ammianus would demand, *pace numinum exorata.*⁷²

Diviners and philosophers in the *Res gestae* fight each other for religious authority, but such tension between the gods' different spokesmen is absent from the *Historia Augusta*. If Alexander embodies perfectly directed religious instincts, we find him equally given to philosophy and divination. Thrasybulus the *mathematicus* was his close friend.⁷³ Naturally he read Plato, and Apollonius of Tyana stood in his chapel.⁷⁴ Both

---

67. "Nata in domo laurus iuxta Persici arborem intra unum annum Persici arborem vicit. Unde etiam coniectores dixerunt Persas ab eo esse vincendos," 13.7. Cf. the Alexander *renatus* of Festus, 22.

68. 56.10. In a dream his father once saw the senate's statue of Victory lifting him to Heaven, 14.1–2. This statue was, of course, a focus of pagan agitation even as the Scriptor wrote. See Straub, *Heidnische*, 146–49. Victory and piety (toward Rome's traditional cults) are inseparable, as the emperor makes clear, "vestrum est supplicationem decernere, ne dis videamur ingrati," 56.9.

69. 57.1.

70. He too was adept at divination: "haruspicinae quoque peritissimus fuit, orneoscopos magnus, ut et Vascones Hispanorum et Pannoniorum augures viceret," 27.6.

71. See above, p. 83.

72. Baynes, *Historia*, 118–44, argued that this *vita* was modeled upon the life of Julian in every respect, including his religious policy, 137. Straub (*Heidnische*, xvi–xvii) examines Bayne's view. Syme (*Ammianus*, 118, 133) also believes that the rendering of Severus Alexander "owed not a little to Julian." While accepting the general validity of this comparison between the two emperors, I would draw attention to their contrasting achievements in religion. The strife and excess described by Ammianus are missing here.

73. 62.2.

74. 29.2, 30.1.

professions have, as they do in the *Res gestae,* their bad men, the *magi* who followed Julianus into *amentia* or the greedy philosopher Apollonius of Chalcis.[75] Diviners are among those Egyptians whom the Scriptor charges with *levitas,* but here I think that maddeningly unstable identities—one could never be sure who these people were or what they were going to become—are his complaint, not that divination itself is by any means wrong.[76] Philosophers receive his most explicit praise: Plato is the *unicum sapientiae munus;* Aristotle and Zeno of Elea rise to Heaven on "every philosophical virtue"; Apollonius of Tyana stands as a "wise man of the most celebrated renown and authority, one of the ancient philosophers, a true friend of the gods, who even yet draws worshippers unto himself as a divinity. . . . For what is holier, more reverend, purer, and more divine among men than that man?"[77] "Vopiscus" even intends to write his own life of Apollonius—following that of Nicomachus Flavianus?[78] Our competition must nevertheless end in a draw, for if philosophers and diviners are each judged according to their actual involvement in the Scriptor's rituals and omens, the former do almost nothing.[79]

When weighing various religions in the *Historia Augusta,* we should first note that the Scriptor has neither Ammianus' interest in, nor his enthusiasm for, non-Roman cults; Rome lives in the light while the rest of the world is dark. Respect for Egyptian religion appears only once and very mildly: Septimius Severus' journey through Thebes, Memphis, the Pyramids, and Serapeum is a *iucunda peregrinatio.*[80] At its worst though, Egypt is a land of doctrinal promiscuity, where devotees of Serapis and Christ wash back and forth. Distinctions between cults have no meaning

---

75. *Antoninus Pius,* 10.5. Cf. Metrodorus whetting the greed of Constantine, *Res gestae,* 25.4.23.

76. From a letter of Hadrian: "[Aegyptum] totam didici levem, pendulam, et ad omnia famae momenta volitantem. Illic qui Serapem colunt, Christiani sunt, et devoti sunt Serapi, qui se Christi episcopos dicunt. Nemo illic archisynagogus Iudaeorum, nemo Samarites, nemo Christianorum presbyter non mathematicus, non haruspex, non aliptes. Ipse ille patriarcha cum Aegyptum venerit ab aliis Serapidem adorare, ab aliis cogitur Christum," *Saturninus,* 8.1–4. "Sunt enim Aegyptii, ut satis nosti, viri ventosi, furibundi, iactantes, iniuriosi, atque adeo vani, liberi, novarum rerum usque ad cantilenas publicas cupientes, versificatores, epigrammatarii, mathematici, haruspices, medici," 7.4. The problem of grasping evanescent identities—"I do not know who you are!"—is one that troubled Ammianus as he observed Julian's *levius ingenium.*

77. *Aurelianus,* 3.5; 24.3, 8.

78. See above, p. 70 and p. 71, n. 3.

79. But for the reverend *imago* of Apollonius, there is only an oracle of Zeus Nicephorius said to be quoted in the works of a *Platonicus,* Apollonius the Syrian, *Hadrianus,* 2.9.

80. *Severus Alexander,* 17.4.

for the unstable Egyptians.[81] Ammianus himself criticizes Egyptian *levitas* but does not allow this censure to touch his praise of their venerable religion.[82] To the Scriptor, anyone who left Rome's temples also departed from the world of well-ordered religion. Rituals outside the city seem to erode his capacity and desire to distinguish between them. He insists that a cult can only achieve complete intelligibility after it has been translated from its foreign or provincial setting to the *Templum totius mundi* and there worked harmoniously into the fabric of Rome's traditional priesthood like Aurelian's Sol.

Christianity will serve as an example of his bias. Severus Alexander could not give a *templum* to Christ and so institute his cult officially at Rome. Elsewhere, the Scriptor displays a pronounced tendency to lump Christians with Jews and Samaritans; he refuses to get identities straight.[83] Such taxonomical *levitas* is, I think, a stylistic device consciously employed to belittle Christianity: that religion fails publicly at Rome, but for beating out a *popina,* and is cast onto the crazy heap of ethnic cults, undistinguishable and unintelligible. But if Aurelian asserted that Christianity had nothing to do with saving the empire, Alexander, the model *princeps*, nevertheless tolerated both it and Judaism. Perhaps the Scriptor then, as Ammianus, would at least concede to Christianity the minimal status of a *religio licita* and, looking to Alexander's *lararia*, grant that Christ himself was a holy man, *anima sanctior*.[84]

. . .

---

81. See above, p. 126, n. 76. Syme correctly assesses the Scriptor's attitude toward Egypt, although in saying so we must pull together comments from both his *Ammianus* (25, 64) and *Emperors* (27–28): the Scriptor does have "a lively interest" in Egypt, but he shows none of the usual esteem for its religion. Contrast this exercise in xenophobia with the *Expositio*'s loving hymn to Egypt (see above, p. 100, n. 69). But Syme may be exaggerating the Scriptor's dislike when he attributes to him the very blackest belief that there was "no religion in Egypt, only frivolity and rabid violence."

82. "Ad singulos motus excandescentes, controversi et reposcones acerrimi," *Res gestae*, 22.16.23.

83. Severus' prohibition against conversion to Judaism or Christianity, 17.1; Elagabalus' inclusion of Jewish, Samaritan, and Christian rites within the cult of his new god, 3.5; Severus Alexander's toleration of Judaism and Christianity, 22.4, and his use of a Jewish or Christian adage, 51.6–7; the critique of Egyptian character in the *Saturninus*, 8.2–7: Christian and Samaritan malcontents; Christians confused with devotees of Serapis; Jews, Samaritans, and Christians as concealed diviners; Jews, Christians, and *omnes gentes* worshipping money as a god.

84. About the role of religion in this work, Syme (*Ammianus*, 73) thinks "religion is patently not among the major preoccupations of the *Historia Augusta*." Momigliano ("Pagan and Christian Historiography," 95) believes that "the *Historia Augusta* is by no means the

Through the fragmentary history of Eunapius (about 414)[85] we enter a religious world about which the *Res gestae* and *Historia Augusta* are silent, that of Theodosius.[86] Both Ammianus and the Scriptor are aggressive pagans who believed in the possible symbiosis of traditional religion and Christianity; to them the *cultus deorum* yet appears politically viable. The *vita* of Severus Alexander, we note, is addressed to "Constantine." Eunapius, however, could not enjoy that illusion in his own time when paganism had obviously been put to flight beyond any help. He has no incentive for moderation. It is not surprising then that the fragments yield in effect two stark icons: an absolutely divine Julian facing the evil Theodosius. And textual gaps notwithstanding, we are able to share his vision of religious decay within the empire. Far from diminishing Julian's religious stature during the Persian expedition as Ammianus does, Eunapius wants to keep him as a *deus praesens*. On the march some god may have told the emperor that the Goths were about to rise against Rome. Helios said that he himself, the divine Charioteer and Ruler of All, was Julian's father, and truly, Eunapius believes, Julian did rise by a golden chain to claim his throne in the sun. In his last crisis the emperor kept his gaze on heaven and communed with the gods—the Roman army would have required no less than a god to succeed him.[87] Apart from such straight panegyric, another route to the adoration of Julian could

---

big anti-Christian pamphlet which some scholars have seen in it"; more recently ("Popular Religious Beliefs," 147) he states that it is "a first class document of the reformed paganism of the fourth century." Straub (*Heidnische*, 188, 193) claims that we have a *Historia adversus Christianos*. Generally, I accept Straub's view. Religion is a most important piece of the puzzle, and clearly it is a militant paganism, although one that does not totally withhold the hand of conciliation from Christianity. Insofar as the Scriptor has a point of view on religion, this is it. But he, as Ammianus, is interested in other subjects as well, and to call his work a veritable *Historia adversus Christianos* begs the question of its total intended impact. Where is the greater *ictus*, politics or religion?

85. For this brief discussion of Eunapius' history, I shall rely on Mueller's fragments without interpolating material from Zosimus, who used much of the lost work for his own history. To rebuild the fragmented religious argument of Eunapius in that way seems insufficiently precise to justify the effort, for—Blockley's opinion (*Classicizing Historians*, 26) notwithstanding—Zosimus pretty clearly omits portions of religious material that Eunapius would have considered important. I am thinking primarily of the Persian expedition, which Zosimus offers shorn of cult and omens. Eunapius could hardly have honored Oribasius' command to piety (above, p. 64) had he so expunged religion from his hero's final *agōn*. Note Mendelssohn's belief (*Historia nova*, xlv–xlvii) that Zosimus did not take his account of the expedition from Eunapius, considering it too rhetorical, "rhetoris prae Iuliani amore insanientis futtilitate." It seems best then to treat the Eunapian fragments and Zosimus separately.

86. See Momigliano, "Popular Religious Beliefs," 148–50.

87. Ff. 22–24.

have lain, as I have suggested before, in shifting blame for the emperor's unhappy fate onto the shoulders of his mentor, Maximus, and there remains an intriguing reference to the thorough inexperience of Maximus and Priscus in political and military affairs.[88] This of course suits Ammianus' criticism of interfering *philosophi*.

The death of Julian freed his enemies to attack *ta theia Hellenika* and philosophy, whose eminence he had restored; so Eunapius understands those mass trials through which Valens exterminated Julian's pagan intelligentsia. Theodorus himself comes off badly as the *notarius* whose suggestibility prepared the immediate ground for this catastrophe. Although Ammianus similarly describes the trials as a general attack upon *docti* throughout the East, he differs significantly from Eunapius in presenting Theodorus as a completely innocent man and dwelling at great length upon the actual ceremony. If, by presenting this oracle, he is somehow inviting Theodosius to recognize the hand of the old gods in granting him *imperium*, for the younger historian these trials left no such divine residue. That Eunapius treats the diviners Hilarius and Patricius simply as victims of the persecution without, apparently, ever mentioning their direct link to the fatal ceremony for which Ammianus makes them responsible reveals a completely different apprehension of the event.[89]

Julian's gifts to Rome were piety and philosophy; those of Theodosius, Christianity and barbarism. As if gazing at reflections captured by a mirror, Eunapius can see in Theodosius the ruin of the state. Barbarians disguised themselves as monks and bishops to plunder Roman citizens, and by feigning Christianity they could move without suspicion among the emperors who professed it.[90] Still Eunapius manages to find a pagan champion among these barbarians, the Gothic general Fravitta, "perfect in virtue," who in return for his victory over Gainas sought only the right to practice traditional Greek religion.[91] No doubt this was a noble request from the point of view of a pagan historian, but Ammianus himself would never have thrust up a barbarian, particularly a Goth, as any spokesman for heroic, civilizing paganism. His own

---

88. F. 19.
89. Ff. 38–40. "[Hilarius] adiecit benivole id Theodorum penitus ignorare," *Res gestae*, 29.1.33. See above, pp. 38–39, 110.
90. F. 48, 55. Ammianus himself may have frequently looked upon Christians as barbarians in disguise, see above, pp. 103–4.
91. Ff. 80, 82. "[Fravitta] leader of those Goths who were dear to the gods and pious . . . , possessed of a soul most nobly disposed to truth and virtue, he pledged himself to worshipping the gods in the old way," f. 60.

vaguely similar barbarian convert, Mederichus, "initiated into certain Greek mysteries," father of Serapio,[92] was thoroughly hostile to Rome and no serious advertisement for the *cultus deorum*. It would simply not have occurred to either Ammianus or the Scriptor to make their arguments for traditional religion so depend upon the great men of barbarian tribes. In this sense the history of Eunapius marks a great shift in apologetic technique.[93]

Zosimus (after 498) is another pagan historian of this newer type, who wants to confront squarely the religious decadence of the Theodosian world, and he feels no attraction to those areas of middle ground occupied by Ammianus, the Scriptor, and epitomators. His predecessor Eunapius had been able to know personally the still hovering radiation of Julian's *eusebeia*, but the glory of Julian feels colder in the *Nea historia*, where his restoration of paganism passes strangely unnoted. Perhaps Zosimus was depressed by the emperor's bad fate. He gives Julian a felicitous vision of Sol at Vienne but openly refuses to discuss those bad signs under which he left Antioch.[94] Unlike Ammianus, who is waiting in suspense for the verdict of Theodosius, Zosimus has seen that moment pass and cannot compensate for Julian's loss with some greater belief that *nomos* might survive.

Religious compromise does not exist in the *Nea historia*. Everyone has withdrawn himself to virtue or vice. Zosimus intends to prove that Providence abandoned Rome from her want of holiness[95] and so at the very outset of his work urges "those who judge events rightly" to see the reason for her decline in a broken connection with God, obviously, religion. It quickly becomes apparent that Christianity is responsible for this rupture. Put succinctly, traditional rites guaranteed the *eumeneia* of God: as long as Rome had continued to celebrate the Secular Games she had held her empire intact, but during the third consulship of Constantine and Licinius (316), the games were neglected and ruin followed.[96] Indi-

92. *Res gestae*, 16.12.25.
93. On the Christian attitudes of Eunapius and his colleague in Theodosian decay, Zosimus, see Blockley, *Classicizing Historians*, 15–22, 86–87.
94. *Nea historia*, 3.9, 12.
95. An *aphoria psychōn*, or want of (divinely inspired) souls, opposed to Rome's former *euphoria psychōn*, 1.1. The problem is a human, "psychic" failure to remain in contact with Providence; souls had become uninspired, estranged, incapable of receiving the descending stream of Logos, and so become barren with nothing to give. Zosimus' particular use of this Platonic and Stoic phrase carries with it the connotation of willful religious estrangement: holiness no longer exists among the Romans of his day. For a contemporary *schema* of the different grades of souls and their distances from the gods, see E. Dodds, ed., *The Elements of Theology*, by Proclus (Oxford, 1963), 185.
96. 2.7.

vidual fates are also bound to cult. Dike and Adrasteia take revenge for murder as they do in the *Res gestae,* but Zosimus, unlike Ammianus, explicitly represents Dike making attacks upon those who profaned pagan shrines.[97]

Divine activity proceeds vaguely by turns from a supreme Tyche—no doubt following his stated Polybian conceit—*Theos, to Theion,* or *ho Daimōn,*[98] and the historian's approach to theology may generally be described as agglutinative rather than analytic with comparatively little interest shown in distinguishing one deity or type of deity from another. The flaccid etiology, "Whether Moirai, stars, or will of God,"[99] is an example. Murky theology aside, he does direct our attention to specific deities, particularly through an important and lengthy religious digression on the Secular Games: the Sibylline Oracle demands worship for Zeus, Hera, Apollo, Leto, Artemis, Moirai, Demeter, Hades, Persephone, and the Eileithyiai.[100] This stands well beside Ammianus' inscription from the obelisk, for it too offers a list of deities whose favor is worthy to be sought by the pious. Both speak to imperial *felicitas:* through piety Rameses ruled the earth as did those Roman emperors, until Constantine, who celebrated the Secular Games.[101] That traditional deities are vital participants in *to Theion* is proven by Athene's appearance on the Acropolis, the oracle delivered to Julian by Sol, and the miraculous preservation from fire of two statues of Athene and Zeus Dodonaeus in the *curia* of Constantinople.[102]

Zosimus turns his religious presentation about a very simple idea: one impassable wall divides the pagan friends and Christian enemies of divine *eumeneia.* Christian sins include Constantine's flight to Christianity after murdering Crispus and Fausta—not in the war against Maxentius, his suppression of divination, his looting of sacred objects, Gratian's refusal to be *Pontifex maximus,* the withdrawal of public money from the old cults by Theodosius, and Pope Innocent's frustration of pagan ceremonies that might have saved Rome from Alaric.[103] As in the *Res gestae,* there are frequent reminders of Christian ferocity like the lethal riot-

97. For Constans, 2.49, and Sopater, 2.81; against the impious Bargus, 5.10, Stilicho and Serena, 5.38.
98. 1.1, 58; 2.37, 49; 4.4; 5.14, 18, 24; 6.7.
99. 1.1.
100. 2.1–7.
101. Victor, 28.2, also employs such an abeyance of the Secular Games, not held in the *annus centesimus* after Philip's celebrations, to comment upon religious neglect. See above, pp. 115–16.
102. 3.9; 5.6, 24.
103. 2.29, 31, 36; 4.59; 5.41.

ing in support of John Chrysostom that filled the churches of Constantinople with bodies, or the times when holy sanctuary was waived to murder Eutropius, the Gothic *foederati*, and Stilicho.[104] Against these sins appear pagan miracles and felicitous acts of devotion: the true prophecy of Sol to Julian, Achilles' deliverance of Athens from an earthquake, her deliverance from Alaric by Athene, the unscathed statues of Athene and Zeus, Praetextatus' victorious defense of the Eleusinian Mysteries before Valentinian, the refusal of Roman senators to obey Theodosius' request that they become Christian, the similar refusal of Fravitta, and Generid's procurement of religious toleration for himself and his army.[105]

With the exception of these last two instances in which barbarians are somehow posed as champions of the *cultus deorum*, a device alien to Ammianus' method of apology, Zosimus sketches out that same idea of pagan virtue found more intricately rendered in the *Res gestae*. But his tone and argument are strident and coarse by comparison. The free-flowing rage of the *Nea historia* betrays, I believe, its author's own awareness that any argument for traditional religion was now purely academic. The opponents of paganism had not been interested in compromise or reprieve for more than a century, and whether Zosimus was restrained or not made no difference to them: screaming was easier when no one would hear.

For Ammianus, Jupiter had promised Rome she would be eternal, a personal belief whose corollary was the unceasing political viability of the *cultus deorum*. When in the *Nea historia*, however, Alaric brings on the ransom stripping of the golden statue of Virtus, we know the final, literal, dismemberment of Ammianus' conception of heroic paganism, the saving Pharos.[106]

· · ·

The tension penetrating every aspect of religious presentation in the *Res gestae* suggests that Ammianus was moving close to the edge of a precipice. If he backed away, he would join Festus, Eutropius, and Victor, those eager to placate the Christian regime. Victor was still solicitous

---

104. 5.18, 19, 23, 34.
105. 4.3, 18, 59; 5.21, 46. Cf. Tertullus' successful invocation of heroes, the Castores, during a similar revolution of the elements, *Res gestae*, 19.10.4.
106. "Truly when this statue was destroyed, whatever remained of courage and virtue among the Romans was extinguished, just as those men learned in the ancient religion and its rituals prophesied at the time," 5.41.

for *religiones antiquissimae*, but both he and Eutropius praised Constantine, an impossible concession for Ammianus. Such men improperly subordinated *nomos* to *ethos*, the religion of a world to the *felicitas* of one. If the Scriptor was another who directed encouraging remarks to the house of Constantine, his pagan fervor and critical attitude toward Christianity were strong. As "Aurelian" clearly asserted, there would be no Roman victory until the emperor and senate together found religious concord under the aegis of traditional cult. He also shared Ammianus' willingness to tolerate: the ascendancy of the *cultus deorum* would occur as a natural result of its superior virtues, not through the persecution of other religions. Accordingly, in that ideal *speculum* raised by Severus Alexander—Julian's superior in this respect—there is no strife between cults. All receive some form of imperial support, and even Christianity finds a niche within the emperor's chapel.[107] But if Ammianus chose to go beyond his ideological precipice, leaving behind the Scriptor and epitomators, he would enter the far different world of Eunapius and Zosimus, strident pagans without hope and so without restraint.

107. "Ammianus as a source and inspiration of the *Historia Augusta*, that is something solid," Syme, *Ammianus*, 72.

· CONCLUSION ·

ROME

The moment was here again. In June 389, Theodosius entered Rome after defeating Maximus the previous July. What would be the religious significance of this particular *adventus*? Rome had received Constantius and stunned him with the architectural *miracula* of her old religion. At his order a new Pharos rose in the Circus. If no one had originally wished for the quasi-triumph which that monument commemorated,[1] they could see a great prayer to Sol. Many in Antioch, however, had wanted the *adventus* of Julian, an emperor of more majesty and promise, a *sidus*. But he left only a blighted legacy to religion there; Antioch became no Pharos. As a great capital again went out to meet an emperor, there were new opportunities to secure the safety of paganism. That Theodosius had already made Nicomachus Praetorian Prefect of Italy was a good auspice, one he would later augment by making two other pagans, Symmachus and Flavius Eutolmius Tatianus consuls.[2] At the *curia*, Latinius Pacatus Drepanius, a Gallic senator, seductively laid the hands of pagan heroes and gods upon the newly arrived emperor: Crete bore Jupiter; Delos, Apollo and Diana; Thebes, Hercules. But here was Spain, the Mother of Emperors—and *clarissimi vates*. The military virtues of Theodosius called to his mind Alexander, Scipio Africanus, and Hannibal, or the Curii, Coruncani, and Fabricii who placed triumphal laurel on the

1. "Populo haec vel simile quicquam videre nec speranti umquam nec optanti," 16.10.2.
2. They would be consuls in 391. For more detailed descriptions of the political and religious environment of this event and Theodosius' religious policy in general, see Piganiol, *L'Empire chrétien*, 255–79; Ensslin, "Die Religionspolitik," 64–67, 71–86; Martroye, "La Repression," 689–92; Matthews, *Western Aristocracies*, 227–37; Matthews, "Symmachus," 175–95; Holum, *Theodosian Empresses*, 14–15.

Conclusion: Rome   135

knees of Jupiter Capitolinus. As the Castores had come to aid Postumius, so immortal God intervened for Theodosius against Magnus Maximus.[3] Ammianus no less than the panegyrist undoubtedly believed that his own task during such a momentous occasion should be to lead the emperor's vision to *sacrae aedes* and *dicata numini summo delubra*—to show again that Rome's history, glory, and religion were inseparable, irresistible.[4] Nicomachus gave him entry to the palace: if he had any patron among those senators who applauded his recitations of the *Res gestae*,[5] it would have been Theodosius' own prefect, whose biography of Apollonius and history dedicated to Theodosius place him squarely across the ideological path of Ammianus.[6] Through him the historian could well have been brought to the emperor's notice, possibly for a recitation from the *Res gestae* of his father's triumphant campaign against another rebel, Firmus.[7] And if Theodosius reacted as many other listeners had, he would want more.

Suppose that in Rome this Christian emperor received at least these two pagan testimonials; each, nevertheless, would have lain differently in his hand. Pacatus not only drew Theodosius up through the ranks of

---

3. *Panegyrici Latini*, ed. R. Mynors (Oxford, 1964), 2.45, 8.4–5, 9.5, 21.1, 39.4.

4. In the opinion of Matthews ("Ammianus," 1120) Theodosius' visit was "an opportunity surely not to be missed by an ambitious historian looking for an appreciative public."

5. In 392, Libanius addressed a congratulatory letter to *Markellinos*, Ammianus, (Foerster, *Opera Libanii*, 1063), which attests to his popularity at Rome; but it should be remembered that the date of writing might well have been far removed from the events actually described. On this letter, see Sabbah, *La Méthode*, 245–49; Syme, *Ammianus*, 10–11; Cameron, "Review," 262; Cameron, "Roman Friends," 18–19; Matthews, "Ammianus," 1120.

6. Refer to the two Roman memorials in H. Dessau's *Inscriptiones Latinae selectae* (Berlin, 1892), vol. 1, which mention this history: (*Virio Nicomacho Flaviano*) *historico disertissimo*, 2947 (A.D. 394); *cuius in eum* (*Flavianum seniorem*) *effusa benevolentia, et usque ad annalium, quos consecrari sibi a quaestore suo voluit* (*Theodosius*), *provecta, excitavit livorem improborum*, 2948 (A.D. 431). Because the *Annales* of Nicomachus are lost, it is impossible to gauge its influence upon Ammianus with any precision, but most critics accept the existence of some active area of contact between the two histories. See Thompson, *Historical Work*, 39; Sabbah, *La Méthode*, 116, 118, 121; Momigliano, "Lonely Historian," 133; Cameron, "Roman Friends," 23–24; Cameron, "Paganism and Literature," 9; Trankle, "Ammianus Marcellinus," 27. There is no agreement on whom specifically Ammianus knew in Rome, and Cameron's caveat ("Roman Friends," 28) should be accepted: "Caution therefore is requisite in using Ammianus as a witness to the attributes and aspirations of the senatorial aristocracy of Rome." Still, I will put forward Nicomachus on the evidence of his religious militancy and precise literary interests.

7. 29.5.4–56. Note that the elder Theodosius returns to Sitifis, *triumphanti similis*, 29.5.56. Obviously, Ammianus would not have selected the "unwanted" triumph of Constantius for such an occasion. See above, p. 110, n. 113.

gods and their inspired heroes but, inevitably for his genre, let him surmount them: Spain was *greater* than Crete or Delos; those lands bore gods whom men knew only by report, she, a god they could see. And why did anyone pay attention to old stories about the labors of Hercules or Liber's conquest of India when he might be honoring the emperor's deeds in his temples and fora? Rome, really, did not consecrate Theodosius so much as he, it.[8] Whatever purchase the senator gained upon Theodosius through such hyperbole, he lost by making the gods seem minuscule figures clinging to the emperor's mantle. Why should Theodosius need them when he possessed the greater power of blessing? If Pacatus had meant rather that the emperor should see himself as the fulfillment of all those ancient deeds of heroes and gods, the tip of an obelisk but fully part of it, in reality his panegyric absolved Theodosius of any particular need to feel obliged to the heroic past or its religion. On the other hand, Theodosius would never have received such an erroneous encouragement to cut free of *aeterna* if he listened to Ammianus: history, *virtus,* and empire began forever *iussu deorum.* Had the emperor finally spared Rome's traditional cults, the historian alone, not the panegyrist, would have been responsible.[9]

But their moment passed quickly, for the year of *adventus* was followed by the year of slaughter. When the people of Thessalonica murdered their German overlord, Butheric, Theodosius condemned them to universal execution.[10] His own subsequent condemnation by Ambrose, Bishop of Milan, compelled him to an extreme act of penitence before Christ. In February 391, he strengthened the imperial bans against pagan worship, and he never again entered the *Templum totius mundi.* Although Roman paganism had yet to follow its political trajectory from this point to the far bank of the Frigidus in 394, no Thessalonica, Ambrose, ultimate edicts, or Frigidus exists in the *Res gestae.*[11] We are entitled to this belief not only from the lack of internal evidence for any event beyond 390—Ammianus would surely have mentioned the final destruction of

---

8. 44.5. "Non publica tantum opera lustraveris sed privatas quoque aedes divinis vestigiis consecraris," 47.3.

9. Sabbah (*La Méthode,* 323–25) discusses the relationship between Ammianus and Pacatus.

10. And so strangely fulfilled the counsel of Libanius: "As for me, if a general or any other army officer had suffered such a thing, I would only think it your duty to come to grips with his butchers," *On Avenging Julian,* 24.29.

11. On the revolt of Eugenius, the restoration of pagan leadership in Rome, and Theodosius' second invasion of Italy, see Matthews, *Western Aristocracies,* 238–50; Piganiol, *L'Empire chrétien,* 261–68; Wytzes, *Der letze Kampf,* which contains a useful collection of primary sources; and Vera, "La Carriera," 35–37.

the Serapeum—but from what we know of the historian's personal character.[12]

I have argued that Ammianus was a thoughtful, aggressive pagan, who came to Rome with the expectation of revealing his religion, not concealing it. Absorbed in the moderate aspects of his character, we may forget that Ammianus was essentially an aggressive man, a *miles* seeking attention among the *patres*. He deliberately courted publicity for his views, religious and political, by committing himself to the production of a literary masterwork that was certain to arouse public interest and the inevitable requests for readings—no larval epitome; who would want a recitation from one of those? His severe portrayal of Rome's many supine nobles is misleading in this respect, for Libanius proves, if nothing else, that Ammianus succeeded in finding a warm senatorial audience, one that probably included the great Nicomachus.

If Ammianus was so completely a soldier of the spirit, we must ask ourselves whether such a man would have been silent while his religion was being actively destroyed in 391. That is impossible; we should better ask what peculiar circumstances have given us a text that its author would surely have revised within a year of completing it. Ammianus could not have been faithful to his ideal of heroic paganism had he only believed and not acted. In *miles quondam et Graecus*, a phrase redolent of heroes— similarly "Greek warriors of old"—he is Jason on the Black Sea, envisioning himself at one with those specially bound by the gods to strenuous labor in a strange land.

12. Matthews ("Ammianus," 1117), Gimazaine, and Cameron (see above, p. 110, n. 113) think Ammianus probably finished his *res gestae* by 391. This is my conclusion as well; we have him just before the storm, not after. More, however, have chosen a date nearer 395, after the fall of Eugenius. See Glover, *Life and Letters*, 32; Maenchen-Helfen, "Date of Ammianus Marcellinus' Last Books," 384–99; Thompson, "Ammianus," 150–52; Syme, *Ammianus*, 6; Jannacone, *Ammiano Marcellino*, 114; and Demandt, *Zeitkritik*, 148–52. See Neri's survey of the question, "Ammiano," 71–86.

BIBLIOGRAPHY

Alfoldi, A., and E., eds. *Die Kontorniat-Medaillons.* Berlin, 1976.
Angliviel de la Beaumelle, L. "Remarques sur l'attitude d'Ammien Marcellin à l'égard du christianisme." *Mélanges W. Seston.* Paris, 1974.
Athanassiadi-Fowden, P. *Julian and Hellenism.* Oxford, 1981.
Barnes, T. *The Sources of the Historia Augusta.* Brussels, 1978.
Barrow, R. *Prefect and Emperor.* Oxford, 1973.
Baynes, N. *The Historia Augusta, Its Date and Purpose.* Oxford, 1926.
Beckley, H., ed. *Anthologia Graeca.* Munich, 1965.
Bidez, J., ed. *Historia ecclesiastica,* by Philostorgius. Berlin, 1981.
———, ed. *Historia ecclesiastica,* by Sozomen. Berlin, 1960.
———, ed. *Letters of Julian.* Paris, 1924.
———, and Cumont, F. *Les Mages Hellénisés.* Paris, 1938.
Blockley, R. *Ammianus Marcellinus, A Study of His Historiography and Political Thought.* Brussels, 1979.
———. *The Fragmentary Classicizing Historians of the Later Roman Empire.* Liverpool, 1981.
———. "Tacitean Influence on Ammianus Marcellinus." *Latomus* 32 (1973): 63–78.
Boer, W. den. *Some Minor Roman Historians.* Brussels, 1972.
Boissier, G. *La Fin du paganisme.* Paris, 1894.
———. *La Religion Romaine.* Paris, 1900.
Bouché-Leclercque, A. *Histoire de la divination dans l'antiquité.* Paris, 1879–82.
Bowder, D. *The Age of Constantine and Julian.* London, 1978.
Bowersock, G. *Greek Sophists in the Roman Empire.* Oxford, 1969.
———. *Julian the Apostate.* Cambridge, Mass., 1978.
Bregman, J. *Synesius of Cyrene.* Berkeley and Los Angeles, 1982.
Brown, P. *The Making of Late Antiquity.* London, 1979.
———. *Religion and Society in the Age of Augustine.* London, 1972.
Browning, R. *The Emperor Julian.* London, 1975.
———. "History." In *Cambridge History of Classical Literature,* edited by E. Kenney. Cambridge, England, 1982.
Cameron, A. *Claudian.* Oxford, 1970.

———. "Paganism and Literature in Late Fourth Century Rome." *Foundation Hardt* 23 (1976): 15–28.
———. "Review of *Ammianus and the Historia Augusta*, by R. Syme." *Journal of Roman Studies* 61 (1971): 255–67.
———. "The Roman Friends of Ammianus." *Journal of Roman Studies* 54 (1964): 15–28.
———, and A. Cameron. "Christianity and Tradition in the Historiography of the Later Empire." *Classical Quarterly* 58 (1964): 316–28.
Camus, P.-M. *Ammien Marcellin, témoin des courants culturels et religieux à la fin du IVe siècle.* Paris, 1967.
Chesnut, G. *The First Christian Historians.* Paris, 1977.
Clark, C., ed. *Res gestae*, by Ammianus Marcellinus. Berlin, 1910–15.
Conduché, D. "Ammien Marcellin et la mort du Julien." *Latomus* 24 (1965): 359–80.
Dautremer, L. *Ammien Marcellin, étude d'histoire litteraire.* Lille, 1899.
D'Elia, S. "Ammiano Marcellino e il cristianesimo." *Studies in Religion* 10 (1962): 372–90.
Demandt, A. *Zeitkritik und Geschichtsbild im Werk Ammians.* Bonn, 1965.
Des Places, E., ed. *De mysteriis Aegyptorum*, by Iamblichus. Paris, 1966.
Dill, S. *Roman Society in the Last Century of the Western Empire.* 2d ed. London, 1910.
Dillon, J. *The Middle Platonists.* London, 1977.
Dodds, E., ed. *The Elements of Theology*, by Proclus. Oxford, 1963.
Du Labriolle, P. *La réaction païenne.* Paris, 1948.
Eadie, J., ed. *Breviarium*, by Festus. London, 1967.
Ensslin, W. "Die Religionspolitik des Kaisers Theodosius der Gross." *Sitzungsberichte der Bayerischer Akademie der Wissenschaften* 2 (1953): 1–88.
———. *Zur Geschichtsschreibung und Weltanschauung des Ammianus Marcellinus.* Leipzig, 1923.
Festugière, A.-J. *Antioch païenne et chrétienne.* Paris, 1959.
Foerster, R., ed. *Opera Libanii.* Leipzig, 1909–27.
Fontaine, J. "Ammien Marcellin, historien romantique." *Bulletin de l'Association Guillaume Budé* 28 (1969): 417–35.
Fowden, G. "The Pagan Holy Man in Late Antique Society." *Journal of Hellenic Studies* 102 (1982): 33–60.
———. "The Platonist Philosopher and His Circle in Late Antiquity." *Philosophia* 7 (1977): 359–83.
Fränkel, H., ed. *Argonautica*, by Apollonius Rhodius. Oxford, 1961.
Funke, H. "Majestäts- und Magieprozesse bei Ammianus Marcellinus." *Jahrbuch für Antike und Christentum* 10 (1967): 145–75.
Geffcken, J. *The Last Days of Greco-Roman Paganism.* Translated by S. MacCormack. New York, 1978.
Giangrande, J., ed. *Vitae sophistarum*, by Eunapius. Rome, 1956.
Gibbon, E. *History of the Decline and Fall of the Roman Empire.* 8th ed. London, 1925.
Gimazaine, J. *Ammien Marcellin, sa vie et son oeuvre.* Toulouse, 1889.
Glover, T. *Life and Letters in the Fourth Century.* Cambridge, England, 1901.

Bibliography 141

Greundel, R., ed. *Caesares,* by Aurelius Victor. Leipzig, 1970.
Hahn, I. "Der ideologische Kampf und der Tod Julians des Abtrunnigen." *Klio* 38 (1960): 225–32.
Halsberghe, C. *The Cult of Sol Invictus.* Leiden, 1972.
Henry, P., and H.-R. Schwyzer, eds. *Enneads,* by Plotinus. Oxford, 1964.
Holum, K. *Theodosian Empresses.* Berkeley and Los Angeles, 1982.
Homo, L. *De Rome païenne a la Rome chrétienne.* Paris, 1950.
Jannacone, S. *Ammiano Marcellino.* Naples, 1960.
Jones, C. "An Epigram on Apollonius of Tyana." *Journal of Hellenic Studies* 100 (1980): 190–94.
Jonge, P. de. *Sprachlicher und historischer Kommentar zu Ammianus Marcellinus.* Groningen, 1935–53.
Kayser, C., ed. *Vita Apollonii,* by Philostratus. Leipzig, 1870.
Kennedy, M. *The Literary Work of Ammianus.* Lancaster, Pa., 1912.
Klein, U., ed. *De vita Pythagorica,* by Iamblichus. Stuttgart, 1975.
Lacombrade, C., ed. *Works of Julian.* Paris, 1964.
Laistner, M. *The Greater Roman Historians.* Berkeley and Los Angeles, 1966.
Liebeschuetz, J. *Antioch, City and Imperial Administration in the Later Roman Empire.* Oxford, 1972.
―――. *Continuity and Change in Roman Religion.* Oxford, 1979.
Loyen, A., ed. *Epistulae,* by Sidonius Apollinaris. Paris, 1970.
MacCormack, S. *Art and Ceremony in Late Antiquity.* Berkeley and Los Angeles, 1981.
MacKail, J. *The Last Great Roman Historian.* London, 1925.
MacMullen, R. *Enemies of the Roman Order.* Cambridge, Mass., 1966.
―――. *Paganism in the Roman Empire.* New Haven, 1981.
Maenchen-Helfen, O. "The Date of Ammianus Marcellinus' Last Books." *American Journal of Philology* 76 (1955): 384–99.
Martroye, F. "La Répression de la magie et la culte des gentils au IVe siècle." *Revue de l'Histoire du Droit Francais* 4, no. 9 (1930): 669–701.
Matthews, J. "Ammianus Marcellinus." In *Ancient Writers, Greece and Rome,* edited by T. Luce. New York, 1982.
―――. "Symmachus and the Oriental Cults." *Journal of Roman Studies* 63 (1973): 175–95.
―――. *Western Aristocracies and Imperial Court, A.D. 364–425.* Oxford, 1975.
Maurice, J. "La terreur de la magie au IVe siècle." *Comptes rendus de l'Académie des Inscriptions et Belles-Lettres* (1926): 182–89.
Mazza, M. "L'Intelletuale come ideologo, Flavio Filostrato ed un speculum principis del II siecolo." *Passatopresente* 2 (1982): 93–121.
Meineke, A., ed. *Geographica* by Strabo. Leipzig, 1877.
Mendelssohn, L., ed. *Historia nova,* by Zosimus. Leipzig, 1887.
Migne, J. P., ed. *Historia ecclesiastica,* by Socrates Scholasticus. Paris, 1864.
―――, ed. *Works of Gregory Nazianzen.* Paris, 1886.
Misson, J. *Recherche sur le paganisme de Libanios.* Paris, 1914.
Momigliano, A. "The Lonely Historian Ammianus Marcellinus." In *Essays in Ancient and Modern Historiography,* edited by A. Momigliano. Oxford, 1977.
―――. "Pagan and Christian Historiography in the Fourth Century A.D." In

The Conflict between Paganism and Christianity in the Fourth Century, edited by A. Momigliano. Oxford, 1963.

―――. "Popular Religious Beliefs and Late Roman Historians." In *Essays in Ancient and Modern Historiography,* edited by A. Momigliano. Oxford, 1977.

Mommsen, T., and P. Meyer, eds. *Codex Theodosianus.* Berlin, 1905.

Mueller, K., ed. *Fragmenta historicorum Graecorum.* Paris, 1841–72.

Mynors, R., ed. *Panegyrici Latini.* Oxford, 1964.

Nauck, A., ed. *Porphyrii opuscula.* Leipzig, 1896.

Naudé, C. "Fortuna in Ammianus Marcellinus." *L'Antiquité Classique* 7 (1964): 70–88.

Neri, V. "Ammiano e il cristianesimo, Religione e politica nelle 'Res gestae' di Ammiano Marcellino." *Studi di Storia Antica* 11 (1985).

Niebuhr, B., ed. *Cedrenus.* Bonn, 1838.

Nilsson, M. "Pagan Divine Service in Late Paganism." *Harvard Theological Review* 38 (1945): 63–71.

Nock, A., ed. *De deis et mundo,* by Sallustius. Cambridge, England, 1926.

―――. "The Emperor's Divine *Comes.*" *Journal of Roman Studies* 37 (1947): 103–16.

Pack, R. "The Roman Digressions of Ammianus Marcellinus." *Transactions of the American Philological Association* 84 (1953): 181–89.

Parmentier, L., ed. *Historia ecclesiastica,* by Theodoret. Berlin, 1954.

Parthey, G., ed. *Epistola ad Anebonem,* by Porphyry. Berlin, 1847.

Pearson, A. *The Fragments of Sophocles.* Cambridge, England, 1917.

Peter, H., ed. *Scriptores Historiae Augustae.* Leipzig, 1884.

Petit, P. *Libanius et la vie municipale à Antioch dans la IVe siècle.* Paris, 1955.

Pharr, C. "The Interdiction of Magic in Roman Law." *Transactions of the American Philological Association* 63 (1932): 269–95.

Piganiol, A. *L'Empire chrétien.* Paris, 1972.

Rochefort, G. "La Démonologie de Saloustios et ses rapports avec celle de l'empereur Julien." *Lettres d'Humanité* 16 (1957): 53–61.

Rougé, J., ed. *Expositio totius mundi et gentium.* Paris, 1966.

Roullet, A. *The Egyptian and Egyptianizing Monuments of Imperial Rome.* Leiden, 1972.

Ruehl, J., ed. *Breviarium,* by Eutropius. Leipzig, 1919.

Russell, D., and N. Wilson, eds. *Menander Rhetor.* Oxford, 1981.

Sabbah, G. *La Méthode d'Ammien Marcellin.* Paris, 1978.

Scala, R. von. "Doxographische und stoïsche Reste bei Ammianus Marcellinus." *Festgeben zu ehren Max Büdinger.* Innsbruck, 1898.

Scott, W., ed. *Hermetica.* Oxford, 1924.

Seeck, O., ed. *Epistulae,* by Symmachus. Berlin, 1883.

Selem, A. "Considerazioni circa Ammiano ed il cristianesimo." *Rivista di Cultura classica e medioevale* 6 (1967): 224–62.

Seyfarth, W. "Glaube und Aberglaube bei Ammianus Marcellinus." *Klio* 46 (1966): 373–85.

Solari, A. "Particolarismo religiosa Bizantino di Ammiano." *Rendiconti della Classe di Scienze morali, storiche e filologiche dell'Accademia dei Lincei* 8, no. 4 (1949): 502–8.

Straub, J. *Heidnische Geschichtsapologetik in christlichen Spätantike.* Bonn, 1965.

Syme, R. *Ammianus and the Historia Augusta*. Oxford, 1968.

———. *Emperors and Biography: Studies in the Historia Augusta*. Oxford, 1971.

Teuffel, W. *History of Roman Literature*. Translated by G. Warr. Cambridge, England, 1890.

Thompson, E. "Ammianus Marcellinus." In *Roman Historians*, edited by T. Dorey. London, 1966.

———. "Ammianus Marcellinus and the Romans." *Greece and Rome* 11 (1941–42): 130–34.

———. *The Historical Work of Ammianus Marcellinus*. Cambridge, England, 1947.

Trankle, H. "Ammianus Marcellinus als römischer Geschichtsschreiber." *Archäologischer Anzeiger* 11 (1962): 21–35.

Vera, D. "La Carriera di Virius Nicomachus Flavianus e la Prefettura dell'Illirico Orientale nel IV Sec.d.C." *Studi Periodici di Letteratura e Storia dell'Antichità* 61 (1983): fasc. 1, 24–64; 4, 390–426.

Wagner, J., and C. Erfurdt, eds. *Res gestae*, by Ammianus Marcellinus. Leipzig, 1808.

Wallis, R. *Neoplatonism*. London, 1972.

Wardman, A. *Religion and Statecraft among the Romans*. London, 1982.

Willis, J., ed. *Commentarii in somnium Scipionis*. Leipzig, 1963.

Wissowa, G. *Religion und Kultus der Römer*. Munich, 1912.

Witte, E. "Ammianus Marcellinus, quid iudicaverit de rebus divinis" (Diss., University of Jena, 1891).

Wytzes, J. *Der letze Kampf des Heidentums in Rom*. Leiden, 1977.

Yonge, C., trans. *Res gestae*, by Ammianus Marcellinus. London, 1862.

INDEX

Abraham, 123n62
Academy, 74, 82
Achilles, 28n74, 81, 90, 123n62, 132
Adonis, 26, 52
Adrasteia–Nemesis, 11–13, 36, 118, 131
Aegae, Cilician, 81n53, 82
Aesculapius, 81n53, 82, 83, 96
Africanus, governor, 37n3
Alans, 88–89
Alaric, 131, 132
Alexander the Great, 66, 112, 123n62, 134
Alexandria, 60, 73, 82, 97–98, 100n69
Alypius, Faltonius Probus, Prefect of Rome, 110n113
Amantius, diviner, 38n3, 72
Ambrose, Bishop of Milan, 136
Amida, 28, 90, 95, 108
Amphiaraus, 22n48
Amphilochius, tribune, 22n48
Anaxagoras, 58, 73
Anthropophagi, 89
Antioch, 11n6, 19, 26, 41, 47, 52–60, 81n48, 84
Antiochus Epiphanes, 54
Antoninus, philosopher, 86, 98n60
Antoninus Pius, Emperor (A.D. 137–61), 113n6, 121
Apis Bull, 55, 96
Apollo, 27–30, 38, 53–54, 61; in Christian works, 65n50, 66; in the *Historia Augusta*, 119, 122; in the works of Julian, 29, 35, 59; Libanius, 28n74, 34n105, 43; Pacatus, 134; Philostratus, 81; Zosimus, 131
Apollonius of Chalcas, philosopher, 126

Apollonius of Tyana, 20, 74, 80–85, 119–20, 123n62, 125, 126
Apollonius the Syrian, philosopher, 126n79
Aprunculus, governor, 44
Argonauts, 24, 25, 108–9
Aristotle, 73, 126
Armenia, King of (Papa), 19
Arsaces, Parthian King, 94
Asclepiades, philosopher, 54
Aspendus, 84
Athanasius, Bishop of Alexandria, 105
Athene–Minerva, 36, 114n15, 119, 131, 132
Athens, 45, 83, 132
Auchenius, charioteer, 37n3
Audience of Ammianus, 10, 135, 137
Augustus, Emperor (27 B.C.–A.D. 14), 20, 28, 72, 74, 113, 114n17
Aurelian, Emperor (A.D. 270–75), 109n108, 113n6, 118, 119, 122–23
Aurelius Victor, Sextus, historian, 114–17

Babylas, Bishop of Antioch, 66
Babylon, 72n9, 81
Barbatio, general, 11, 38n3
Bargus, tribune, 131n97
Bassianus, secretary, 38n3
Batnae, 61, 63
Bellona, 17, 25–26, 40, 89, 120
Beroea, 63
Besa, god of Abydum, 37, 73
Bezabde, 104
Bishops, 102–4, 106
Black Sea, 108–9

Index

Brahmins, 72, 82, 94
Burgundians, 91–92
Butheric, general, 136

Caesar, 97. *See also individuals by name*
Callinicum, 61
Cambyses, 28n74, 94
Campensis, diviner, 72
Cannae, 50
Capitolium, 114, 121–25 passim, 134–35
Caracalla, Emperor (A.D. 198–217), 114, 115n17
Carrhae, 41n15, 61, 63, 65
Carus, Emperor (A.D. 282–83), 115
Castor and Pollux, 55, 119, 135
Castra Herculis, 24n54
Cedrenus, George, Byzantine chronicler, 65n50
Chalcas, diviner, 64
Chaldaeans, 71, 72, 83, 94
Chionitae, 90–91
Christ, 123n62
Christianity: Ammianus' attitude toward, 100–7, 110, 132–33; in the *Historia Augusta*, 121, 123, 124, 127; and the reign of Julian, 40–41, 49, 50, 54, 66–67, 86; and the reign of Theodosius I, 55n10, 129, 130, 131–32
Chrysanthius, philosopher, 56n16, 64, 77–78, 86
Chryses, 28n74
Cicero, 44n32, 62–63, 123n62
Circus Maximus, 29
Claudian, 100n69
Claudius II Gothicus, Emperor, (A.D. 268–70)
Cleopatra, 98
Coeranius, philosopher, 74n23
Colophon, 82
Commodus, Emperor (A.D. 177–92), 120
Constans, Emperor (A.D. 337–50), 115n20, 131n97
Constantine I, Emperor (A.D. 307–37): Ammianus' attitude toward, 28, 101; law regarding diviners, 55n10; in the works of Eutropius, 113, 114; in the works of Julian, 35; in the works of Victor, 116, 117; in the works of Zosimus, 130, 131
Constantinople, 38n6, 47–49, 56, 60, 131
Constantius I, Emperor (A.D. 305–6), 117, 122

Constantius II, Emperor (A.D. 337–61): at Rome, 28, 30, 32, 52n1; death foreshadowed, 18, 22n48, 42, 46; *genius* of, 20, 22, 23; Julian appropriates an obelisk of, 60; law against pagans, 115n20; superstition of, 102n76, 106n99
Crassus (Dives), 61
Crispus, Caesar (A.D. 317–26), 131
Ctesiphon, 109n109, 115, 118

Damasus, Pope, 102
Daphne, suburb of Antioch, 27n68, 28n74, 53–54, 81, 112n1
Darius, 94
Date of completion of the *Res gestae*, 110n113, 136–37
Delos, 27
Delphi, 27n69, 65n50
Demeter, 47, 131
Demetrius Cythras, philosopher, 37, 73, 74n23
Demiurge, 12n9, 33–34
Deus, supreme deity. *See* Numen
Diana–Artemis, 131, 134
Diocletian, Emperor (A.D. 284–305), 116, 117, 118n35
Diviners: following Julian's reign, 19, 25, 38–39; general discussion of, 71–75; in the *Historia Augusta*, 124, 125–26; and Julian, 53, 57, 62, 65; in the works of Philostratus, 83; in the works of Victor, 115
Domitian, Emperor (A.D. 81–96), 28n72, 80, 113
Domitianus, prefect, 18
Druids, 72n9, 73, 74, 92–93, 118n35
Dura–Europos, 61, 62

Egypt, 29–31, 58, 71, 73, 91–92, 96–100; in the *Expositio totius mundi et gentium*, 100n69; *Hermetica*, 98n60, 99n65; *Historia Augusta*, 126–27; in the works of Eunapius, 98n60; in the works of Iamblichus, 33n101, 72n9, 96n45; in the works of Julian, 35; in the works of Libanius, 57, 98n60; in the works of Philostratus, 82, 83; in the works of Porphyry, 21n47, 33–34; in the works of Sozomen, 86n78; in the works of Victor, 114
Eileithyiae, 131

Index

Elagabalus, the god, 119
Elagabalus, Emperor (A.D. 218–22)
Elements, divine and terrestrial matter, 12–15 passim, 21, 26, 29, 34n106
Eleusinian Mysteries, 47, 72n9, 82, 114, 132
Epidaurus, 82
Epigonus, philosopher, 74n23
Eugenius, Emperor (A.D. 392–94), 137n12
Euhages, 73, 93
Eunapius, 41, 42, 49, 64, 77–78, 85–86, 128–30
Eupraxius, quaestor, 103
Eusebius, Bishop of Nicomedia, 50
Eusebius, philosopher, 77, 86
Eutropius, chamberlain, 132–33
Eutropius, historian, 113–14
Exempla, 24–25
Expositio totius mundi et gentium, 100n69

Fabricius, 21n47, 134
Fatum–moira, 12, 16, 18, 20, 35–36, 118, 131
Fausta, 131
Felix, count, 56
Festus, Rufius, historian, 11n6, 38n3, 112–13
Fetiales, 91n21
Firmus, 104, 135
Flavianus, Virius Nicomachus, 70n3, 86n78, 126, 134, 135
Fortuna–tyche, 16–17, 118, 131
Forum of Theodosius, 38n6
Fravitta, general, 129, 132
Fritigern, Gothic chief, 50n56, 103
Furies, 19

Gades, 83
Galerius, Emperor (A.D. 305–11), 118
Gallienus, Emperor (A.D. 253–68), 114
Gallus, Caesar (A.D. 351–54), 11, 18, 22, 84
Gaul, 24, 92–93
Generid, general, 132
Genii–demons, 16, 19–23, 42, 61, 112
George, Bishop of Alexandria, 48, 53, 98
Germanicus, 96n52
Gordian III, Emperor (A.D. 238–44), 61
Goths, 17, 104, 128, 129, 132
Gratian, Emperor (A.D. 367–83), 29n75, 55n10, 131
Gregory Nazianzen, 45, 66, 67n58
Grumbates, King of the Chionitae, 90–91

Hadrian, Emperor (A.D. 117–38), 53, 114, 124n66, 126n76
Hadrianople, 19, 25–26, 50
Hagistia, 72, 93–95
Hannibal, 50, 134
Heliopolis, 30
Hellenism, 49, 58
Hercules, 24–25, 92, 134, 135
Hermes Trismegistus, 20
Hermetic writings, 33, 34n106, 98n60, 99n65
Heroes, 20, 21, 50, 93, 107–11, 137
Hierapolis, 61, 63
Hierophant of Eleusis, 41, 42, 56n16
Hilarinus, charioteer, 37n3
Hilarius and Patricius, diviners, 25, 38–39, 110, 129
Hippodrome at Constantinople, 22n48, 38n6
Historia Augusta, 117–27
Homer, 20, 23n52, 28, 78, 91n23, 109n109
Huns, 87–88
Hymetius, governor, 38n3
Hytaspes, father of Darius, 94

Iamblichus, 12n9, 33n101, 71–72n9, 86, 96n45
Idmon, diviner, 71
Imbrus, 72n9
Innocent I, Pope, 131
Iris, 14n16
Isis, 120, 124
Iustitia–Dike, 17, 20–21, 36, 118, 131

Jason, 108n105
John Chrysostom, Bishop of Constantinople, 132
Jovian, Emperor (A.D. 363–64), 22, 61, 62n40, 104, 105, 114
Judaism, 56, 101, 124, 127
Julian, Emperor (A.D. 360–63): in Christian works, 41n15, 42, 45, 49, 60, 65n50, 66–67; as exemplifying the heroic emperor, 108–9; his imperial journey through Antioch, 52–60; his imperial journey through Constantinople, 47–49; his imperial journey through Gaul, 40–44; his imperial journey through Naissus, 44–46; his imperial journey through Persia, 61–67; his imperial journey through Pessinus, 49–51; letters of, 41, 43, 45,

Julian, Emperor (*continued*)
49n54, 50, 58, 60, 63, 65; his life as an *indicium* of the pagan gods, 23–32; orations of, *Against the Cynic Heracleius*, 35–36; orations of, *Hymn to King Helios*, 34–35; orations of, *Misopogon*, 58, 59; and the problem of Pagan apology, 39, 66–67; in the works of Eunapius, 41, 42, 49, 64, 128–29; in the works of Eutropius, 114; in the works of Libanius, 24n53, 28n74, 34n105, 39, 41–67 passim, 71n3, 98n60, 136n10; in the works of Philostratus, 84; in the works of Zosimus, 41, 45, 64, 130; victory over *fortuna*, 16n23
Julianus, count, 56, 66
Juno–Hera, 119
Jupiter–Zeus, 14, 31–34, 55, 80, 105n93, 132; in the *Historia Augusta*, 119, 121–25 passim; in the works of Eutropius, 114; in the works of Julian, 35–36, 43; in the works of Libanius, 34n105; in the works of Pacatus, 134, 135; in the works of Victor, 114n15; in the works of Zosimus, 131

Lemnos, 72n9
Leto, 131
Leuce, island, 90
Libanius: on Christian depredations, 55n10; compares Julian to Apollonius of Tyana, 70n3; and Hercules, 24n53; interest in particular deities, 34n105; letter to Ammianus, 135n5; on Julian's imperial progress through Gaul, 41, 43–44; on Julian in Naissus, 45; on Julian in Constantinople, 48–49; on Julian in Pessinus, 50; on Julian in Antioch, 28n74, 54n6, 55–59 passim; on Julian in Persia, 63–64; response to Julian's death, 39, 54n6, 67, 98n60, 136n10
Liber–Dionysus, 82, 136
Liberius, Pope, 102, 105n91
Licinius, Emperor (A.D. 308–24), 117n27, 130
Literary and rhetorical convention: in connection with Julian, Constantius, and Sapor, 44, 91n23, 95n43; deities, 14n16, 25–26, 34n105, 136; excursuses, 8–9, 87; problem of, 8–9

Lollianus, senator, 38n3
Lucius Verus, Emperor (A.D. 161–69), 28
Luna, 95, 118
Lyceum, 82

Macrobius, 10, 19
Magi, 72, 93–95, 120
Magic, 37–39, 79; and Apollonius of Tyana, 73n18, 80; and Didius Julianus, 120; and Julian, 40–41, 46; necromancy, 19, 95
Magnentius, Emperor (A.D. 350–53), 38n6, 67n60
Magnus Maximus, Emperor (A.D. 383–88), 38n6, 134, 135
Mainz, 104
Maras, deacon, 105n91
Marcius, diviner, 71
Marcomanni, 121
Marcus Aurelius, Emperor (A.D. 161–80), 28, 101, 115n17, 121
Marius, 20, 74
Mars–Ares, 21n47, 25–26, 30, 32, 61, 88, 89
Martyrs, 101–2, 103, 117n27
Mater, 29, 49–51, 61, 119, 122
Maximian, Emperor (A.D. 286–305), 117
Maximinus, prefect, 19
Maximus, philosopher, 49, 62, 73, 75–79; lying oracles of, 66; in the works of Eunapius, 11n6, 64, 86, 129
Maximus and Balbinus, Co-emperors (A.D. 238), 121
Mederichus, Alamannic chief, 130
Memphis, 96–97, 126
Menander, comic poet, 20
Menander, rhetorician, 54n9
Mercury–Hermes, 26, 36, 40
Metrodorus, philosopher, 102n75
Milan, 103, 136
Miletus, 71n9
Millennial Games of Philip, 115
Mithras, 35, 49, 120
Mobsus, diviner, 71
Montius, Magnus, quaestor, 18
Musonianus, Strategius, prefect, 102n76

Naissus, 44
Neoplatonism, 13, 14, 31, 33, 34, 106n96
Neoterius, Flavius, consul, 110n113
Neptune, 14n16
Nicomedia, 27, 50, 54

Index

Nile Festival, 97
Numa, 20, 71, 74, 121
Numen, supreme deity, 11, 12, 17, 25, 31–34, 119
Numerius, tribune, 19

Obelisks, 29–30, 38n6, 60, 111
Olympius, philosopher, 86n78
Oribasius, 41, 64–66
Orpheus, 123n62
Orsiloche, 89, 90

Pacatus, Latinius, panegyrist, 134–35, 136
Paganism, 107–11; and Julian, 40, 49, 52–60, 66–67
Palladius, tribune, 104
Palmyra, 123
Pantheon, 99n65, 105n93
Paris, 42
Pasiphilus, philosopher, 74n23
Paul, secretary, 19
Pegasius, Bishop of Ilium, 49n54
Peleus, 96
Perinthus (Heraclea), 24
Persecutions, 101–2, 117n27
Persephone, 131
Perseus, 32
Persia, 81, 93–95, 112, 118, 125
Personified deities, 15–17
Pessinus, 49–50
Phantasiai–imagines. See Specters
Pharos at Alexandria, 98
Philip, Emperor (A.D. 244–49), 115–16
Philosophers, 72–75, 85–86, 125–26
Philosophi, faction in Julian's court, 62
Philostorgius, ecclesiastical historian, 66
Philostratus, 73n18, 80–84
Phineas, diviner, 71
Phoenicia, 72n9
Phrygia, Assyrian village, 67n58
Plato, 58, 72, 74, 80, 94, 125, 126
Plotinus, 20, 21n45, 21n47, 61n35, 74, 79
Pompey, 112n1
Porphyry, 33–34, 79n41
Praetextatus, Vettius Agorius, 132
Priests, pagan, 71–75, 82
Priscus, philosopher, 62n40, 75, 78, 129
Proclus, philosopher, 130n95
Procopius, Emperor (A.D. 365–66), 22, 33n99
Proteus, 57

Pyramids, 126
Pythagoras, 20, 35n108, 58, 71–72n9, 73, 74, 81, 93

Quadi, 88

Rameses, 29, 30, 99
Rando, Alamannic chief, 104
Religio absoluta et simplex, 106–7
Reman and Busan, Mesopotamian forts, 103
Remigius, master of offices, 17
Rome, 83, 98n60, 115, 134–36

Sabinianus, general, 104
Sallustius, Flavius, philosopher and prefect, 12–13, 15, 61
Samaritans, 126n76, 127
Samothrace, 72n9, 82
Sapor, Persian King, 19, 44n31, 95, 103–4, 108n105
Scipiones, 20, 50, 74, 134
Scordisci, 89, 112n1
Scudilo, tribune, 11
Secular Games, 115, 131–32
Seleucia, on the Tigris, 28
Senate of Rome, 10, 63n43, 83, 120, 121–23, 125, 132, 134
Septimius Severus, Emperor (A.D. 193–211), 119, 126, 127n83
Serapeum, 30n81, 86, 97, 100n69, 126, 136–37
Serapis, 124, 126
Serena, wife of Stilicho, 131n97
Serenianus, count, 38n3
Severus Alexander, Emperor (A.D. 222–35), 112, 123–25
Sibylline Books, 27, 29, 50, 56, 115, 118, 122–23, 131
Sidonius Apollinaris, 70n3
Simonides, philosopher, 74n23
Smyrna, 84
Socrates, 20, 74
Socrates, ecclesiastical historian, 42
Sol–Helios, 28–31, 34–36, 66, 95, 98–100, 123, 128
Solon, 58, 73
Sopater (philosopher), 131n97
Sophists, 81n53
Sozomen, ecclesiastical historian, 42, 45, 86n78
Spain, 72n9, 125n70, 134

Index

Specters, 18–19, 119–20
Stilicho, 131n97, 132
Strasbourg, 23
Symmachus, Quintus Aurelius, 32, 55n10, 83, 134
Synesius, Bishop of Cyrene, 111n113

Tacitus, 96n52, 101n72
Tages, diviner, 71
Tarsus, 32
Tatianus, Flavius Eutolmius, consul, 134
Taurica, 89–90
Teiresias, 64
Telesinus, consul, 83n60
Tertullus, Prefect of Rome, 25, 55
Thales, 71n9
Thebes, Egyptian, 28n74, 126
Themis, 13–15, 17, 36
Theodoret, ecclesiastical historian, 41n15, 66
Theodorus, secretary, 78, 129
Theodosian Code, 55n10, 60n33, 115n20
Theodosius, count, 110n113, 135
Theodosius I, Emperor (A.D. 379–95), 28n74, 29n75, 38, 86n78, 110, 129, 131, 134–36
Theodotus, governor, 32, 55
Theologi, 11, 20
Theophilus, governor, 84

Thessalonica, 136
Thrace, 89, 108–9
Thrasybulus, diviner, 125
Titus, Emperor (A.D. 79–81), 28n72
Tolerance, 106n96, 117n27, 124, 127, 132
Trajan, Emperor (A.D. 98–117), 109n110, 111n113, 313
Triptolemus, 47
Trophonius, 82

Valens, Emperor (A.D. 364–78), 17, 22, 25–26, 29, 38, 97, 103, 112
Valentinian I, Emperor (A.D. 364–75), 22, 38n3, 60n33, 105, 132
Valentinian II (A.D. 375–92), 55n10
Venus, 26–27
Vestal Virgins, 119, 120, 121
Victor, general, 63
Victory, statue of, 125n68
Vienne, 42
Virgil, 31, 75, 123n62
Virtus, statue of, 132

Zaitha, 61
Zeno of Citium, 74
Zeno of Elea, 126
Zoroaster, 71, 72, 94
Zosimus, 28n75, 41, 45, 64, 130–32

Compositor:	G&S Typesetters, Inc.
Text:	10/13 Palatino
Display:	Palatino
Printer:	Braun-Brumfield, Inc.
Binder:	Braun-Brumfield, Inc.